Alfred Jacob Miller

Romancing The West

in the Bank of America Collection

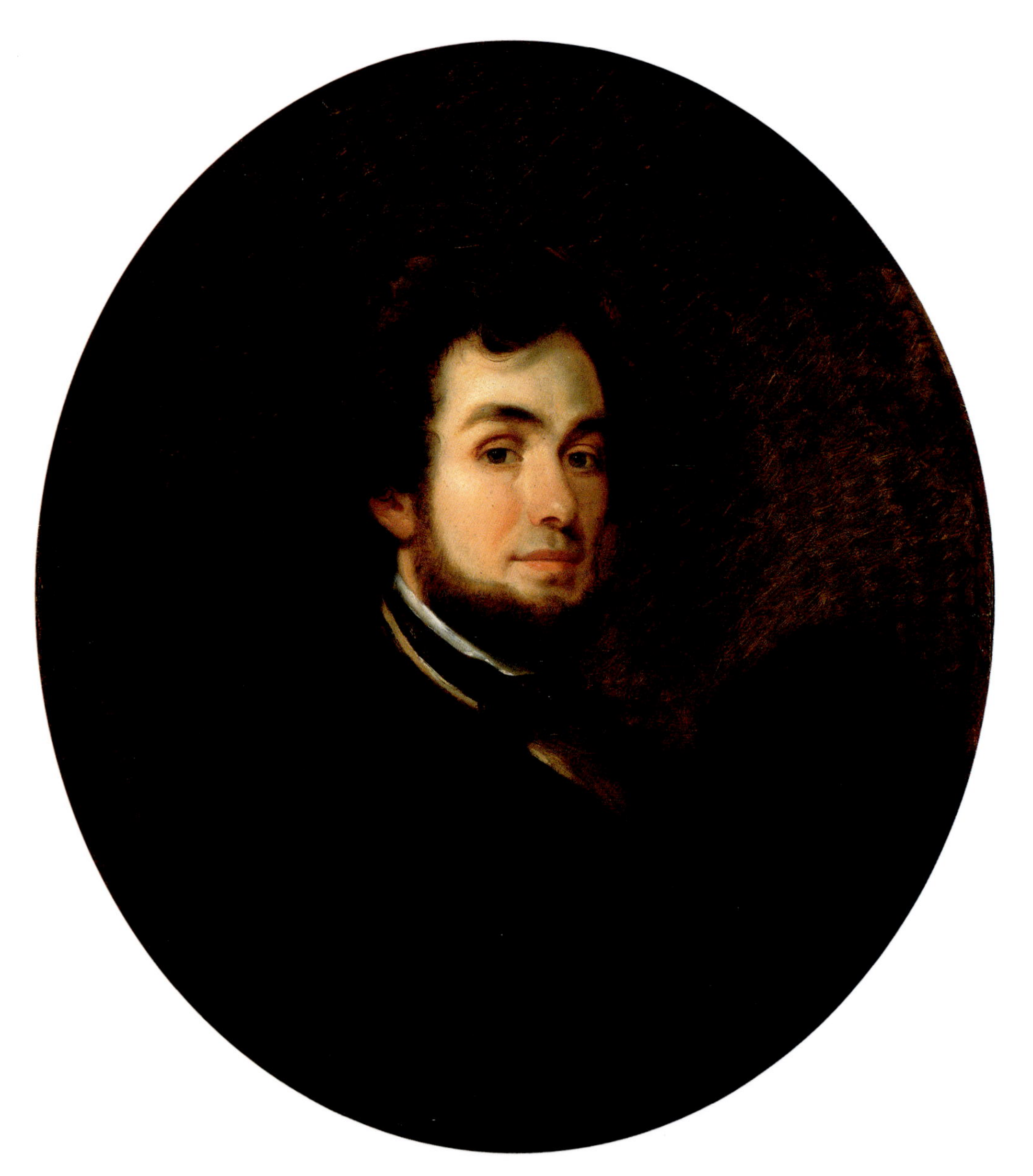

Alfred Jacob Miller

Romancing The West

in the Bank of America Collection

Margaret C. Conrads, editor

Essays by Kathleen A. Foster, Lisa Strong,
and William H. Truettner

Catalogue entries by
Margaret C. Conrads and Stephanie Fox Knappe

The Nelson-Atkins Museum of Art | Kansas City, Missouri

Published on the occasion of the exhibition *Romancing the West: Alfred Jacob Miller in the Bank of America Collection*

Romancing the West: Alfred Jacob Miller in the Bank of America Collection is organized by The Nelson-Atkins Museum of Art and is made possible by the Bank of America Art in Our Communities program.

Exhibition Itinerary

The Nelson-Atkins Museum of Art
25 September 2010–9 January 2011

The Museum of Fine Arts, Houston
5 February–8 May 2011

Philadelphia Museum of Art
4 June–18 September 2011

Distributed by University of Washington Press
P.O. Box 50096, Seattle, WA 98145
www.washington.edu/uwpress

Library of Congress Cataloging-in-Publication Data
Miller, Alfred Jacob, 1810–1874.
Alfred Jacob Miller : romancing the West in the Bank of America collection / Margaret C. Conrads, editor ; essays by Kathleen A. Foster, Lisa Strong, and William H. Truettner ; catalogue entries by Margaret C. Conrads and Stephanie Fox Knappe.
p. cm.
Published on the occasion of an exhibition held at the Nelson-Atkins Museum of Art, Sept. 25–Jan. 9, 2011, the Museum of Fine Arts, Houston, Feb. 5–May 8, 2011, and the Philadelphia Museum of Art, June 4–Sept. 18, 2011.
ISBN 978-0-615-35171-1 (softcover : alk. paper)
1. Miller, Alfred Jacob, 1810–1874—Exhibitions. 2. Frontier and pioneer life in art—Exhibitions. 3. Indians in art—Exhibitions. 4. West (U.S.)—In art—Exhibitions. 5. Bank of America—Art collections—Exhibitions. I. Conrads, Margaret C., II. Foster, Kathleen A. III. Strong, Lisa Maria IV. Truettner, William H. V. Nelson-Atkins Museum of Art. VI. Museum of Fine Arts, Houston. VII. Philadelphia Museum of Art. VIII. Title. IX. Title: Romancing the West in the Bank of America Collection.
ND1839.M54A4 2010
759.13—dc22 2010016098

Front cover: Alfred Jacob Miller, *War Path* (detail), n.d. Oil and glazes over graphite, ink, and possibly watercolor on cream wove paper, 9 × 12¼ in. (22.9 × 31.1 cm). Bank of America Collection (cat. 30)
Frontispiece: Alfred Jacob Miller, *Self-Portrait*, c. 1850. Oil on canvas, 30 × 24 15/16 in. (76.2 × 63.4 cm). The Walters Art Museum, Baltimore

Project director and general editor: Margaret C. Conrads
Copy editor: Fronia W. Simpson
Proofreader: Ted Gilley
Designer: Patrick Dooley
Typeset in Adobe Caslon Pro by Marie Weiler
Color management by iocolor, Seattle
Produced by Marquand Books, Inc., Seattle
Printed and bound in China by C&C Offset Printing Co., Ltd.

Contents

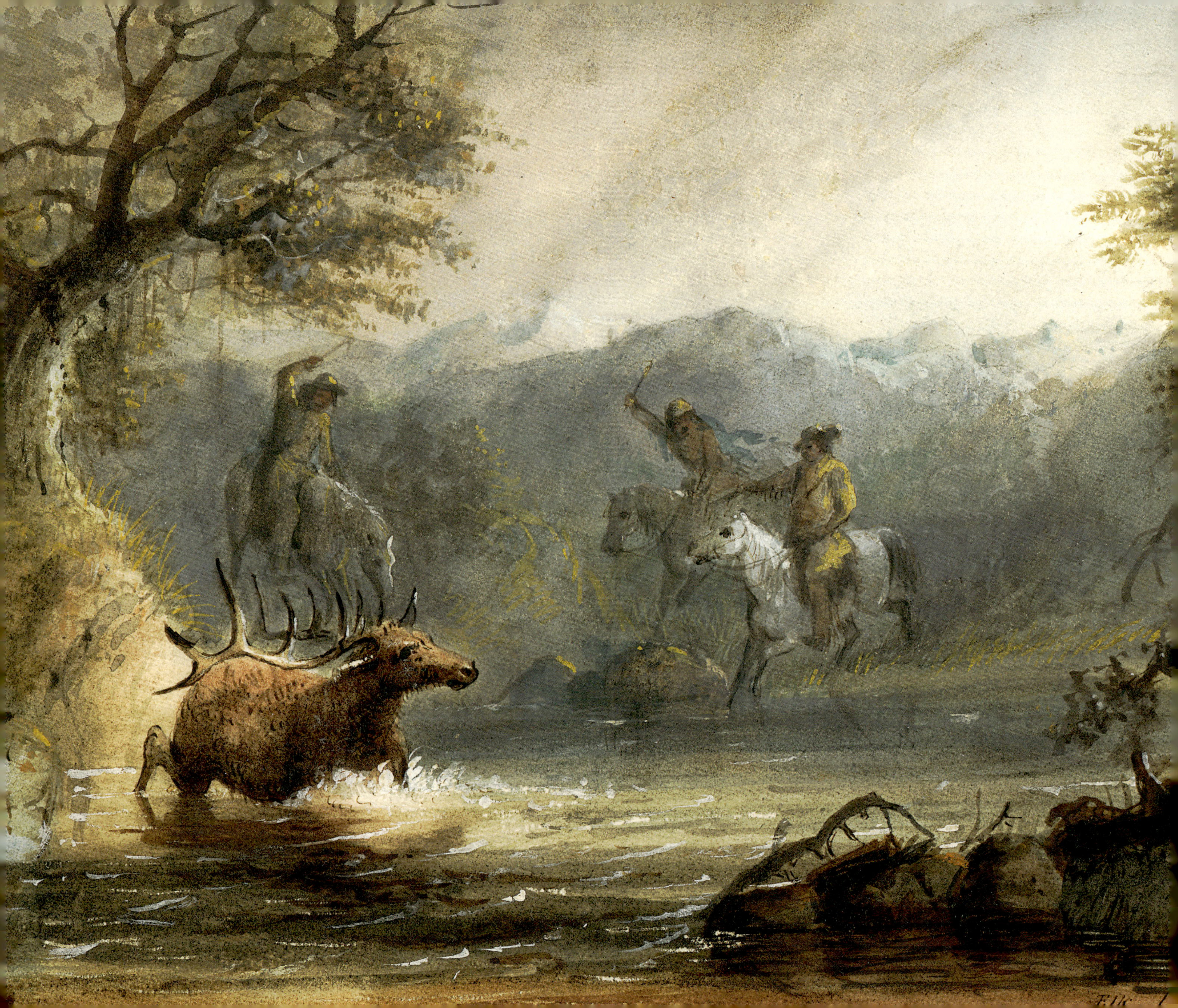
Elk

Sponsor's Statement

Bank of America is honored to serve as the national sponsor of *Romancing the West: Alfred Jacob Miller in the Bank of America Collection*. The exhibition focuses on thirty works on paper that exemplify Miller's understanding of the American West in the mid-nineteenth century. We are delighted to bring this beautiful and revealing group of objects to the wider public for the first time.

Alfred Jacob Miller joined Sir William Drummond Stewart, a Scottish nobleman and adventurer, to chronicle a journey to the Rocky Mountains to attend an annual gathering of the fur trade. In 1837 the expedition left Missouri by wagon train along what is now the Oregon Trail, giving Miller the distinction of becoming the first, and perhaps only, artist to paint the legendary fur trade from firsthand knowledge. Thereafter, Miller based his art on the rich experiences from that trip, which inspired the works in this exhibition.

Bank of America is a major supporter of arts and heritage in the United States and increasingly internationally. Our support is built on a foundation of responsible business practices and good corporate citizenship that improves access to the arts and arts education in local communities nationwide. When we lend to museums from our art collection, we expand cultural resources for the public and provide access to the visual arts, both of which are critical features in the cultural and economic vitality of the communities we serve.

Bank of America extends special thanks and appreciation to The Nelson-Atkins Museum of Art for organizing this outstanding project, including the conservation of important artworks, the development of the exhibition, and the catalogue. Through the diligent and thoughtful work of Margaret C. Conrads, Stephanie Fox Knappe, and Cindy Cart, they have shaped this endeavor from beginning to end to ensure its success.

At Bank of America, we recognize that cultural resources are part of the foundation on which healthy communities are built. We hope you enjoy the exhibition and that you continue to share our passion and enthusiasm for the important role art plays in all our lives.

Allen Blevins
Senior Vice President, Director of Art and Heritage Programs
Bank of America

Alfred Jacob Miller, *Elk Taking the Water*, detail (cat. 10)

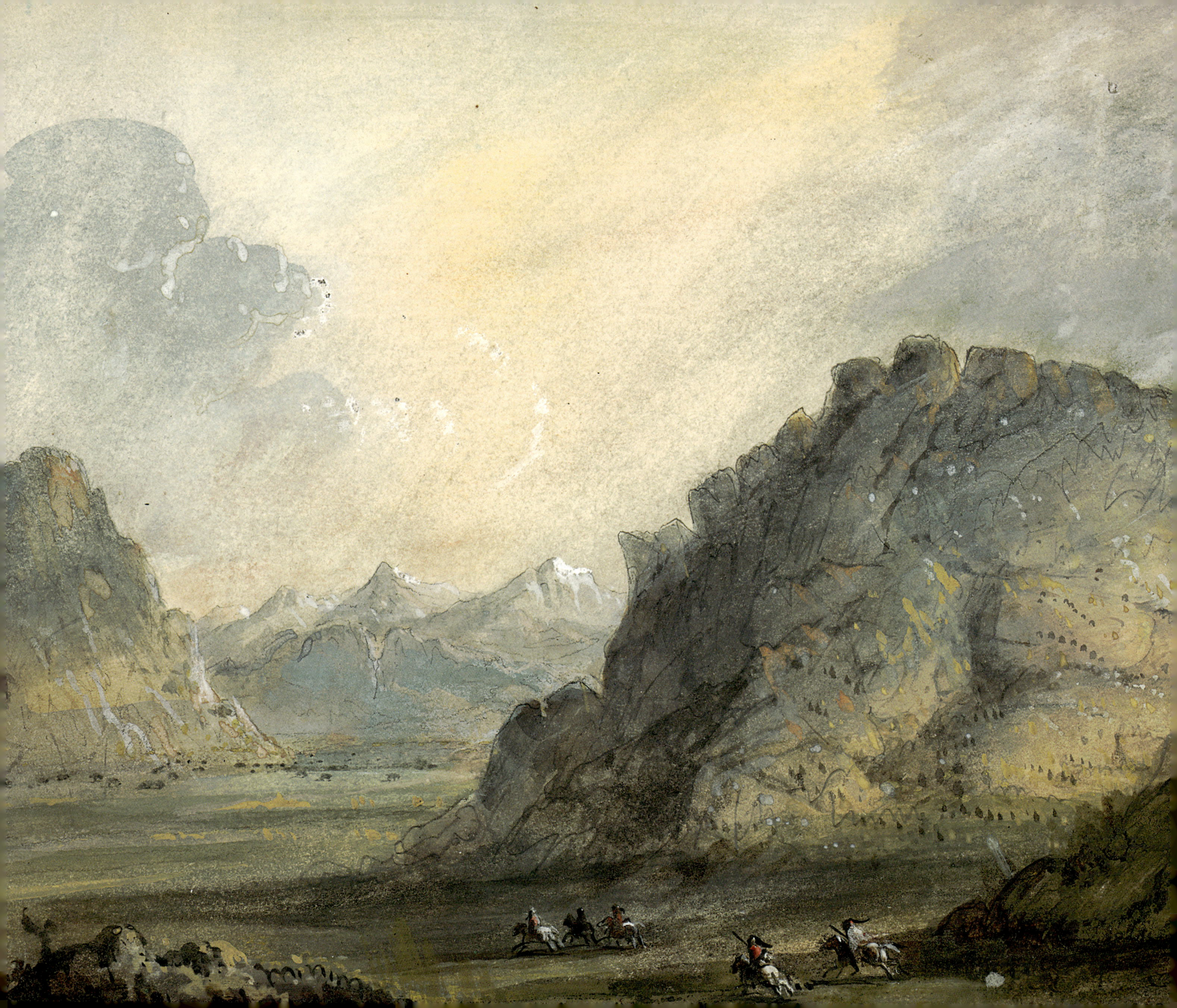

Foreword

Good things do come in small packages. Looking closely at an intimate group from an artist's body of work reaps rich rewards. *Romancing the West: Alfred Jacob Miller in the Bank of America Collection* offers this opportunity in thirty captivating works on paper that span the subjects and techniques that inspired the artist for more than thirty years. Mainly studio works in various stages of completion and in a sometimes unorthodox fusion of media, they provide a window onto not only how Miller worked but how he envisioned the American West. Miller's West was, to be sure, based on the experience of his six-month trek from Missouri to the Oregon Territory in 1837. More important, it is a West that blended fact and fiction—the West he saw combined with an intricate web of perceptions and attitudes of his generation. Far more than just laying out Miller's preferred subjects, the exhibition and this catalogue further elucidate the artist's complex mix of patrons, methods, and underpinnings of his art. There is much to see in these modest works that surprise the eye and encourage us to reconsider our own understandings of the West, past and present.

It is especially heartening to welcome home images whose genesis is rooted, literally and figuratively, in nearby Westport, just blocks from the Nelson-Atkins, where caravans of adventurers and emigrants, including the one that carried Miller and his Scots patron, William Drummond Stewart, gathered before they headed west. We extend our sincerest thanks to Bank of America, in particular Allen Blevins, Senior Vice President, Director of Art and Heritage Programs, for the generous loans to the exhibition as well as sponsorship. We are delighted that our colleagues in Houston and Philadelphia enthusiastically embraced the exhibition for their communities to enjoy.

Romancing the West: Alfred Jacob Miller in the Bank of America Collection was organized at the Nelson-Atkins by Margaret C. Conrads, Samuel Sosland Senior Curator of American Art, who expertly guided the exhibition and catalogue from inception to completion. She was joined in the catalogue by Kathleen A. Foster, Stephanie Fox Knappe, Lisa Strong, and William H. Truettner, all of whom have made important contributions to the literature on the artist. The staff at the Nelson-Atkins has attended to the exhibition with its customary fine care. They and their colleagues at The Museum of Fine Arts, Houston, and Philadelphia Museum of Art are to be commended for bringing to life Alfred Jacob Miller's romance with the West.

Marc F. Wilson
Menefee D. and Mary Louise Blackwell Director/CEO
The Nelson-Atkins Museum of Art

Alfred Jacob Miller, *Rocky Formations near the Nebraska or Platte River,* detail (cat. 25)

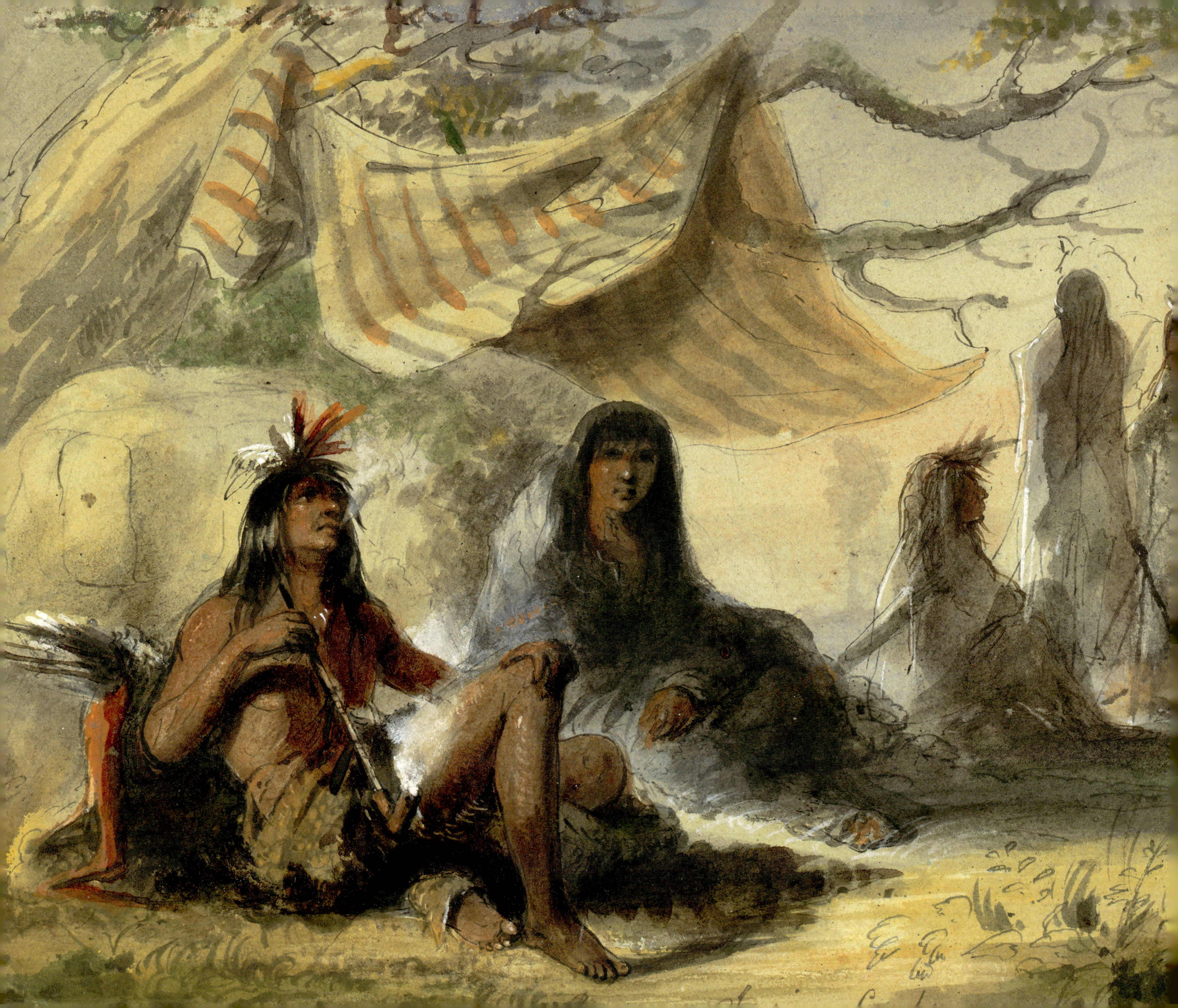

Acknowledgments

Every exhibition has a unique story about its genesis. *Romancing the West: Alfred Jacob Miller in the Bank of America Collection* was born when Allen Blevins, Bank of America's Senior Vice President, Director of Art and Heritage Programs, recognized that the bank's thirty works on paper by Miller deserved serious study and greater visibility and that The Nelson-Atkins Museum of Art was particularly well suited to develop and execute the project. Not only does the Museum have a strong commitment to American art, it also is located in the neighborhood from which Miller and his patron, William Drummond Stewart, launched their trip west in 1837. Additionally, it is in the state where these pictures have resided since 1947, when Boatmen's Bank, now part of Bank of America, acquired the paintings from the artist's family. The Museum welcomed the opportunity to organize an exhibition that had local roots and so seamlessly connected to its mission of displaying the finest visual art, providing greater understanding and enjoyment of the arts for our community, and contributing to art historical scholarship.

We are deeply grateful for the bank's generous support, including the loans from its collection. In addition to Allen Blevins, we also thank Bank of America's helpful team for the project, especially Jeanne Cahill Steiner as well as Lillian Lambrechts, Mary Edith Alexander, Pamela Sak, Heidi Strassner, Toni Eldreth, Shaun McGarry, Brent Prater, and Lisa Lieb.

Alfred Jacob Miller, *Pawnee Indian Camp*, detail (cat. 21)

Our good friends Spence Heddens, Bank of America President in Kansas City, and Linda Lenza, Bank of America Senior Vice President of Corporate Social Responsibility, have championed our endeavors all along the way and ensured our community will enjoy a variety of programs associated with the exhibition.

I could not have asked for better scholarly partners in this project. Kathleen A. Foster, Robert L. McNeil, Jr., Senior Curator of American Art and Director, Center for American Art, Philadelphia Museum of Art; Lisa Strong, independent curator; William H. Truettner, Senior Curator, Smithsonian American Art Museum; and Stephanie Fox Knappe, Assistant Curator of American Art, The Nelson-Atkins Museum of Art, have shared unselfishly their wide-ranging expertise, finely tuned critical eyes, keen insights, and good humor. Their thoughtful contributions to this catalogue expand considerably the foundational writings on the artist by Bernard DeVoto, Marvin Ross, Joan Troccoli, and Ron Tyler as well as Strong's previous scholarship on Miller, on which all of our work has depended. The project was greatly enriched by the careful technical examinations performed by Nancy Heugh, Heugh-Edmondson Conservation Services, Kansas City. Looking closely at Miller's art on paper has revealed previously unknown complexities of his working method. We are also grateful for Heugh-Edmondson's sensitive conservation of many of the works.

The authors depended on many individuals and institutions for information and assistance. For their generous responses, we are grateful to Charles B. Greifenstein, American Philosophical Society, Philadelphia; Jana Hill, Lacey Imbert, Trang Nguyen, and Ron Tyler, Amon Carter Museum, Fort Worth; Anne Marie Menta, George Miles, and Eva Wrightson, Beinecke Rare Book and Manuscript Library, Yale University, New Haven; Maria Murguia-Harding, The Bridgeman Art Library International Ltd, New York; Mindy Besaw and Sean Campbell, Buffalo Bill Historical Center, Cody, Wyoming; Sandra Tansky, C2 Creative, New York; Joan Troccoli, Petrie Institute of Western American Art, Denver Art Museum; Gerald Peters and Debbie White, Alfred Jacob Miller Project, Gerald Peters Gallery; Robert Cross, Michelle Maxwell, and Jeremy Planteen, Gilcrease Museum, Tulsa, Oklahoma; Paula Bailey, The Grosvenor Estate, Chester, England; Andrew Harrison, The Alan Mason Chesney Medical Archives, The Johns Hopkins Medical Institutions, Baltimore; Tom Edmondson, Heugh-Edmondson Conservation Services, Kansas City; Louise Brownell, Jenny Ferretti, and Francis P. O'Neill, Maryland Historical Society, Baltimore; Mr. and Mrs. Decatur H. Miller; Victoire Autajon, Musée Calvet, Avignon, France; Wesley Dunn, Museum of Indian Culture, Allentown, Pennsylvania; Gina Garden, Museum of Nebraska Art, Kearney; Lizanne Garrett Reger, National Portrait Gallery, Smithsonian Institution, Washington, D.C.; John DeFeo and Alex Morganti, New Britain Museum of American Art, Connecticut; Stephan Saks, Rare Books Division, The New York Public Library; Geinette Godward, Public Archives of Canada, Ottawa; Genevieve Ellerbee, Sheldon Museum of Art, University of Nebraska–Lincoln; Richard Sorenso, Smithsonian American Art Museum, Washington, D.C.; Mary Vesty, Stark Museum of Art, Orange, Texas; Peter Nabokov, Department of World Arts and Culture, University of California, Los Angeles; Jim Deagon, American Heritage Center, University of Wyoming, Laramie; Ruth Bowler, Betsy Dahl, Liz Flood, Joy Peterson Heyrman, William R. Johnston, and Elissa O'Loughlin, The Walters Art Museum, Baltimore; and Colleen E. Curry, Yellowstone National Park, Wyoming.

We are delighted that the exhibition will be seen in both Houston and Philadelphia. Emily Ballew Neff, Curator of American Painting and Sculpture at The Museum of Fine Arts, Houston, and Kathleen A. Foster at the Philadelphia Museum of Art are to be thanked for their collaborative spirits and careful shepherding of the exhibition in their respective institutions. In Houston we are also grateful to Peter Marzio, Director; Karen Vetter, Chief Administrator, Exhibitions & Curatorial, as well as Julie Bakke, Gwendolyn H. Goffe, Willard Holmes, and Amy Purvis. In Philadelphia we appreciate the commitment of Timothy Rub, The George D. Widener Director and Chief Executive Officer; and Suzi Wells and Zoe Kahr, Director and Assistant Director of Special Exhibition Planning, along with both museums' dedicated staffs of educators, registrars, art handlers, and designers.

It is a special pleasure to acknowledge my colleagues at The Nelson-Atkins Museum of Art, all of whom give each exhibition their full attention. I greatly appreciate the constant support of Marc Wilson, Menefee D. and Mary Louise Blackwell Director/CEO. In the American Art department, I am especially grateful to Stephanie Fox Knappe as well as Betts Coup, Project Assistant, and former staff members Randall Griffey, Ann Morganthaler, Jillian Murphy, and Erin Olm-Shipman for their steadfast assistance. Simon Kelly, Associate Curator of European Painting and Sculpture; Ian Kennedy, Louis L. and Adelaide C. Ward Curator of European Painting and Sculpture; and especially Gaylord Torrence, Fred and Virginia Merrill Senior Curator of American Indian Art, provided lively conversation regarding influences on Miller and his depiction of American Indians. Cindy Cart, Curator of Exhibition Management, has adeptly attended to the mechanics of the exhibition, and Michele Boeckholt, Beth Byers, Amber Mills, Susan Patterson, and Clint Paugh of our Design Department have guaranteed that the installation and related exhibition materials beautifully reflect the spirit of Miller's art. Angela Bell-Morris, Christine Droll, Ann Erbacher, and Julie Mattsson in our Registrar's office; John Laney, Mark Milani, and Julia Stroud, art handlers; and Elisabeth Batchelor and Steve Bonham in our conservation lab have made sure the art is well cared for at every stage of the project. John Lamberton and Lou Meluso have ensured the photographic images accurately represent Miller's art. Emily Black, Adam Johnson, Melissa Kleindl, Helen Meyer, Christine Minkler, and Sarah Hyde Schmiedeler have generously collaborated on the educational materials and programs accompanying the exhibition. Marilyn Carbonell, Karen Harrell, Zachary Meek, Stacey Sherman, Mona Vassos, Roberta Wagener, and Jeffrey Weidman provided library services and reproduction requests with their usual speed and collegiality. Randy Attwood, Shannon Stone, and Toni Wood have ensured that news of the exhibition has reached our community and beyond. I also appreciate the assistance of Karen Christiansen, Chief Operating Officer; Janet Mark, Manager of Corporate Development, and our colleagues in our external affairs office; Jennifer Byers, Department Assistant, American Indian Art; Harland Hunt, Assistant Director, Finance; Kerry Peak, Manager, Donor and Information Services; Mark Zimmerman, Director, Administration; and former staff members Hal Prestwood and Deborah Emont Scott.

Finally, I am ever grateful to Fronia W. Simpson, who edited this volume with her customary fine wordsmithing, grace, and wit. The handsome design of this catalogue is the result of the considerable talent of Patrick Dooley, Professor of Design, University of Kansas. Marquand Books has adeptly managed the book's production under the watchful eyes of Sara Billups, Jeremy Linden, Adrian Lucia, Keryn Means, Brynn Warriner, and freelancer Marie Weiler.

Margaret C. Conrads
Samuel Sosland Senior Curator of American Art
The Nelson-Atkins Museum of Art

In early 1837 Alfred Jacob Miller was asked to join William Drummond Stewart on an expedition to the Rocky Mountains. In late April Miller met Stewart in St. Louis, Missouri, but their journey truly began in Westport, the premier jumping-off site for travels west, and which today is surrounded by Kansas City. The first leg of the journey was a five-week trek to Fort Laramie, at the confluence of the Laramie and North Fork of the Platte rivers. The caravan departed Fort Laramie about 27 June, arriving on 18 July at the fur traders' rendezvous already under way on Horse Creek in the Green River valley in present-day Wyoming. The rendezvous is said to have concluded sometime between 5 and 10 August, but Stewart and his party had left before then for the Wind River Mountains, where they camped, hunted, and fished for several weeks at the headwaters of the New Fork River. Miller was back in New Orleans, returning via St. Louis, by the early autumn.

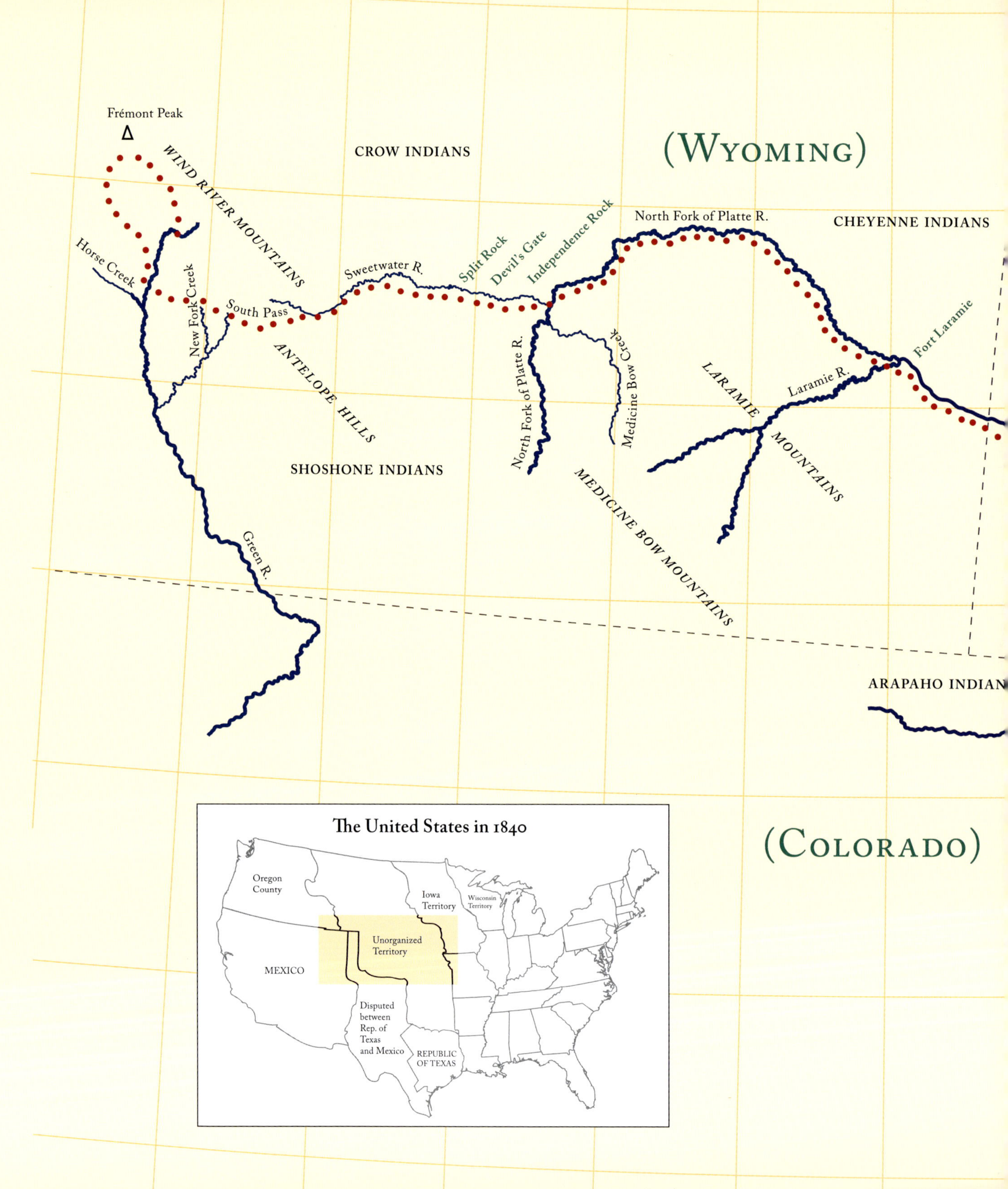

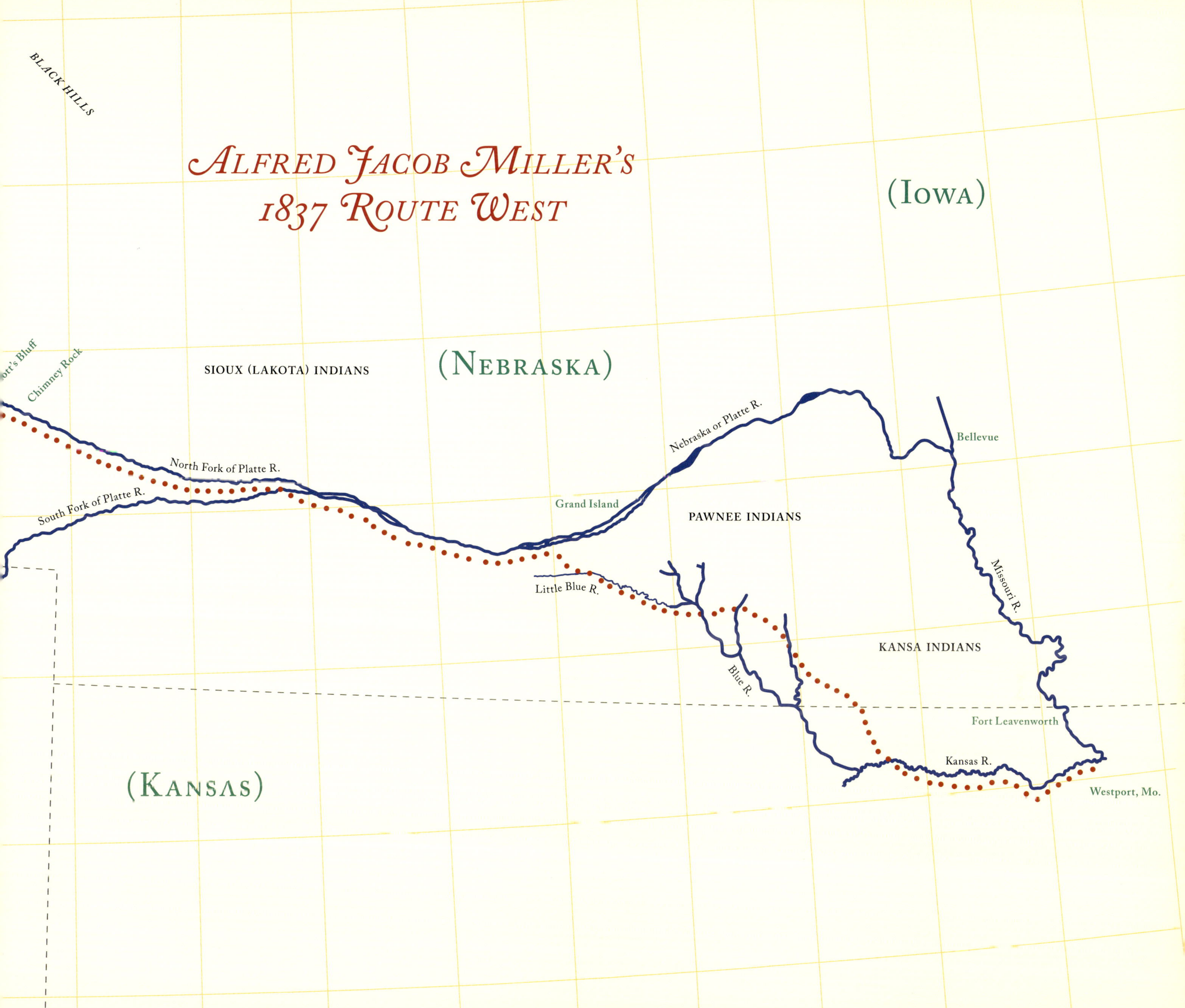

Alfred Jacob Miller's
1837 Route West
Black Hills
(Iowa)
(Nebraska)
(Kansas)
Sioux (Lakota) Indians
Pawnee Indians
Kansa Indians
Chimney Rock
North Fork of Platte R.
South Fork of Platte R.
Nebraska or Platte R.
Grand Island
Bellevue
Little Blue R.
Blue R.
Missouri R.
Fort Leavenworth
Kansas R.
Westport, Mo.

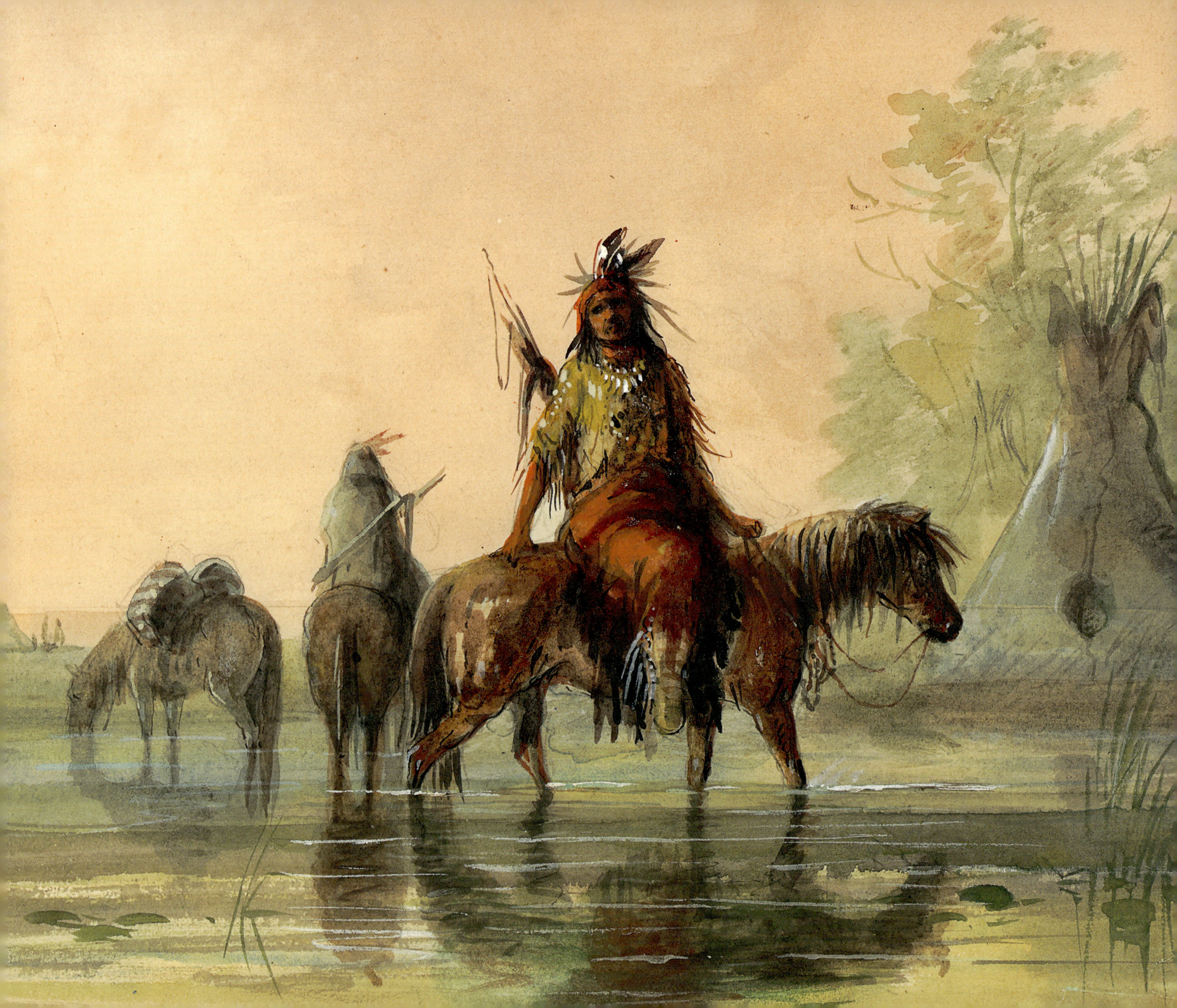

Locating Alfred Jacob Miller's West

WILLIAM H. TRUETTNER

LONG AFTER THE WORK OF GEORGE CATLIN AND KARL BODMER HAD EARNED FROM SCHOLARS AND COLLECTORS A MEASURE OF recognition, Alfred Jacob Miller's numerous watercolors and paintings of the West lay relatively unknown in private collections, mainly in Baltimore, Miller's hometown, and at Murthly Castle in Scotland, the residence of Miller's major patron, Sir William Drummond Stewart. To some extent, the difference is explained by the circumstances that led to the formation of the first two collections: Catlin went west on his own in the 1830s to create a visual and written account of what he considered a vanishing race—some forty-eight tribes of Indians, then located on remote stretches of the Great Plains and the eastern slopes of the Rocky Mountains. Catlin's prediction of doom, however, was not necessarily shared by others of that time. Or perhaps it's safer to say that it was not uppermost in the minds of the few white observers who preceded or immediately followed him through the same territory—explorers, fur trappers, and an occasional missionary. Most of them seemed to think that these same tribes, especially those that lived along or near the Upper Missouri River, were, if not flourishing, still decades away from having to contest white control over their homelands. But Catlin, raised on the border of New York State and Pennsylvania and familiar with the steady pressure to remove remnants of the Iroquois and Delaware from that area during the early decades of the republic, was perhaps more farsighted than most. He saw Upper Missouri tribes threatened by impending westward expansion long before others did.

Bodmer, a Swiss artist, with little or no knowledge of the American West, and with a less inquiring mind than Catlin's, was in the employ of a German prince, Maximilian von Wied-Neuwied, a dedicated amateur scientist keen to test his theories about the social mobility of "primitive" peoples in the Americas. If Bodmer's role was secondary to that of Maximilian, it was, in other ways, a match made in heaven, with Bodmer quickly and skillfully adapting to Maximilian's program while the two traveled up and back down the Missouri River in 1833–34, spending the winter at the Mandan village. What Maximilian most wanted to know about Upper Missouri Indians was not necessarily how soon they would be subject to expansionary pressure but how to gauge their anthropological status—whether they were evolving or devolving in their remote wilderness circumstances. Could they move up the ladder of human development (at the top of which was Western European culture), or would such colorful tribes as the Mandan, Sioux, Assiniboine, Blackfoot, and Crow turn out to be static societies, permanently underdeveloped or even degenerating? Were they, in effect, a seed planted long ago that had failed to generate progressively stronger offspring?[1]

Despite somewhat different objectives, Catlin and Bodmer-Maximilian followed similar field programs. At the heart of each was a

Alfred Jacob Miller, *Indian Village,* detail (cat. 17)

deep concern for scientific inquiry, best understood in today's terms as a passion for describing and cataloguing the salient characteristics of the numerous tribes they encountered. In doing so, they would loosely follow the Linnaean system, which had previously been applied to flora and fauna in the West (on the Long expedition, 1819–20, for example) but not necessarily to Indian life on the Great Plains. Ethnography, along with carefully detailed field notes, would thus play a major role in the artistic efforts of Catlin and Bodmer. The result—the inevitable summary of findings—would be turned into elaborately illustrated publications, both to make the observations of the two parties available to a wider audience and to help offset the cost of their travels. One might even say that publication of such material was predetermined, so basic was it to the scientific protocol that had led Catlin and Bodmer to Indian country to begin with.

The format in which such publications were issued at the time was almost always as illustrated travelogues. (Alexander von Humboldt's travel journals, published 1805–34, and Darwin's *Voyage of the Beagle*, 1839, were the models.) Yet there were differences; each author's summary was to some extent a reflection of method and mission. Catlin preferred a rambling journalistic style, replete with anecdotes, miscellany, and a fair amount of truth-stretching. For all his faults, however, he produced a landmark two-volume account of his travels, *Letters and Notes on the Manners, Customs, and Condition of the North American Indians* (1841). Maximilian, as might be expected, was a more concise reporter: his publication, entitled *Travels in the Interior of North America in the Years 1832 to 1834*, reads like a scientific journal. Published originally in German in 1839–41 (with beautifully hand-tinted plates), and in English and French in 1843, none of the editions circulated widely in midcentury Europe or the United States (not nearly as widely, for example, as Catlin's *Letters and Notes*). But Maximilian's *Travels* got a small boost when it was included as volumes 22–25 of Reuben Gold Thwaites's comprehensive *Early Western Travels*, published in 1906.

One could argue, of course, that neither of these publications prevented the work of Catlin and Bodmer from dropping into relative obscurity during the late nineteenth and early twentieth centuries; the West the public was enthralled with during those years was a Wild West, created by such legendary figures as Theodore Roosevelt, Buffalo Bill, and the artists Frederic Remington and Charles M. Russell. The West of the 1830s was seen mostly through their eyes; thus, it was considered a distant warm-up for the more vivid cowboy-and-Indian West that followed. Yet the work of Catlin and Bodmer managed to stay alive among art and history specialists through the first half of the twentieth century. Then, from 1954 to 1984, it came roaring back, with major exhibitions at the Smithsonian Institution and, after 1962, those organized by the Joslyn Art Museum.[2]

Miller, by contrast, was not as preoccupied with scientific illustration as Catlin or Bodmer, nor did Stewart, his patron, care much for a publication that would gather and highlight truly memorable scenes of the mountain-man West of the 1830s. Lacking a channel to a potential audience, Miller's work suffered almost total neglect until 1947, when Bernard DeVoto, historian, critic, and son of the New West (he was born in Ogden, Utah, in 1903), published *Across the Wide Missouri*, his widely acclaimed study of the fur trade.[3] The book featured numerous Miller watercolors (along with a few works by Catlin and Bodmer) as an imaginative sidebar to the equally compelling story DeVoto told, almost as a first-person narrative. Most of the watercolors came from Mae Reed Porter, an aspiring Miller collector and scholar, and resident of Kansas City, who had purchased the watercolors from the artist's family in Baltimore, where they had quietly passed down through several generations. They were rarely shown even at local exhibitions.[4]

Just how much did DeVoto see Miller's watercolors as a visual complement to his own account of the fur trade? On the surface, DeVoto seems to have accepted them as a fairly accurate (if sometimes "Romantic") version of his detailed description of the Rocky Mountain

West in the 1830s—indeed he called them (along with works by Catlin and Bodmer) "The Look of the West in the 1830s."[5] And he delighted in Miller's occasional depiction of legendary fur trade characters, such as Jim Bridger, who appeared at the 1837 fur trade rendezvous (something like a trade fair) wearing an ancient suit of armor (fig. 1).[6] But DeVoto's interest in Miller seems to have gone well beyond the artist's supposedly truthful illustrations of fur trade activities; what apparently also impressed DeVoto was the way Miller pictured pioneering accounts of wilderness enterprise, such as a trapper's lonely contest to win from nature an independent livelihood (see cat. 5). And Miller, like DeVoto, was a compelling storyteller. Most subjects painted by Miller on the 1837 trip (and later) have an implied chronology: one could almost arrange the album of watercolors he did for his patron Stewart, who displayed it at Murthly Castle as a coffee-table memoir of his western adventures, or those in a similar series commissioned in 1858 by William T. Walters, a Baltimore collector, as frames in a moving narrative, not unlike the colorful sequence of descriptions that formed the basis of DeVoto's own literary style. Characters, events, and places parade across DeVoto's pages as a formidable accumulation of facts and details, tightly woven into an extended human drama.

If we can assume, then, that the subject and style of Miller's work attracted DeVoto—caused him to recognize what one might call an affinity of interests—can we go on to link this to an Old West that DeVoto was trying to resuscitate in 1947, the year *Across the Wide Missouri* was published? The one apparent answer is that DeVoto was seeing Miller's image bank as the visual equivalent of firsthand accounts of mountain men that DeVoto had read in preparation for writing his book. What Miller had pictured, in other words, was a West DeVoto longed to see embodied in the makeup of post–World War II America. After all, the nation had entered a war that the Allies were on the verge of losing and turned the tide. Some part of that will to survive, DeVoto believed, had ultimately come from its western adventure—from a lot of old trappers,

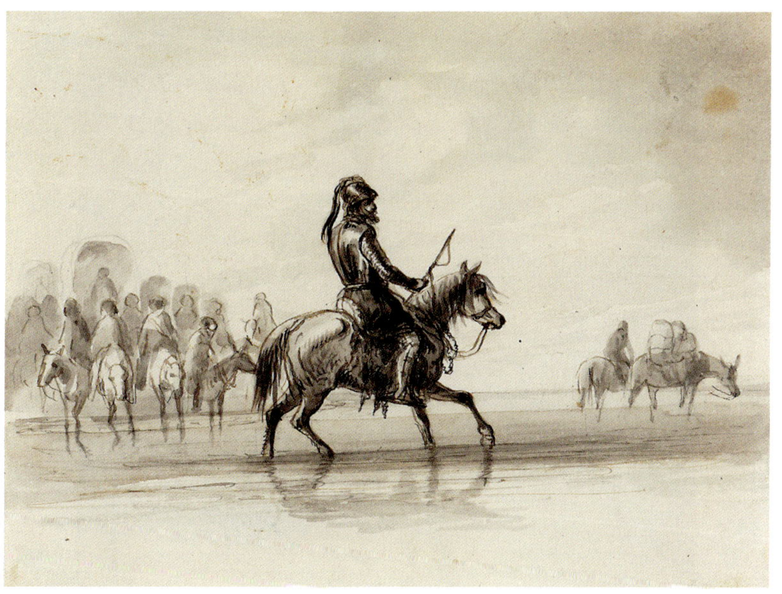

FIGURE 1. Alfred Jacob Miller, *Jim Bridger, in a Suit of English Armor*, n.d. Pen and ink and wash on paper, 5¾ × 7¾ in. (14.6 × 19.7 cm). Joslyn Art Museum, Omaha, Nebraska, InterNorth Art Foundation Collection

for example, who had often faced overwhelming odds but had never given up, never surrendered their commitment to living or dying on their own terms. One can almost hear DeVoto saying, Let the nation show the same determination. If this sounds a bit too strong, one has only to thumb the pages of *Across the Wide Missouri* to recognize DeVoto's deep convictions about nationhood, realized in the form of trappers whose spirit and courage had been nourished in the western mountain wilderness. On a lesser scale, with a disposition not quite as morally reassuring as that of white men, were the Indian inhabitants of the same landscape. Yet Miller was seemingly reluctant to represent his Indians as fully realized Others, while Catlin and Bodmer did so with less hesitation. Again, science surely accounts for some of the difference. Despite the willingness of the latter two artists to study and promote Indian life, and to recognize

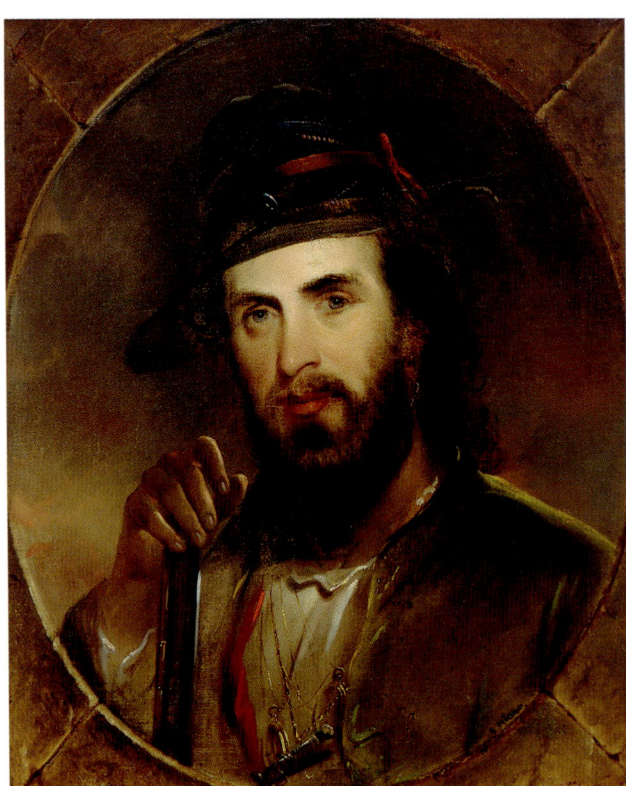

FIGURE 2. Alfred Jacob Miller, *Portrait of Captain Joseph Reddeford Walker*, n.d. Oil on canvas, 23⅜ × 19½ in. (59.4 × 49.5 cm). Joslyn Art Museum, Omaha, Nebraska

the sublime aspect of Upper Missouri topography, the western world they represented seems more rooted in the anthropological codes of the East than in the freewheeling, mountain-man culture of the West in the 1830s. Was Miller's West therefore more inspirational to DeVoto? One gathers as much from the selection of works DeVoto illustrated. Miller's work is not only more "on subject" but is also a more evocative national model on which DeVoto could superimpose his hopes for a vigorous and resourceful post–World War II America.[7]

The Fur Trade West

Such comparisons bring us back to the core question of this essay. How do we reconstitute Alfred Jacob Miller's West, or, more generally, how do we deal with a succession of Wests that historians have constructed over the years, especially those in more recent times? We might begin with a few direct questions. How much was known about Rocky Mountain geography in the 1830s; who were the principal white men and Indian tribes involved in the fur trade; how did the trade operate, both in the field and as a national industry; how did it affect the concurrent pace of westward expansion; and how can we judge the accuracy of Miller's painted western world? The last question perhaps touches on all the others. Was the West of the 1830s a series of heroic encounters between man and nature (or between white men and Indians) that Miller and DeVoto describe, or was there a more everyday West, characterized by subsistence-level activities in which mountain men dealt with nature, geography, native peoples, and the business of fur trapping in a more unremarkable and entrepreneurial way? What comes down to us, of course, is more of the former than the latter: accounts from the journals of the trappers themselves reveal that they were inclined to self-style their rugged existence. At the same time, they *were* loners, men who preferred a solitary life, roaming the mountains as "free" trappers or on behalf of fur trade principals, such as Manuel Lisa, William H. Ashley, Jim Bridger, Joseph Reddeford Walker (fig. 2), Jedediah Strong Smith, William Sublette, and Kit Carson. But we must also probe at another level: do these accounts, varied as they may be, ever really match Miller's description of the people and places he recorded in the series of watercolors done during and after his trip west with Stewart? Is Miller's West mostly in the mind's eye, a fabulous invention that art historians in more recent times have proposed as an Arcadia in which heroic trappers mixed with "noble red men," the latter more often referred to as exotics than real Indians?[8]

The answer, of course, is that history cannot stay alive as either invented image or relentlessly factual narrative; it must draw carefully from both sides. If Miller's West has a certain fantasy atmosphere, it is also, as Lisa Strong reminds us, a West conjured by Miller (along with Stewart, and a succession of later historians like DeVoto) with some very real objectives in mind.[9] That tells us, in turn, that we should first try to see Miller's West in context, a West that features Miller and/or DeVoto as principal narrators, true, but also as lesser figures on a much larger regional stage. The time, the decade of the 1830s, culminates in the 1837 fur trappers' rendezvous in the Wind River Mountains, which Miller attended with his patron, Stewart. The place, the eastern slopes and river valleys of the Rocky Mountains, extends from as far north as the forty-ninth parallel (not yet an official boundary separating the United States and Canada), south to Taos and the Mexican frontier, in present-day northern New Mexico. Within that area lived the greatest number of marketable, fur-bearing animals (especially beaver) anywhere in the world. Moreover, the fur trade was still a principal engine in the United States economy, and would be for another decade. But fur trappers, it turns out, were not only preoccupied with trapping; they were also restless explorers who by the end of the 1830s had crossed the mountains to Oregon and California, in some cases following trails more by instinct than instruction. Alta (or Upper) California, as it was called, still belonged to Spain, and Oregon was more under the control of Britain than the United States, even though in 1803 John Jacob Astor had launched his Pacific Fur Company, a short-lived effort to establish a trade depot at the mouth of the Columbia River, from which he hoped to ship furs both around Cape Horn to the East Coast and west to Canton, where wealthy Chinese would use them to trim their robes.

The most frequently traveled routes leading west at this time were up the Missouri River, provided that hostile tribes along the way allowed river traffic to pass, and along the trails that proceeded west from Independence, Missouri, at first following the Platte River for hundreds of miles and then branching north, crossing the continental divide at South Pass in present-day Wyoming. From there one could carry on to Oregon or California, through lesser ranges that by the 1830s were an additional trapper's heaven. Lewis and Clark had more or less previewed this later exploration. Assisted initially by the young Shoshone mother Sacagawea, they crossed the northern Rockies, then (on foot and in canoes) made their way along the Snake River to the upper reaches of the Columbia. A long float down the Columbia brought them to the river's mouth, where they spent the damp, cold winter of 1804–5. But they were by no means the first to travel the Upper Missouri route to the Pacific, or to investigate the surrounding fur country. On the return trip to St. Louis, after Clark rejoined Lewis at the confluence of the Missouri and Yellowstone rivers, they passed "not fewer" than eleven parties that had, for several years, been traveling the same route into the mountains.[10]

One of our great misconceptions about the pre–Lewis and Clark West is that we assume it was a forgotten wilderness until they "discovered" it. Moreover, we seemingly will it to be that way, so that we can imagine it as virgin territory, empty of white men, inhabited only by primitive tribes of Indians.[11] Thus, it has become a tabula rasa on which we seek to imprint the last great phase of national expansion. History tells us, however (more so now than ever before), that for a century before the 1830s, the Missouri had been the principal highway and trade route to the West, servicing tribes who lived along or near the river and a vanguard of white men, mostly trappers, who were indeed the first of their kind to plunge solo into the wilderness, with very little of the corporate support that would back trappers in the 1830s. Miller's trip west with Stewart in 1837 is a good example of how times had changed, how travel to the fur country had become less of a hardship. In *Departure of the Caravan at Sunrise* (cat. 1), for example, Stewart's equipment train is shown stretching to a far-off horizon. And no wonder. All told, his party consisted of forty-five mounted men, numerous extra horses, pack animals, and twenty-two wagons, over which the Scotsman (who as a

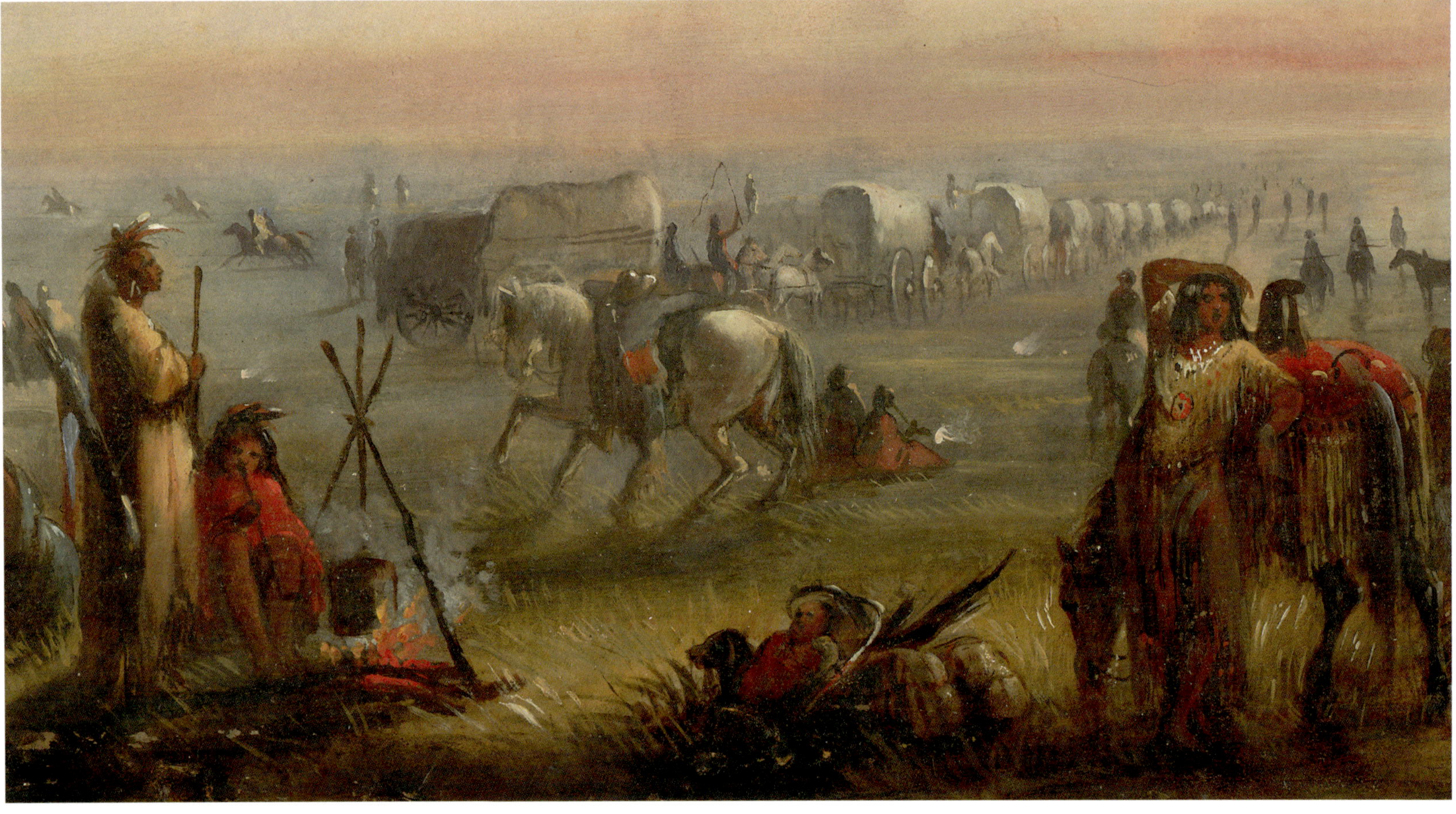

Alfred Jacob Miller, *Departure of the Caravan at Sunrise,* detail (cat. 1)

young lieutenant had fought with Wellington at Waterloo), ruled day and night with military precision.[12] The route west Stewart chose was fairly tame (perhaps by necessity); for two-thirds of the way he more or less followed the nascent Oregon Trail. When the party reached the Wind River Mountains and proceeded up the Green River, however, the trail grew rough and steep. Their destination was a mountain valley in which surrounding native tribes and numerous itinerant trappers, both eager to unload a year's accumulation of beaver pelts, came together on temporarily sociable, if not quite friendly, terms.

Gatherings such as the 1837 rendezvous, not uncommon in the intermountain West of the 1830s, encourage us to think of such events as more or less multicultural, shared as a matter of convenience by both Indians and white men, although not in equal numbers. Beyond the campfires of the rendezvous, the former greatly outnumbered the latter. Hence, the first concern of the trappers was to strike a bargain with neighboring tribes. Gifts were offered by some in exchange for access to native trapping grounds; others, so inclined, would take an Indian wife, whether or not there was another back home. In either case, the "bargains" probably also entailed sharing the proceeds from the annual rendezvous. Furs, the basic currency at these events, were exchanged for supplies that would enable free trappers, company men, or various groups of Indians to continue gathering furs through the following winter. What each drew from St. Louis supply wagons was, of course, somewhat different. The trappers acquired food staples, camp equipment, and sometimes alcohol (which usually didn't last the duration of the rendezvous), enough for a subsistence livelihood, plus items for occasional trades with Indian hosts. The Indians, many of whom lived in more comfortable circumstances than the trappers, were interested in English rifles, metal cook pots, and colorful fabrics and beads—items that over time made them dependent on a white economy, despite the hostility with which many tribes observed the increasing presence of white men in their world.

If Miller's visit to the 1837 rendezvous was his sole western experience, it was not so with Stewart. The latter had traveled extensively up and down the Rockies during the four years that preceded the 1837 rendezvous, following fur trade activities as far north and west as Astoria, at the mouth of the Columbia River, and as far south as Taos. He apparently also led groups of trappers on an interim basis, for one company or another, but his principal tie was with Sublette and Campbell, a St. Louis firm in which he may have had a stake.[13] In 1843 Stewart returned for his last western extravaganza, having by then succeeded his brother, who had died a year earlier, to the family seat at Murthly Castle.

Stewart's penchant for exploring the West was shared by others in the fur trade. In addition to crisscrossing the Rocky Mountains numerous times, Jedediah Strong Smith took a side trip over the Sierra Nevada range in 1826–27, the first American to reach the California coast via an overland route. The Santa Fe Trail had opened a few years earlier, marking a significant increase in trade with northern Mexico. At the same time, the hide and tallow trade, vividly described by Richard Henry Dana in *Two Years before the Mast* (1840), was flourishing along the coast of Upper California. No less remarkable was the pace of overland travel to Oregon. In 1843, the same year as Stewart's last trip west, 875 migrants crossed the Rockies in covered wagons, heading for well-advertised farmland in the fertile Willamette Valley.[14] In 1840 the national census revealed that seven million people, or 40 percent of the United States population, lived west of the Appalachians and across the Mississippi.[15] One could argue that settlement of the West over the preceding and following years was a selective process; immense stretches of unoccupied wilderness still remained. But by the time the last of the mountain men died or settled into retirement, most of the area west of the Rockies had been explored, some of it mapped, and even the smaller ranges, connecting valleys, and less-trodden paths were known and named by those who lived in the vicinity. Another decade and they would rise from geographic limbo, taking their rightful place on maps that appeared in newly issued travel guides and government survey reports.

The Indian West

At the same time we revise and extend the white man's West of the 1830s, claiming that it was a more active national space than we might have imagined, we should also look more carefully at the Indian West of Miller's time. Here, though, we encounter other problems. We assume that the history we write today is to some extent based on firsthand reporting and/or original sources and documents. But when addressing Indians, our knowledge of their history is usually once removed, that is, most of it is told by the whites who interacted with them in one way or another, not by the Indians themselves. Few of those white men had ethnographic training or even an ethnographic instinct (Catlin and Bodmer-Maximilian were perhaps the notable exceptions). Lacking such perception, they had a difficult time assessing a society in which beliefs and values differed greatly from their own. More often, they tolerated Indians as necessary accomplices in the fur trade. Through such connections, whites were able to tap into an extraordinary trail network over which Indians had traveled for generations, first on foot, then, after about 1680, on horseback. One need only recall that Lewis and Clark depended on Indian guides to cross the formidable range of mountains that lay between the Missouri River and the upper reaches of the Columbia. Indeed, for all the fighting that went on between the two sides and between the tribes themselves, there seems to have been a clearinghouse that operated above everyday hostile encounters to apprise whites and Indians of how to get on with their not-so-separate lives. One group may have stolen horses from the other the night before, but news continued to circulate and connect the various communities.

To probe further into an Indian West, however, and to avoid the endless replays of bloody encounters, remarkable escapes, and occasional gestures of goodwill and friendship, we must turn to anthropologists (again mostly white) who in recent years have written about tribes involved in the fur trade in the 1830s. A standard assumption about these tribes is that they had occupied more or less permanent villages along the Upper Missouri or across the southern Great Plains for generations, and although they frequently fought among themselves, their home territories were never at stake. This turns out to be not quite true. The disposition of tribes along the Upper Missouri, for example, had been in flux for most of the century preceding Miller's arrival, owing most likely to rapid colonial expansion. As settlement moved inland from the Atlantic coast, tribes were pushed westward, over the Appalachians, either into the Ohio Country or farther south, into the upland valleys of Kentucky and Tennessee. Tribes long resident in the mid-South, such as the Creek and Cherokee, were also affected by white settlement in their area, especially after President Andrew Jackson took office. Refusing to acknowledge a Supreme Court decision that granted the Cherokee sovereignty over lands they owned within the state of Georgia, Jackson ordered a roundup of the tribe in 1838 and forced them to embark on the infamous Trail of Tears, which ended on an arid, marginally productive reservation in eastern Oklahoma.

More germane to Miller's West was the pressure put on the Eastern Sioux and tribes to the west by Indians leaving the Ohio Country and by remnants of the Iroquois Confederacy who followed them, seeking land to replace their former home territory, which had spread across colonial New York from Albany to Buffalo. After the Revolution (which had gone badly for the Iroquois, allies of the British), most Confederacy land had been claimed by the New York State government and sold to white settlers. The Iroquois and other uprooted tribes in the East carried west with them up-to-date rifles supplied to them by the British through most of the eighteenth century. These at first gave them an advantage over the Northern Plains tribes, whose muskets, Spanish cast-offs that had come north through New Mexico, were no match. Rifles or not, it was pressure from the east that prompted the Plains Ojibwa, on the eastern edge of the Great Plains, to move against their neighbors to the west, the Assiniboine and Cree, who in turn supplied rifles to tribes farther upriver, such as the Blackfoot. Even the powerful Sioux moved west during the first half of the eighteenth century, to buffer themselves from neighboring tribes and to take advantage of "global" Indian markets that had opened up among northern tribes engaged in the fur trade.[16] Thus, tribes along the Upper Missouri were shifting, trading, and harassing each other up to and beyond the 1830s, when the U.S. Cavalry began appearing in greater numbers to protect wagon trains and commercial traffic on routes west, which further destabilized the region. The cavalry also encouraged wholesale destruction of the surrounding buffalo herds, the staple of life for most Upper Missouri tribes. As the nature of the conflict changed, Indians ceased fighting each other to band together against the whites, winning an occasional battle but slowly losing a war of attrition.

Even before such hostilities took over the northern Plains, however, certain Upper Missouri tribes were uneasy about white river traffic and white presence in their hunting territories. The Arikara, for example, were likely to direct a fusillade of arrows and bullets at fur company keel boats whenever they came within range. Farther up the river, around Fort Union, where the Yellowstone flows into the Missouri, the Crow were friendly and helpful, allowing trappers to work the streams surrounding their campsites. The Blackfoot, however, the next tribe upriver, were sworn enemies of the Crow and also fought intermittently with other neighbors, such as the Assiniboine and the Cree. Almost on cue for Bodmer and Maximilian was a wild battle they witnessed between the Blackfoot and the Assiniboine, outside the gates of Fort Mackenzie, a fur trade fort at the northernmost extension of their trip up the Missouri. Bodmer restaged the battle in a well-known print (fig. 3) made for Maximilian's publication. Unstable relations between Upper Missouri tribes caused problems not only for the fur trade but also for the explorers who followed Lewis and Clark, whether it was mountain men, the few enterprising settlers who had begun to cross the Rockies in the 1830s, or official exploring parties, such as those headed by Zebulon Pike (1805–6), Stephen H. Long (1819–20), and John C. Frémont (1843–44). The last, an intrepid journey across the Sierra Nevada range to California, eventually landed Frémont at the center of the Bear Flag Revolt, which became the first step toward United States annexation of California.

In addition to monitoring the constant, low-grade warfare between tribes, the government in Washington, especially during the Monroe Administration, when John Quincy Adams was secretary of state (1817–24), was keeping close watch over British traffic south of the forty-ninth parallel, which was challenging the United States' "rightful" ownership of that portion of the Louisiana Purchase. Then as now, treaties were guaranteed by occupation or considerable off-site power, and the United States had only a modest military presence on the Upper Missouri,

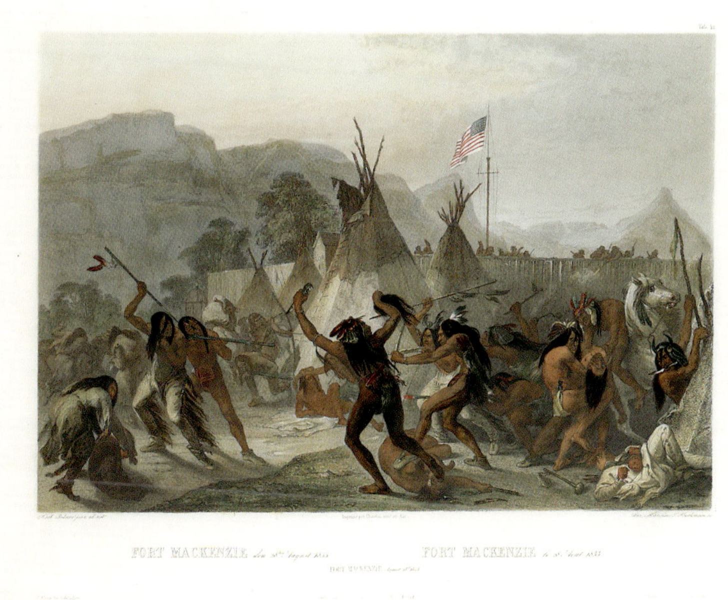

FIGURE 3. After Karl Bodmer, *Fort Mackenzie, August 28th 1833*, c. 1839. Engraving with hand-coloring, 16¼ × 21½ in. (41.3 × 54.6 cm). The Nelson-Atkins Museum of Art, Kansas City, Mo., Gift of Whitney and Betty MacMillan in honor of Estelle and Morton Sosland, 2007.16.4

mostly dispensed by General Clark (of Lewis and Clark) at St. Louis or from Fort Atkinson, near present-day Council Bluffs, Iowa, still far to the south and east of territory frequented by agents of Hudson's Bay, the giant Canadian fur company closely tied to the British government. When a delegation of Osage, a major western tribe that lived seven hundred miles west of St. Louis, visited the Jefferson White House in 1804, the president wrote to Robert Smith, his secretary of the navy, "We shall endeavor to impress [the Osage] . . . not only with our justice and liberality, but with our power . . . because in their quarter, we are miserably weak."[17] Conditions improved somewhat over the next several administrations (John Quincy Adams, Madison, and Monroe); still, each

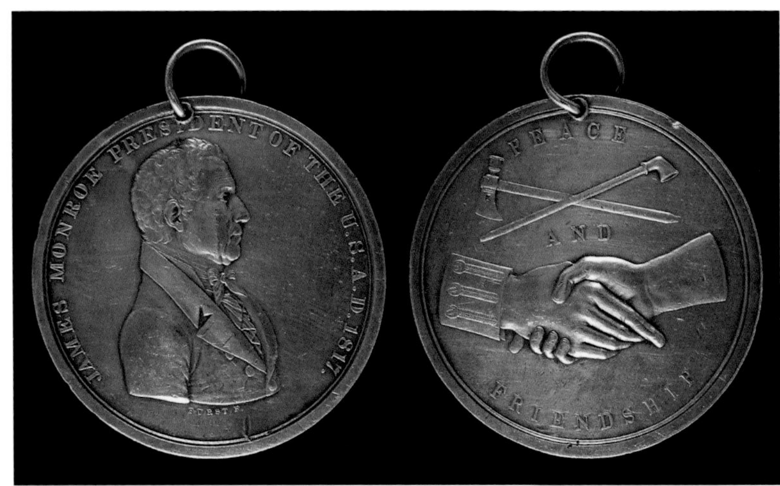

FIGURE 4. Moritz Furst and John Reich, *James Monroe*, recto and verso, 1820. Silver, 2½ in. (6.3 cm) diameter. National Portrait Gallery, Smithsonian Institution; gift of Betty A. and Lloyd G. Schermer, NPG.99.110

of these presidents sanctioned a program that rounded up delegations of Indians from Upper Missouri tribes and brought them to Washington, where they were alternately stroked and intimidated by a finely tuned government program, initiated by Thomas L. McKenney, head of Indian affairs under Monroe. Each Indian visitor went home with a peace medal, on one side of which was an image of the sitting president, while on the other was a sign of friendship (fig. 4). In retrospect, the medals send a deeply ambivalent message. By the time they were dispersed, the balance of power had already begun to shift, with western Indians slowly ceding more and more land to white settlers.

If the Indian population was vanishing, however, Miller and Stewart had nevertheless caught Upper Missouri tribes at a moment when their way of life was still immensely impressive and colorful. One fascinating on-site report from William Marshall Anderson, a lawyer turned mountain man, recounts the flavor of this high moment of Indian life. Present at a camp near the site of the 1834 rendezvous (which Stewart probably attended), Anderson writes,

> *I was very much interested in witnessing the meeting of two friendly parties of Indians to day—A small party of 20 or 30 galloped in sight, whooping, singing and beating their rude drum. At the distance of about a half mile they were met by a gaudily dressed savage handsomely mounted, who was the soldier of the encamped village—they were all halted when he arrived, the leader advanced and after a seeming parley, the soldier returned, and placing himself at the head of a nearly equal number, of the best dressed fellows in the village, advanced on foot to meet the others—When within forty or fifty yards of each other they mutually halted—the horsemen dismounted and disarming themselves placed their weapons on the ground—both sides now slowly advanced in single file, till their leaders met, who took each other by the left hand, their right placed over their hearts—stood at arms length looking one another in the eyes and uttering not a word for about 2 minutes—then passed to the left—till the same silent ceremony was performed successively by all. After the first had become last and the last first, they entered together into the lodges, visitors and friends.*[18]

Even if Anderson exaggerated a detail here and there, he must have witnessed something very close to what he described. Such ritual was, to some extent, consistent with the well-being of Upper Missouri tribes at that time. Buffalo, still abundant on the Great Plains, and deer, found in nearby mountain valleys, supplied robes and hides that Indian women trimmed and decorated with gorgeous bead patterns. From large numbers of horses that ran wild on the plains, Indians selected the best, training them for hunting and warfare (see cat. 26). A variety of game, scarce only during hard winters, supplied them adequately with food. Some tribes supplemented their diet of dried and smoked buffalo meat with produce from small agricultural plots. The Mandans, for example, raised squash, corn, and beans. Other tribes, more heavily invested in the fur trade, acquired manufactured goods – new rifles, cookware, beads, and textiles, which surely raised their lives above subsistence level, if not quite into prosperity. Frequent visits to the forts and trading posts along the Upper Missouri – rustic social centers in their way, where even hostile tribes exchanged goods with one another and with whites – must have also provided moments of peace and stability in an otherwise turbulent existence.

The same year Anderson witnessed the meeting of two friendly tribes in the Wind River Mountains, Catlin was traveling across the southern Great Plains with a contingent of dragoons under the command of Colonel Henry M. Dodge, a veteran of the Black Hawk War. Dodge and his men, on a mission to persuade the Comanche to stop raiding local ranches and traders on the Santa Fe Trail, rode deep into northwestern Oklahoma, where the tribe lived at the base of the Wichita Mountains. As they approached the camp, a lone rider dashed out to meet them, with a display of horsemanship that left Dodge and his officers stunned. That was only the beginning. An equally impressive follow-up by the Comanche reminds one of Anderson's description of Indian ritual farther north in high moments of the 1830s. As Catlin describes the scene (and later pictured it; fig. 5), the lone rider asked Dodge to delay his entrance to the village until the Comanche could offer a suitable welcome. We dismounted for "an hour or so," Catlin writes, while the Indians caught their horses. "At length," he continues,

> *several hundreds of their braves and warriors came out at full speed to welcome us, and forming in a line in front of us, as we were again mounted, presented a formidable and pleasing appearance. As they wheeled their horses, they very rapidly formed in a line, and "dressed" like well-disciplined cavalry. The regiment was drawn up in three columns, with a line formed in front, by Colonel Dodge and his staff . . . my friend Chadwick and I . . . had a fine view of the whole manoeuvre, which was picturesque and thrilling in the extreme.*[19]

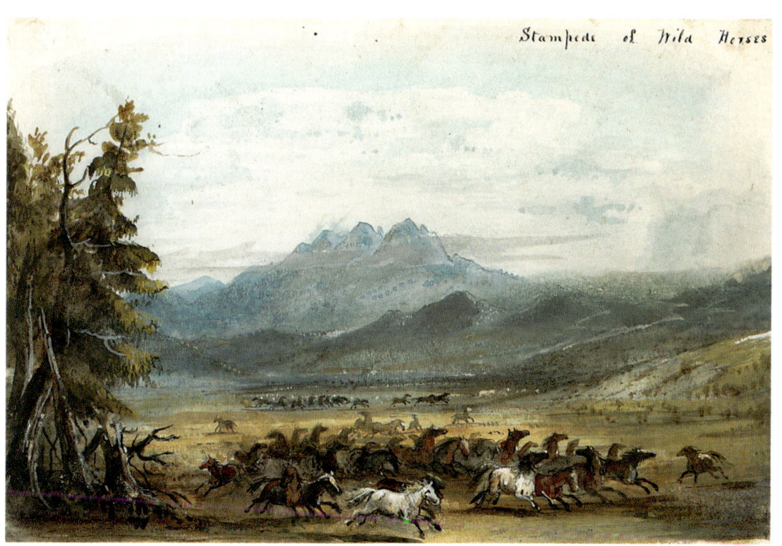

Alfred Jacob Miller, *Stampede of Wild Horses* (cat. 26)

Perhaps the Comanche were only preoccupied with demonstrating their wealth and power, in a manner not dissimilar to the encounter farther north that Anderson relates. But there was also an obvious difference. The face-off Catlin describes was between Indians and white men, an exercise that seemingly lacked the spontaneous interchange between the two groups of Indians Anderson observed. Catlin depicts instead two rigid lines of warriors, drawn up in parade formation, but the composition also turns back to eighteenth-century views of opposing armies preparing for battle. With that in mind, can we say that Catlin, probably quite unintentionally, fixes a moment when the ritual dictating the meeting between the dragoons and the Comanche provides an ominous look into the future? What remains under control inside the picturesque valley where

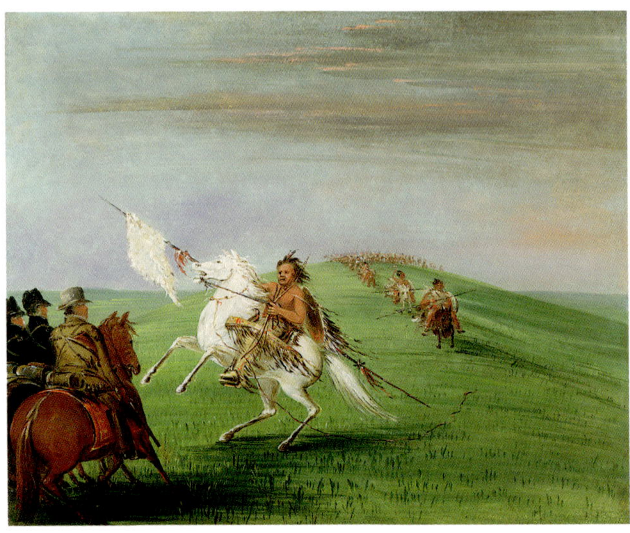

FIGURE 5. George Catlin, *Comanche Meeting the Dragoons*, 1834–35. Oil on canvas, 24⅛ × 29⅛ in. (61.3 × 74 cm). Smithsonian American Art Museum, Gift of Mrs. Joseph Harrison, Jr.

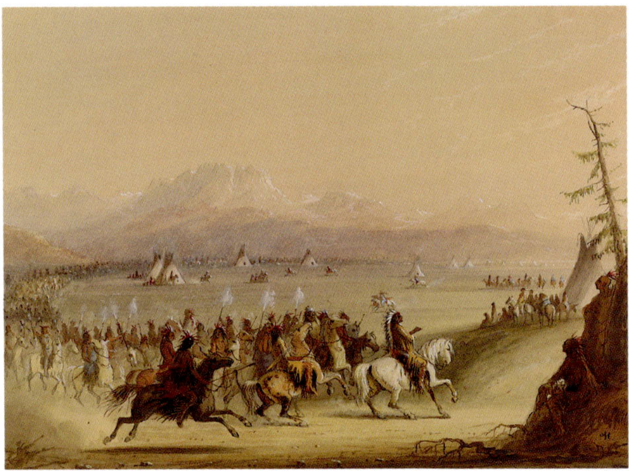

FIGURE 6. Alfred Jacob Miller, *Cavalcade*, 1858–60. Watercolor on paper, 10⅞ × 14 15/16 in. (27.6 × 38 cm). The Walters Art Museum, Baltimore

the two parties meet is not a guarantee of safety outside the valley, where tensions were mounting.

To carry the argument a step further, does the degree of ritual practiced by northern and southern Plains tribes during the 1830s send another signal? Does it represent a moment when their cultures, heavily dependent on spectacle to project regional power, are no longer as secure as they once were? Indeed, if we turn the clock ahead to 1837, only three years after Anderson and Catlin witnessed noteworthy displays of hubris on the part of Plains Indians, and when Miller saw a similarly impressive scene at the fur trade rendezvous (fig. 6), the destruction of Plains culture was already under way. That same year, 90 percent of the Mandan tribe, including the great chief Four Bears, a close friend of Catlin and Bodmer, died in a smallpox epidemic, brought upriver by American Fur Company employees. In the Southwest, the impact of white contact was less abrupt, but by the mid-1830s, white southern farmers and their slaves came to Texas by the thousands, pushing the Comanche farther west and south into Mexico, where they became renegades, wreaking vengeance on those who occupied their former homeland.

All of this takes place outside the frame of Miller's West, of course; his Indians encounter no such reversals of fortune. If they are slowly being disenfranchised by fur trade activities and by subsequent white exploration and settlement, that is not the part of their life Miller wishes to depict. He sees them instead as savages, if not quite innocent, then still deeply a part of an exotic and beautiful world. But with this caveat: they role-play for Miller, who sets them up for Stewart as founding members of the manly club of fur traders and trappers who operate out of St. Louis but are more comfortable in the mountains, living the lives of Indians. Whatever tangled identity this implies, traders and trappers are indeed part of a gendered world, not simply because few white women were involved, but because most of the Indian women who appear in Miller's scenes are either a working subset of the fur trade, fulfilling the role of helpmates (fig. 7), or they are wanton camp followers, to be used or disposed of at will.

The Scenic West

Given these circumstances, one might think that the white males who dominate Miller's West would not be a particularly thoughtful or sensitive group. Yet, individual captions Miller wrote over time to accompany the watercolors done for Walters almost willfully suggest that these mountain men may also have been under the spell of sublime scenery (as well as complementary feelings of retrospection and loss), whether or not they were fully aware of it. Describing one of several pristine lakes set beneath snow-covered peaks in the Wind River range, Miller writes: "Silence reigned supreme over this beautiful sheet of water, only at long intervals broken by the descent of an avalanche, crashing through the trees and among the rocks. As we viewed these lakes, a single line of Keats' occurred to us wherein he says, 'A thing of beauty is a joy forever.'" Or perhaps not forever, if one understands a continuing series of avalanches as an inadvertent reference to the future. When Miller continues, his forecast is chilling but delivered with barely discernible regret: "It would require but a slight stretch of imagination to fancy the myriads of people in the next generation flocking to see these sublime scenes . . . the whirring of car wheels through the 'South Pass' are a foregone conclusion."[20]

Putting aside for the moment Miller's vision of a future West (which he may have regarded as the inevitable consequence of progress), it seems difficult to dismiss the first part of the passage as an exclusive response by Miller to a mountain paradise. Rather, it seems that he is extolling mountain scenery on behalf of mountain men who cannot quite give voice to their own feelings and who were probably ambivalent about proclaiming the merits of what was also an unforgiving wilderness. Joseph Reddeford Walker (see fig. 2), with his self-confident gaze and hat cocked at a fashionable angle, looks like a man who would not be indifferent to his natural surroundings. One can also find, between lines of descriptive prose, an implicit regard for nature in the journals of those

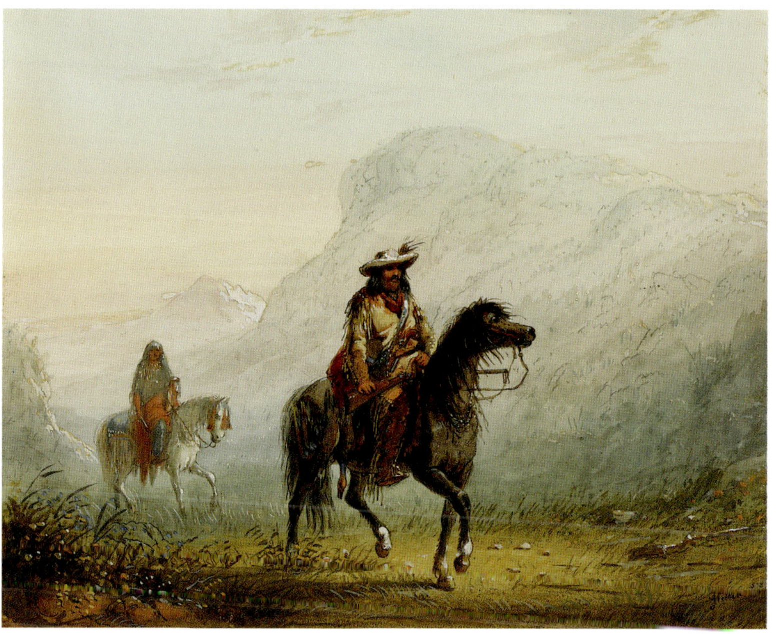

Figure 7. Alfred Jacob Miller, *Bourgeois W——r, and His Squaw*, 1858–60. Watercolor on paper, 9⁵⁄₁₆ × 11¹¹⁄₁₆ in. (23.7 × 29.7 cm). The Walters Art Museum, Baltimore

who took part in the fur trade (although, admittedly, those who kept such journals were probably better educated than the majority of their colleagues). Daniel Potts, for example, a veteran attached to several of William T. Ashley's expeditions, writes from the Big Horn Valley in the middle of July 1826:

> *After crossing [the head of the Sweet Water] . . . we took a more westerly direction over high rolling Prairies to a small branch of a considerable river [known as the Green River] . . . supposed to discharge itself into the Bay of California. This river has a bold running current, 80 or 90 yards wide, and bears a S. E. direction. It falls from the Rocky Mountains in many small rivulets,*

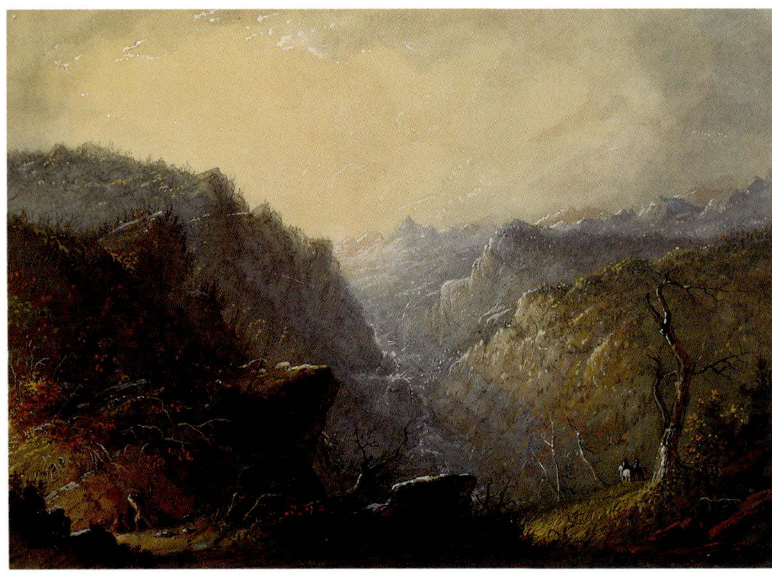

FIGURE 8. Alfred Jacob Miller, *Wild Scenery (Making a Cache)*, 1858–60. Watercolor on paper, 9¼ × 12¹³⁄₁₆ in. (23.5 × 32.5 cm). The Walters Art Museum, Baltimore

> *on which were considerable beaver. This valley, like all the others I have seen in this country, is surrounded by mountains, those to S. W. and N. are covered with eternal snow, near the tops. Columbia Mountain [in the Wind River range], lying N. is the highest I ever saw; and is perhaps the highest in North America [Mount McKinley, then undiscovered, is the highest peak in North America]. It stands rather detached and majestic, beginning abruptly towards the E. and terminating towards N. W. Its tops are the repository of eternal winter. In clear weather its appearance is truly sublime and reflects the brilliancy of the diamond in its various colours. — This mountain gives rise to many streams, the principal are the Yellow Stone and Wind River.*[21]

Potts, understandably, is more concerned with "mapping" the region he is describing than Miller ever was in painting landscapes of similar subjects. The best one can say about Miller's topography is that it bears a generic resemblance to high country in the Wind River Mountains. Miller almost never puts a geographic name on his views (they are more often given vague titles, such as "Lake Scene — Mountain of the Winds"), nor, one suspects, did he even wish to. Stewart was probably more interested in having Miller's mountains outshine anything in Scotland; they were, as far as he was concerned, part of the stage on which his great western adventure was taking place. Hence the backgrounds of such watercolors as *Stampede of Wild Horses* (see cat. 26) are somewhat interchangeable with others that can be found in the Walters collection. None, it should be obvious, is untouched by formulas for recording wild scenery that Miller brought with him from the East. The relationship between landscapes such as *Wild Scenery* (fig. 8) in the Walters collection and works by Thomas Doughty or especially Thomas Cole (fig. 9) that Miller might have seen on exhibit in New York cannot be overlooked, although Doughty and Cole were more likely to take the measure of an actual place than Miller was. Yet one could also claim that Miller's views of the Wind River Mountains would never have achieved such breadth and scale had he not seen the imposing scenery Potts describes in the passage above.

The West Miller painted was not only a panorama of stirring landscapes. More often, his views included Indians as strategic complements to the landscape, as if their thoughts and feelings about nature might be similar to those of the artist. Whether they were or not, Miller recognized the value of Indians, rather than grizzled trappers, in such pictures; the former, he must have assumed, were a less intrusive human presence. More important to the artist (and patron) than landscapes of exacting verisimilitude (like Bodmer's) was conveying to audiences the image of a West that signaled place more obviously than time — a West that could pass as a fabled land, never before witnessed by white men. So instead of white men, Miller staffed such landscapes with Indians. After all, they and their surroundings were the West before white men arrived.

The West Shared by DeVoto and Miller

Perhaps the highest accolade Bernard DeVoto ever received came from his friend Wallace Stegner, whose novels and histories about the West (such as *Angle of Repose* and *Beyond the Hundredth Meridian*) still rank among the best in each category. In a tribute written in 1963, five years after DeVoto's death, Stegner called DeVoto's "grandly conceived" trilogy of western history, consisting of *The Year of Decision, 1846* (1943), *Across the Wide Missouri* (1947), and *The Course of Empire* (1952), worthy successors to books written by the nineteenth-century giants William H. Prescott, George Bancroft, Henry Adams, and Francis Parkman.[22] Would that appraisal hold up today? Probably not, but DeVoto still looms large as an author who influenced subsequent narrative histories of the West. William Goetzmann's Pulitzer Prize–winning *Exploration and Empire* (1966) is written in a similar way, as is Stephen Ambrose's *Undaunted Courage* (1996). All three share a fundamental belief in the nation-shaping, character-building impact of westward expansion on subsequent United States history (a West, in other words, indebted to Frederick Jackson Turner). And all three feature the early exploration of the West as a qualified exercise in imperialism.

DeVoto seems always to have had a soft spot in his heart for the West, although his defense of the region was often mixed with attacks on its insularity and on its perverse willingness to sell itself out to others. At an early age, DeVoto became an indefatigable reader of western history, geography, exploration, and travel, then went off to Harvard, where he gained perspective but never gave up his passion for history as fact.[23] After Harvard, he became a teacher and writer, first in Salt Lake City, then in New York, where in the 1930s he made a name for himself as a critic. In the 1940s he turned to writing history, and in the 1950s he became an ardent conservationist, an outspoken foe of Joseph McCarthy, and a close friend of Adlai Stevenson.

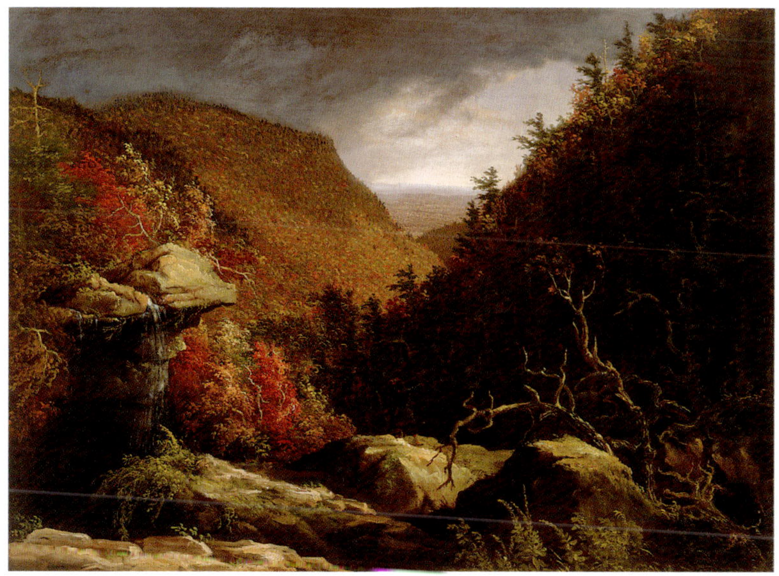

Figure 9. Thomas Cole, *The Clove, Catskills*, c. 1827. Oil on canvas, 25 × 35 in. (63.5 × 88.9 cm). New Britain Museum of American Art, Connecticut

Altogether DeVoto had a remarkable career, but looking back at it often makes one wonder how all the pieces fit together, unless one assumes that many of his later interests, theories, and passions are somehow tied to his formative years in the West. That at least gives us a starting point for his subsequent investigation of the fur trade and his embrace of Miller's art. If both were part of a broader concern, perhaps in this case we can focus more narrowly on his career-long obsession with trying to discover how a new West had evolved from an older West. Or, to tighten up even more, to discover how he could preserve what was solid and enduring about the makeup of the early West, and to discourage the empty rhetoric and stereotypes that had, over time, diminished it. As a New York critic, he had taken on Van Wyck Brooks and others who had

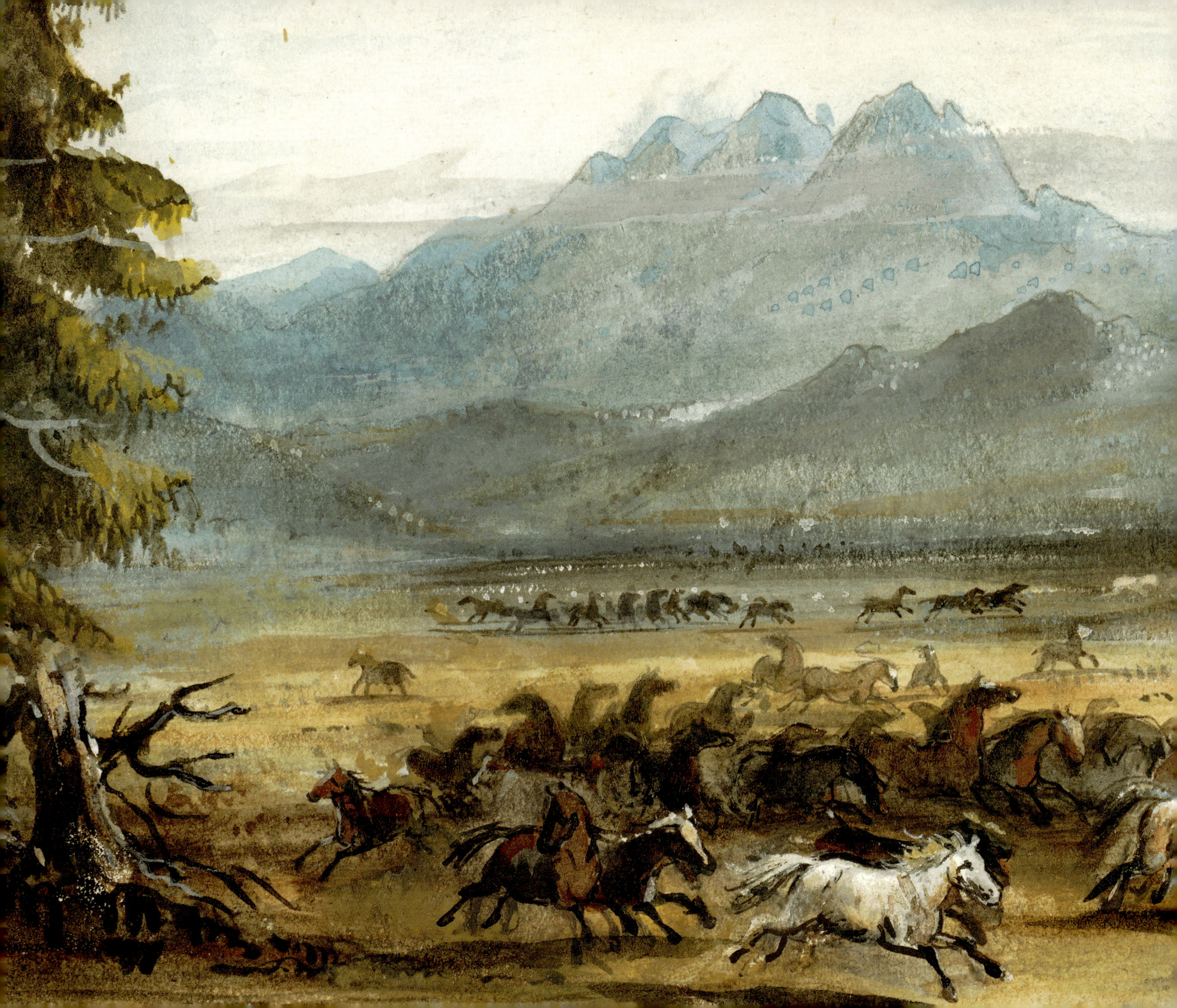

claimed that the average western frontiersman was devoid of culture, sentiment, and feelings—"every good thing" that had come from civilization. DeVoto replied that the frontier was not a person but many different places, in many different stages of development.[24] But he couldn't let it go at that. What he sought was a belief or a theory that might link them, if not totally explain them, and World War II seems to have sharpened his quest. After the war, writing to the historian Catherine Drinker Bowen, he put it this way, addressing not only the era of westward expansion but the whole span of American history:

> *Ours is a story mad with the impossible, it is by chaos out of dream, it began as a dream and has continued as a dream down to our last headlines you read in a newspaper. And of our dream there are two things above all to be said, that only madmen could have dreamed them or would have dared to—and that we have shown a considerable faculty for making them come true.*[25]

Such a vision is born of survival, one might argue, born of a generation that acquired a certain ruthless courage while living through the dark days of World War II. Is that the mind-set DeVoto wished to apply to the mountain men of the 1830s? Equally germane to our search, is that a frame we can also wrap around Miller's West? Which brings us to the real problem: regardless of the unknowns on both sides, DeVoto's West and Miller's West don't quite align, at least from our perspective in 2010. But does their difference create a more complex, multivalent West, one that Miller must have helped fashion for DeVoto, as something more nuanced than the image of testy old mountain men carried forward to 1947? On one side of this difficult equation, we have DeVoto's unexpurgated, tough-minded old West, an example of which he delivers in his disturbingly abrupt account of the death of an old trapper named Bill Williams: "He died as a mountain man should," DeVoto writes, "in an all-out battle with the Sioux, taking enough of them to hell with him to pay his toll."[26] The other side of DeVoto's West, the mad dream somehow realized, is told quite differently in Miller's highly sentimentalized commentary attached to a picture of an Indian camp (see fig. 31) that only obliquely signals the underlying issue. Miller is not quite as ready to dispatch Sioux as DeVoto, but he realizes what is in store for them. He works through the problem visually in a way that might have softened DeVoto's bluster, made him understand the transition from one West to another, not as a dream realized in violence, but as a message conveyed through artistic sleight-of-hand. Thus, we might say that Miller threw DeVoto a lifeline—or, to put it more generously, showed DeVoto a way of dealing with historical change that absolved him from hammering it home with brutal accounts of life in the old West. "At no distant date," Miller remarks, seemingly with the intent of rendering less permanent the Indian camp he pictures, "the mountains and the prairies of the Far West will no longer be a place of refuge from the onward march of civilization, & . . . will the last Indian stand upon the verge of the Pacific seas and his sun will have gone down forever."[27]

If Miller's approach seems less harsh than DeVoto's, it does not mean that the artist and the historian are on separate wavelengths. Keep in mind that both are looking beyond the West of the 1830s (or Miller's West) at a post-Indian America, with trappers, not Indians, as the more resilient and enterprising lead to that future. Miller, in the 1830s, can afford to plot a sympathetic and generous exit for the Indians. Time is on his side. DeVoto in 1947 cannot. Two years after the end of World War II, he is determined to see the United States standing firm as a free and independent nation. No need to worry about the few Indians who got dispatched along the way. He wants a West that will frame a larger picture for America, a West as America, if you will, "mad with the impossible," with a "considerable faculty" for making dreams come true. But doesn't that also tell us that DeVoto, in his own way, is again paying tribute to Miller's art as an inspiring complement to his own? First he "rediscovers" it, after it has been neglected for years, then he encourages it to rise

Alfred Jacob Miller, *Stampede of Wild Horses,* detail (cat. 26)

phoenixlike from the pages of *Across the Wide Missouri*, with a life as vivid and meaningful as his own narrative.

That event also seems to have been the beginning of Miller scholarship; in 1951 (a later edition appeared in 1968) Marvin Ross's fully illustrated catalogue of the Miller collection at the Walters Art Museum appeared, followed by Dawn Glanz's remarkable book (*How the West Was Drawn: American Art and the Settling of the Frontier*, 1978), which first explored the rich symbolic content of Miller's work. William Goetzmann's *The West as Romantic Horizon* (1981), a salute (in part) to the newly acquired Miller collection at the Joslyn Art Museum, came next. From that point, the Amon Carter Museum became a major sponsor of Miller scholarship, first with Ron Tyler's impressive catalogue raisonné of Miller's work (*Alfred Jacob Miller: Artist on the Oregon Trail*, 1982), and five years later with *American Frontier Life: Early Western Paintings and Prints*, which included several pages on Miller's genre paintings. In 1990 Joan Carpenter Troccoli added to the bibliography *Alfred Jacob Miller: Watercolors of the American West,* an important thematic survey of Miller holdings in the Gilcrease Museum. More recently, in 2008, the Amon Carter sponsored the first major retrospective of Miller's work and published Lisa Strong's new book to accompany the show. Together, the show and the book are yet another indication that scholarship in the field of early western art has reached remarkable new heights. Perhaps even DeVoto, a true believer in Miller's work from the beginning, would be surprised at how far Miller has risen in art and history circles since his work first emerged from the basement of the Peale Museum in 1935.

Notes

1. William H. Goetzmann, "The Man Who Stopped to Paint America," in *Karl Bodmer's America* (Omaha: Joslyn Art Museum and University of Nebraska Press, 1984), 5–6.

2. In July 1965 the National Collection of Fine Arts opened *George Catlin's Indian Gallery*, an exhibition that included all 445 oil paintings by Catlin in the collection, plus watercolors, prints, and several cases of memorabilia. Extensive wall texts were written for the exhibition, as well as an informative brochure by Marjorie Halpin, a docent in anthropology at the Smithsonian. The NCFA staged another major Catlin show, called *George Catlin: The Artist and the American Indian*, in June 1981. A visit to the show from President Reagan and a favorable review in *Time Magazine* helped bring further attention to Catlin's work. The Bodmer watercolors debuted even earlier, in 1954, while still belonging to Karl Viktor Prinz zu Wied, a descendant of Maximilian. Under the auspices of the Smithsonian Institution Traveling Exhibition Service, they toured U.S. museums for the next two years, accompanied by a short catalogue (*Carl Bodmer Paints the Indian Frontier*) written by the eminent Smithsonian anthropologist John C. Ewers. In 1962 InterNorth, Inc. purchased the Bodmer collection and placed it on permanent loan at the Joslyn Art Museum, where it was selectively shown in newly designed western art galleries. InterNorth added to its western art collections twice more and featured the new purchases, along with the original Bodmer collection, in a generously illustrated catalogue, *The West as Romantic Horizon* (1981), with a lead essay by William Goetzmann. In 1984 the Bodmer collection was again circulated, this time to four major U.S. museums, including the Smithsonian. This second exhibition tour was accompanied by a more extensive catalogue, called *Views of a Vanishing Frontier*, to which John Ewers, along with three western art experts at the Joslyn, contributed important essays.

3. Total neglect, that is, after Miller died. Until then, patrons had responded enthusiastically to his work, especially those who lived in and around Baltimore, his hometown. Miller also showed western subjects at major venues in New York, Philadelphia, and Boston (the National Academy of Design, American Art-Union, Pennsylvania Academy of the Fine Arts, and Boston Athenæum, among others). Entries for these may be found in Marvin Ross, *The West of Alfred Jacob Miller* (Norman: University of Oklahoma Press, 1968), lv; and in Ron Tyler, ed., *Alfred Jacob Miller: Artist on the Oregon Trail* (Fort Worth: Amon Carter Museum, 1982), 451.

4. With one exception. MacGill James, director of the Peale Museum in Baltimore, organized a show of Miller watercolors at the museum in 1933. These were apparently on loan from various Miller family members. Mae Reed Porter "discovered" the same group of watercolors in 1935 at the museum (a hundred "sketches" in a box), purchased them from the family, and removed them to her home in Kansas City. See Mae Reed Porter, foreword to Bernard DeVoto, *Across the Wide Missouri* (Boston: Houghton Mifflin, 1947), xvi–xvii. Porter briefly repeats the story in Porter and Odessa Davenport, *Scotsman in Buckskin: Sir William Drummond Stewart and the Rocky Mountain Fur Trade* (New York: Hastings House, 1963), 275.

5. DeVoto, *Across the Wide Missouri*, xxi and opp. pl. 34.

6. The armor, presented by Stewart to his friend Bridger in an elaborate ceremony, was apparently an example of mountain-man humor. Bridger otherwise dressed in animal skins and fur. See Porter and Davenport, *Scotsman in Buckskin*, 150–51.

7. Arthur M. Schlesinger Jr., "The Citizen," in *Four Portraits and One Subject: Bernard DeVoto* (Boston: Houghton Mifflin, 1963), 57–62.

8. Herman J. Viola, "The American Indian Genre Paintings of Catlin, Stanley, Wimar, Eastman, and Miller," in *American Frontier Life: Early Western Paintings and Prints* (New York: Abbeville Press, 1987), 156–64.

9. Lisa Strong's important new thoughts about Miller's work are summed up in her recently published book, *Sentimental Journey: The Art of Alfred Jacob Miller,* exh. cat. (Fort Worth: Amon Carter Museum, 2008).

10. William R. Swagerty, "History of the United States Plains until 1850," in *Handbook of North American Indians*, ed. Raymond J. DeMallie, vol. 13 (Washington, D.C.: Smithsonian Institution, 2001), 275–76.

11. See Henry Nash Smith, *Virgin Land* (Cambridge, Mass.: Harvard University Press, 1970), 3–4. All of us raised on this seminal text critique it with great trepidation. But as the title suggests – along with further references to a "vacant continent" and "free land" in the prologue – the Indian presence in the early West is not of great concern to the range of authors Smith investigates.

12. Porter and Davenport, *Scotsman in Buckskin*, 134.

13. Letters from Stewart to William Sublette (who started out with William H. Ashley in 1823, and later set up a major St. Louis firm with Robert Campbell), written 28 February 1836, 1 March 1838, 27 August 1838, and 17 December 1838, request withdrawals ranging from $700 to $1,800, suggesting that Sublette was Stewart's banker during his American travels. Missouri Historical Society, St. Louis.

14. John Logan Allen, "The Eagle Screams, 1840–1865," in *The Story of the West: A History of the American West and Its People*, ed. Robert M. Utley (New York: DK Publishing, 2003), 179.

15. Robert V. Hine and John Mack Faragher, *The American West: A New Interpretive History* (New Haven: Yale University Press, 2000), 159.

16. Swagerty, *Handbook of North American Indians*, 261–75.

17. Ellen Miles, *Saint-Mémin and the Neoclassical Profile Portrait in America,* exh. cat. (Washington, D.C.: Smithsonian Institution Press for the National Portrait Gallery, 1994), 142–43.

18. Dale L. Morgan and Eleanor Towles Harris, eds., *The Rocky Mountain Journals of William Marshall Anderson: The West in 1834* (San Marino, Calif.: Huntington Library, 1967), 147.

19. George Catlin, *Letters and Notes on the Manners, Customs, and Condition of the North American Indians* (London, 1841; reprint, New York: Dover Publications, 1973), 2:61.

20. Ross, *The West of Miller,* opp. pl. 93.

21. Dale L. Morgan, ed., *The West of William H. Ashley* (Denver: Old West Publishing Company, 1964), 148.

22. Wallace Stegner, "The Personality," in *Four Portraits*, 106–7.

23. Ibid., 92–93.

24. Catherine Drinker Bowen, "The Historian," in *Four Portraits*, 19–20.

25. Ibid., 25.

26. DeVoto, *Across the Wide Missouri*, 375.

27. Ross, *The West of Miller*, opp. pl. 153.

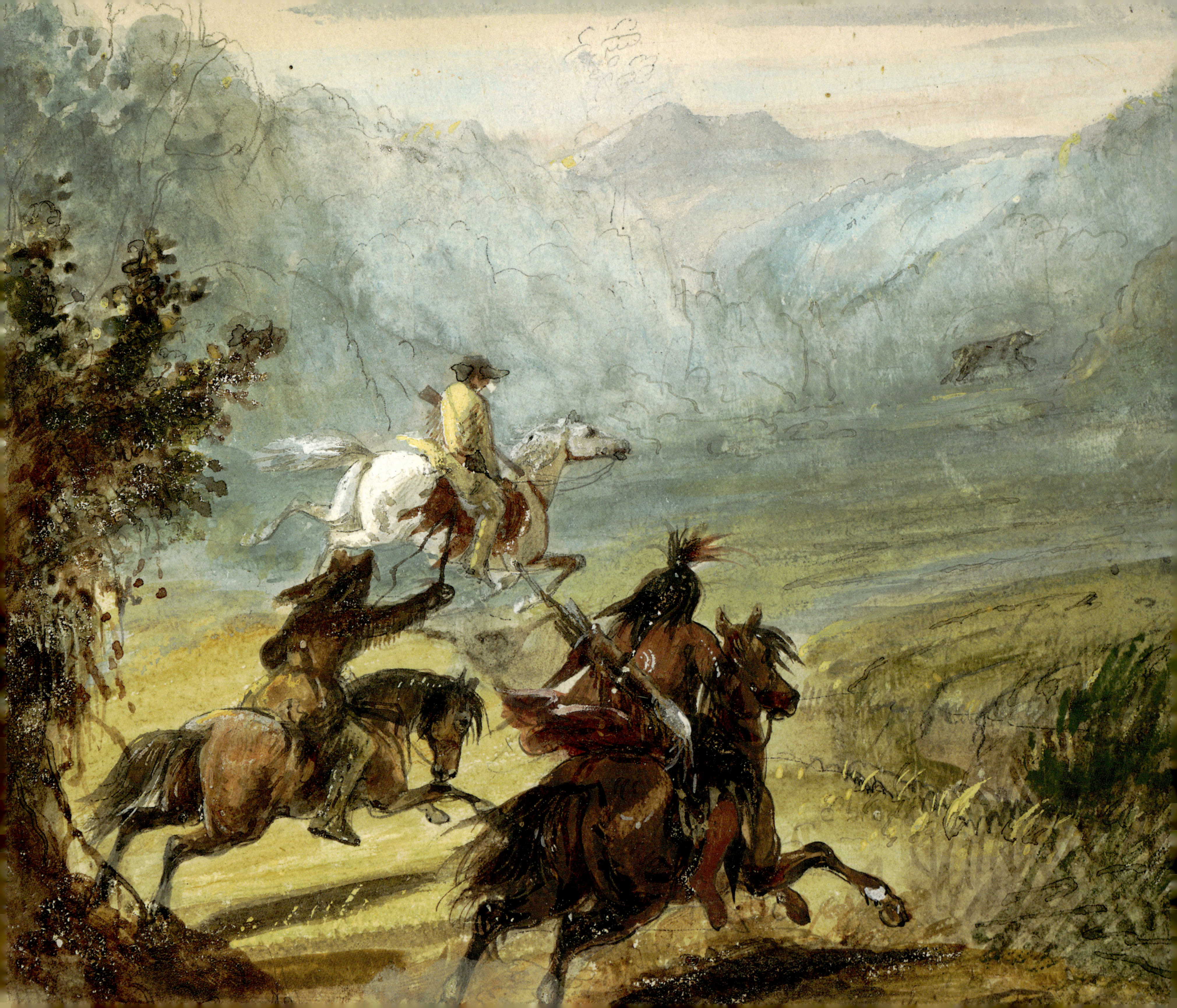

Alfred Jacob Miller

and the Bank of America Collection

Lisa Strong

Imagine a small but elegantly furnished parlor in a Baltimore town house. Books and curios fill an étagère, and the walls are hung with an assortment of large and small oil paintings by the house's owner, the artist Alfred Jacob Miller (1810–1874). Seated on a red plush sofa flanked by marble-topped tables is William H. Graham, partner in the international banking and mercantile firm Alexander Brown and Sons.[1] Before him is a stack of portfolios and scrapbooks filled with sketches of western America: scenes of Indians, trappers, and buffalo, many bearing a number discreetly inscribed in the upper corner. As Miller tells Graham anecdotes about each sketch, his guest selects by number the ones he would like reproduced for Alexander Hargreaves Brown, heir to the English branch of the Baltimore-based firm Alexander Brown and Sons. Miller carefully records the selections on two sheets of paper with blue lines to which he affixes a small card that reads, "Mr. Miller will please make forty of his Indian water sketches as per selection for $1,000. / ordered by Mr. William H. Graham, March 26, 1867."[2]

The commission Miller undertook for Brown at the behest of Graham was the last of the artist's large orders; he had given up his studio five years earlier, and in 1872 he would retire.[3] It was a fitting end to his career. More than thirty years earlier, after a trip to the Rocky Mountains with his first major patron, the Scots baronet William Drummond Stewart, Miller had produced a series of watercolor sketches of Indian scenes that formed the template for his later watercolors, many of which were bound into scrapbooks and kept in the artist's studio. It was from these that Graham made his selection that afternoon in March 1867.

The scene just described and the account book, commission records, and estate papers that document it provide a snapshot of Miller's busy and lucrative career as a painter of western genre. Miller made only one six-month trek to the Rocky Mountain region in 1837, but his sketches from that adventure were the source for at least a thousand paintings in both oil and watercolor.[4] He completed at least three large commissions for watercolors: an album of eighty-seven watercolor or pen and ink and wash sketches for Stewart between 1837 and 1839; two hundred western-themed watercolors for the Baltimore collector William T. Walters in 1858–60; and the forty watercolors for Brown in 1867. Every finished picture was preceded by several working sketches in his studio portfolios and scrapbooks. In addition, there were many unique compositions. A visitor to Miller's studio in the decades following his trip must have been met with a dizzying array of plaster casts, copies after paintings by the old masters, dramatic scenes in oil of buffalo hunts, quaint genre paintings and sketches of his native city of Baltimore, and portfolios filled with watercolors in various stages of completion from which one could select subjects that Miller would execute in oil or watercolor in any number of sizes.[5]

Alfred Jacob Miller, *Chase of the Grizzly Bear, Black Hills*, detail (cat. 11)

The collection of Alfred Jacob Miller's paintings owned by the Bank of America represents a cross section of the artist's studio production. His will listed no fewer than fourteen scrapbooks, one lot of sketches, and eighty-two oil paintings.[6] These passed from the childless Miller to his unmarried sister Harriet to their brother Decatur's children, Decatur and Eugenia. Family lore has it that at some point, the portfolios were opened up and spread across a large dining room table for the grandnieces and -nephews to choose from.[7] Some of these sketches remained in family hands, but many, such as the thirty sketches now owned by the Bank of America, were sold in small batches over the years. Those in the bank's collection were purchased in 1947, directly from Miller's niece, Eugenia Miller Whyte (1858–1949) or his grandniece Louise Whyte Norton (1887–1975).[8] This essay places them within the context of Miller's oeuvre to understand how they contributed to his successful career in mid-nineteenth-century Baltimore.

Alfred Jacob Miller, Baltimore Artist

Alfred Jacob Miller was born in Baltimore, the son of a prosperous grocer and tavern keeper. He was educated at an elite private boys' school, where he made some of his earliest sketches. While still a youth, Miller determined to become an artist and likely received training from a number of sources. According to a student of Miller's, the artist studied briefly with Thomas Sully while Sully worked in Baltimore. Miller surely studied works by the Peale family at Baltimore's Peale Museum, as well as the excellent private collections in the city compiled by Robert Gilmor Jr. and Dr. Thomas Edmondson. In 1832 Gilmor and a number of local businessmen, perhaps including the merchant Johns Hopkins, who did business with Miller's father, put up the money to send Miller to Europe to study.[9]

Miller was sufficiently aware of trends in European art to choose Paris and Rome as his destinations, making him part of the first generation of American artists to study on the Continent, rather than in London. In Paris, Miller enrolled as an auditor at the École des Beaux-Arts, where he was able to draw from a live model. The rigorous training he received, which would not have been available to him in Baltimore, enabled him to draw figures more convincingly. In Paris, and later in Rome and Florence, Miller could study old master paintings, which he diligently copied. According to Miller, his copies of Raphael were accomplished enough that they fooled customs agents at the Franco-Italian border, who stopped him for theft.[10] Miller's later works, such as his *Caravan en Route* (fig. 10) show the enduring influence of his European training in the delicate pastels and brilliant crimsons of his Raphael-inspired palette. Scholars have supposed Miller also found an important touchstone in the work of Eugène Delacroix, elements of whose *Barque of Dante* (1822; Musée du Louvre, Paris) he copied at the Luxembourg Palace while in Paris. Delacroix's vivid colors, spiral compositions, and loose, flowing lines likely appealed to Miller because they offered him an expanded range of formal expression. Moreover, Delacroix's trip with the comte de Mornay to Morocco in 1832 may have provided an intellectual model, if not a direct source, for Miller's later interpretations of his Rocky Mountain material.[11]

However, more influential for Miller was the less radical French Romantic painter Horace Vernet. Miller met Vernet in Rome while the French artist served as director of the French Academy there. One contemporary critic compared Miller's work with Vernet's, and Miller himself mentioned Vernet admiringly in his journal.[12] Vernet's images of horses, particularly his widely reproduced series of paintings illustrating Lord Byron's 1819 poem, "Mazeppa" (fig. 11), offered a possible model for Miller's series of paintings of a battle retreat, two of which are in the Bank of America collection: *On the Warpath – Running Fight* (cat. 29) and *War Path* (cat. 30). The French Romantics' subjects, drawn from literature and folk tales, also suggested to Miller a way to handle the kinds of literary sources, such as eighteenth-century British sentimental novels, those

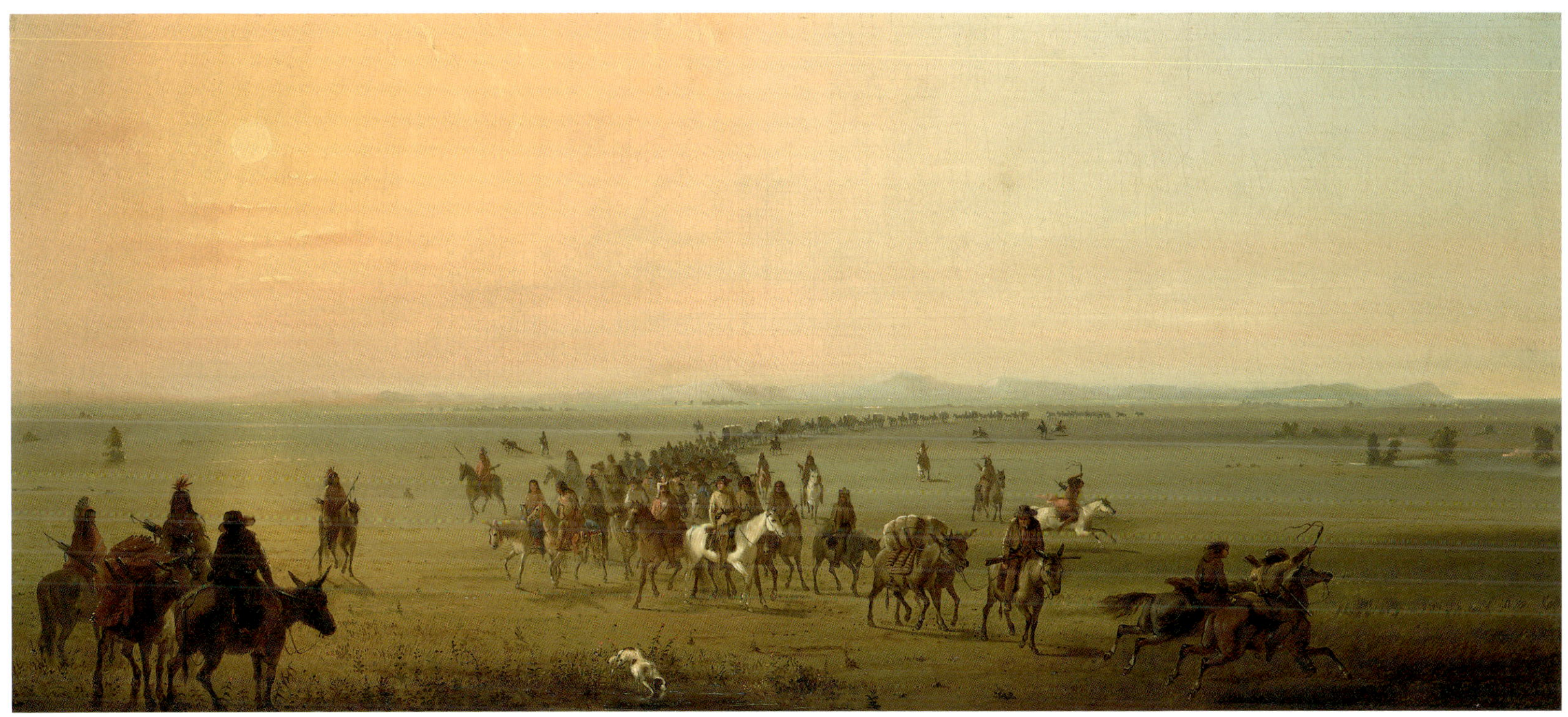

FIGURE 10. Alfred Jacob Miller, *Caravan en Route*, 1849. Oil on canvas, 21 × 47 in. (53.3 × 119.4 cm). Bank of America Collection

of Charles Dickens and Sir Walter Scott, and the poems of Lord Byron, that interested him throughout his career.

Miller returned to Baltimore in 1834 and established himself as a painter of old master copies and portraits, some of which he sold to Johns Hopkins. In 1836 Miller's father died, followed by his mother the next year. As the eldest son, Miller became executor of his father's estate and spent the next year straightening out his father's affairs and paying off debts.[13] Miller left little record of this period in his career, nor are there many works of art that can be documented to this time. In December 1836, however, believing his fortunes lay in the pursuit of his art, he left his seven younger siblings in the care of his eldest sister, Harriet, and moved to New Orleans. There, as one of the few portraitists in the city, he enjoyed what he later recalled was a lively business painting portraits.[14]

It was in New Orleans in the spring of 1837 that Miller had his fateful meeting with William Drummond Stewart. While at work on a landscape of Baltimore's Loundenslager's Hill (now known as Butcher's Hill in East Baltimore), Miller was interrupted by the arrival of a man who

> *at first glance . . . seemed to me to be a Kentuckian—he had on a grey suit with a black stripe worked on the seam of his pantaloons, and held himself as straight as an arrow.—to be*

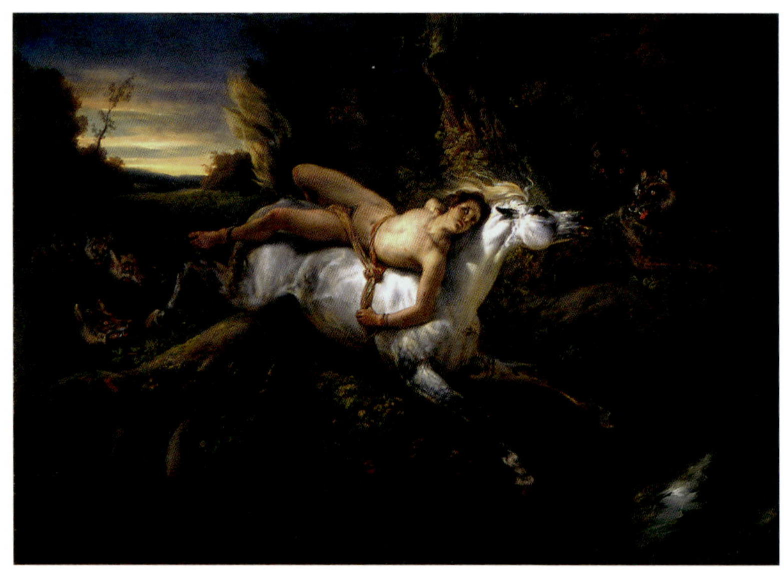

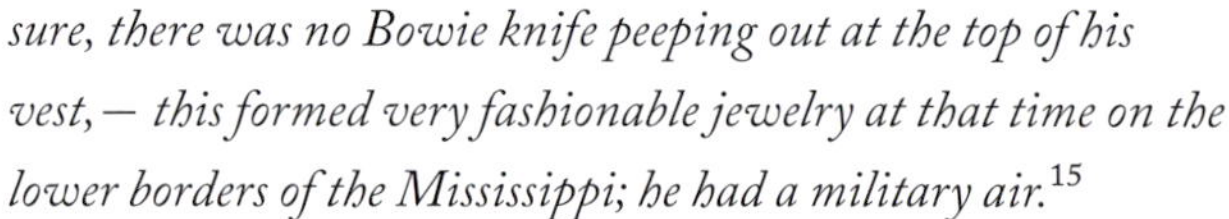
FIGURE 11. Horace Vernet, *Mazeppa and the Wolves*, 1826. Oil on canvas, 38¼ × 53½ in. (97 × 136 cm). Musée Calvet, Avignon, France

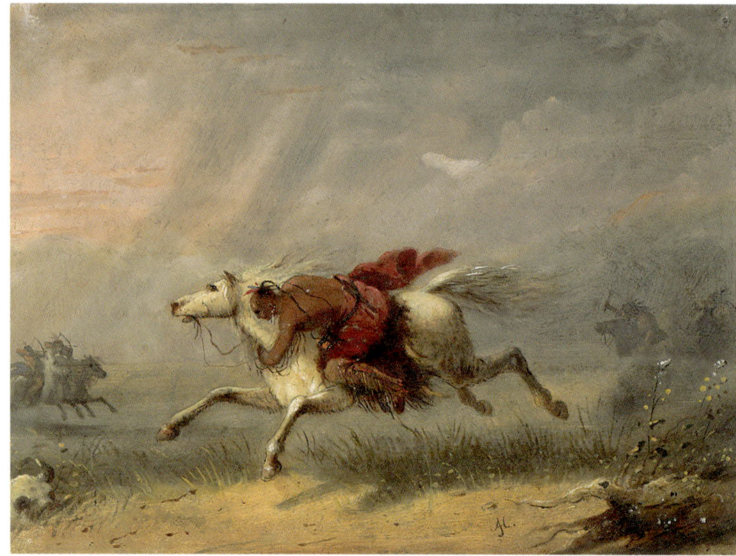

Alfred Jacob Miller, *War Path* (cat. 30)

> *sure, there was no Bowie knife peeping out at the top of his vest, — this formed very fashionable jewelry at that time on the lower borders of the Mississippi; he had a military air.*[15]

According to Miller, the visitor looked at the works of art on view, complimented the landscape on the easel, and left, only to return with an offer that Miller could not refuse. Stewart explained that he had been traveling in the West since 1832, spending each summer, and one arduous winter in 1833, hunting bison, bear, and elk and visiting the annual fur traders' rendezvous. The second son of a Scots aristocrat, Stewart had reason to believe that his 1837 jaunt would be his last. His older brother, who had inherited the family estate, was gravely ill and without an heir. If he died, Stewart would then inherit and be obligated to return to his ancestral home, Murthly Castle, in Perthshire, to assume his familial duties. Stewart invited Miller to accompany him on this trip. They would travel with several wagons, a large personal entourage, and casks of brandy and delicacies. Their party would enjoy the safety of accompanying the annual caravan of traders from St. Louis en route to the Rocky Mountains to meet with trappers and Native Americans at a pre-appointed location along the Green River to exchange a season's worth of beaver pelts for supplies.[16]

The West was still a place of mystery for most easterners. George Catlin had toured many American cities with his collection of Native American portraits, artifacts, and even some willing Native Americans in 1836 and 1839. He published his illustrated volume, *Letters and Notes on the Manners, Customs, and Condition of the North American Indians*, in 1841, and a few other illustrated scientific and government survey texts on the West were available. But there were few paintings of the Rocky

Mountain region and no fully realized genre scenes of the fur trade. For Miller, Stewart offered not only a thrilling adventure but an opportunity to develop a niche subject matter on which to build his career.

Stewart and his party left St. Louis in late April and traveled along the Kansas and Little Blue rivers to the Platte, stopping for about two weeks at Fort Laramie to rest and resupply. They followed the Platte northwest, through the South Pass to Horse Creek, a tributary of the Green River, where the rendezvous had already been under way for at least a week.[17] After they left, perhaps before the rendezvous had concluded, they traveled into the Wind River Mountains in search of rich trout streams and game, returning to St. Louis by October.[18]

Miller closed up his studio in New Orleans and returned to Baltimore later that fall. By 1839 he had completed what would prove to be the most important of his commissions, eighty-seven sketches of scenes from the 1837 trek.[19] The sketches were mostly monochrome, rendered in pencil, pen and ink, wash and watercolor, on an assortment of papers and tinted cards, numbered, and, in some cases, titled. Some were completed in New Orleans, and the rest were finished in Baltimore between 1837 and 1839.[20] All the sketches, along with eighteen oil paintings, were shipped to Scotland.[21] Once at Murthly, the sketches were richly bound in a portfolio and prominently exhibited in the drawing room.[22]

The sketches sent to Scotland were composed while the trip was fresh in Miller's mind and were based on recollection and the sketches he made in the field. Although Miller's fieldwork represented a range of subjects, including sketches of Fort Laramie and many colorful genre scenes of the trappers, such as *A Rocky Mountain Trapper, Bill Burrows* (see fig. 30), the works painted for Stewart's album present a carefully constructed view of their trip. Almost entirely absent are views of trappers. There are no scenes of the fur trade business actually being conducted, nor do we see trappers hunting beaver.[23]

The album does show, however, Stewart and Native American visitors to the rendezvous involved in what would have been the traditional activities of the Scottish aristocracy. Stewart and his Indian companions hunt a variety of big game: mountain sheep, bear, elk, and, of course, bison. They also race horses, engage in diplomacy, socialize, and participate in a tournament-style competition with bows and arrows (fig. 12). In the years following his American travels, Stewart wrote two novels based on his adventures: *Altowan: or, Incidents of Life and Adventure in the Rocky Mountains, by an Amateur Traveler* (1846) and *Edward Warren* (1854). *Altowan* contains a scene very like the one Miller depicts in *Trial of Skill*, which concludes with a statement by the eponymous Altowan: "What are the pleasures of civilized life to me, who am already blooded in the wild Indian chivalry? There is no war among the whites, where I could rise to command, but by land and servile submission; there is no tourney, there is no hunting field among them, where danger is courted, and manhood holds a place such as here is accorded to its prowess."[24]

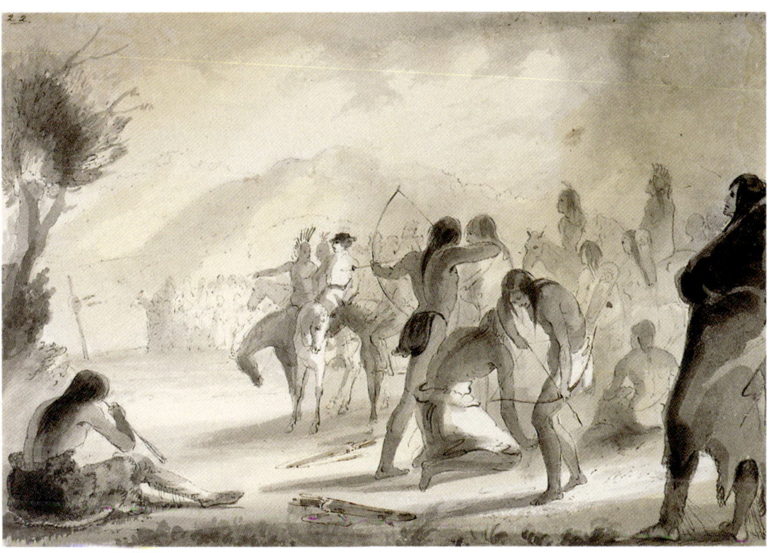

FIGURE 12. Alfred Jacob Miller, *Trial of Skill—with Bow and Arrow*, c. 1837. Pen and ink with gray and yellow washes on paper, 7⅜ × 10¼ in. (18.7 × 26 cm). The Walters Art Museum, Baltimore

Stewart's narrative suggests that he believed in an idea expressed by a number of European aristocrats of the period. Native Americans did not represent a noble savagery, naturally good because free from the corruption of society's laws and class distinctions.[25] Rather, they embodied a savage nobility. New World aristocrats naturally expressed the traits of a European nobility. Warriors ruled by what Europeans perceived as an inherited chiefdom. They engaged in such traditional aristocratic pursuits as hunting, horse racing, and gambling, and, most important, they were untouched by the petty professional concerns of the bourgeoisie.[26]

In the spring of 1840 Miller had the opportunity to experience European aristocratic life firsthand when he traveled to Murthly Castle to join Stewart. He had his own studio next to the library, where he could peruse Stewart's collection of old master prints. He enjoyed the elegant, multicourse dinners, balls, parties, and visits from neighboring gentry. He walked the extensive grounds and fished in the rich streams. When not entertaining himself on the estate, he painted. Stewart commissioned two major oils, *The Trapper's Bride* (1841; location unknown), a romantic scene of a frontier marriage that Miller would reproduce at least six more times, and *Attack by Crows* (1841; Anschutz Collection), a dramatic history painting that portrayed an encounter between Stewart and the Crow in 1833. Miller also painted oil versions of watercolors that Stewart selected from the sketch album, as well as several religious scenes. After his stay at Murthly, Miller traveled to London, where he took a studio near the British Museum. He set sail for Baltimore in 1842.[27]

Back in Baltimore, Miller faced a very different patronage situation from the one he enjoyed in Scotland. Stewart's practice was traditional for the aristocracy. During the time he supported Miller, Miller painted only for him. No price was agreed on beforehand; Stewart simply paid Miller what he thought the artist deserved for each work. In Baltimore, by contrast, Miller was thrown into a highly developed, but fickle, commercial market. The city of Baltimore had a long and illustrious history of private patronage. In the early nineteenth century, Robert Gilmor Jr. had amassed a large collection of old masters, Dutch genre scenes, and works by American artists, including Thomas Cole and William Sidney Mount.[28] Thomas Edmondson also had a large collection, which included works by European artists, the Hudson River School, and local Baltimore artists.[29] William T. Walters also had built a substantial collection of American art before the Civil War.[30] These patrons purchased a few works from a large number of different artists and could not be depended on to support a career. In these circumstances, Miller had to find ways to market his works to many of Baltimore's elite.

Miller shrewdly took a studio in the Law Buildings, next to the Courthouse and Mercantile Exchange in the heart of commercial Baltimore.[31] Scholarship on Miller has treated the artist's years in Baltimore as something of a coda to his earlier career as a western artist. The similarity of subject matter and composition of the works Miller completed for Sir William Drummond Stewart has encouraged writers to discuss and interpret such works against a shared context of western history. Yet Miller's Baltimore milieu inflected his western works with local and personal associations, and his paintings, in turn, appear to have functioned as a kind of social currency in Baltimore society.

An account book Miller kept from 1846 to 1872 documents his successful career in Baltimore and records his cadre of patrons.[32] Although Baltimore's elite were a diverse mix of industrialists, merchants in domestic and international trade, and landed gentlemen who made their incomes from property rentals, Miller's Baltimore patrons came principally from one distinct social group, domestic wholesale merchants.[33] Merchants played a significant role in Baltimore history. Baltimore's rise as the new republic's third-largest city was fueled in part by the financial successes of shipping merchants who operated as privateers during the War of 1812. Though the first generation of merchants after the war suffered from their inability to adapt to new financial markets, the second and third generations, to which Miller's patrons belonged, prospered by finding new sources and markets for their goods in the trans-Allegheny and, later, the trans-Mississippi West. Many Baltimoreans, including Miller himself and particularly many of his merchant patrons, such as the partners of Alexander Brown and Sons, Johns Hopkins, and Patrick Henry Sullivan, invested heavily in the Baltimore and Ohio Railroad (B&O) in hopes that the line would reach far into the West and expand existing markets for their goods.[34] By 1860 the B&O had linked Baltimore to Chicago, and by 1870 to St. Louis. It is not surprising, then, that many of the purchasers of Miller's western scenes had business ties in the West. Although coffee and sugar from the West Indies were two of Baltimore's most lucrative commodities, Miller's patrons were not sugar or coffee merchants. Rather, they specialized in goods traded to and from the West, such as flour, lard, and wholesale groceries.

Miller painted one version of his best-known oil, *The Trapper's Bride* (fig. 13), for the grocery wholesaler Johns Hopkins in 1846, the year before Hopkins took over as director of the B&O Railroad. *The Trapper's Bride* has been interpreted as picturing the peaceful reconciliation of Indian and white cultures through intermarriage.[35] Yet the painting's emphasis on trade goods such as the bead necklace in the woman's hand and Miller's own textual description of the subject as a seduction enacted by the woman and her family to get trade goods from the trapper explicitly commercialize the painting's themes.[36] Hopkins's financial ambitions for the western region, especially his and other B&O investors' hopes of uniting Baltimore merchants with western markets, also cast the painting in a mercantile light. The trapper literally stands at the vanguard of white civilization commercially as well as existentially. In the painting, the development of a new market for goods seems as natural as love and marriage and, perhaps, Miller hints, as essential to that wedded bliss as affection itself.

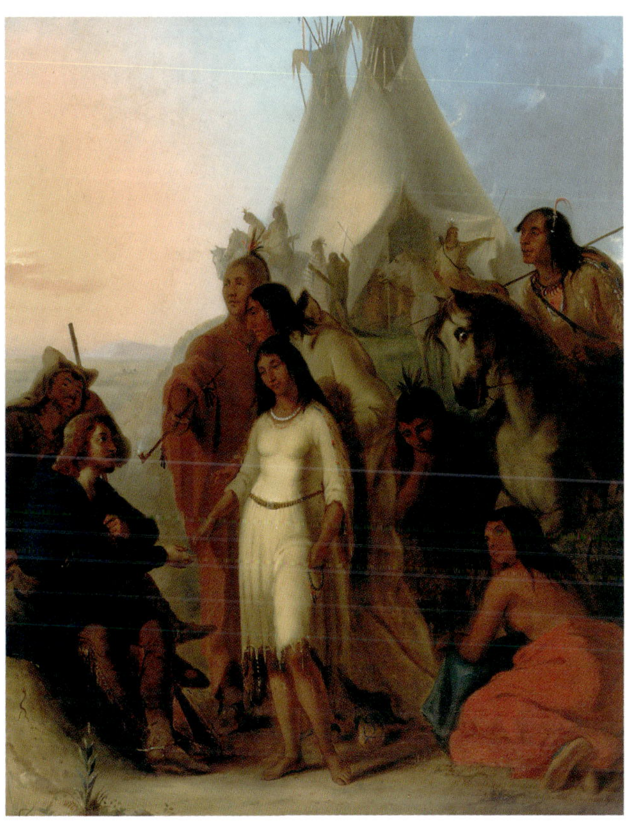

FIGURE 13. Alfred Jacob Miller, *The Trapper's Bride*, n.d. Oil on canvas, 35½ × 28½ in. (90.2 × 72.4 cm). Courtesy of The Alan Mason Chesney Medical Archives of The Johns Hopkins Medical Institutions, Baltimore

If Miller's western images offered his patrons the promise of new markets in the West, the appeal of such images increased during the sectional strife leading up to and culminating in the Civil War. Miller took on two large commissions for a total of 237 watercolors between 1858 and 1860. In 1864 and 1865 he doubled his annual average for western scenes in oil, painting twelve and thirteen respectively. In total Miller sold 282 western scenes from 1858 to 1865.[37] The history of Baltimore and its merchant elite in this period suggests one possible explanation for this surge of interest in western works. As a border state, Maryland was deeply divided over the Civil War. Baltimore, in particular, saw an acrimonious

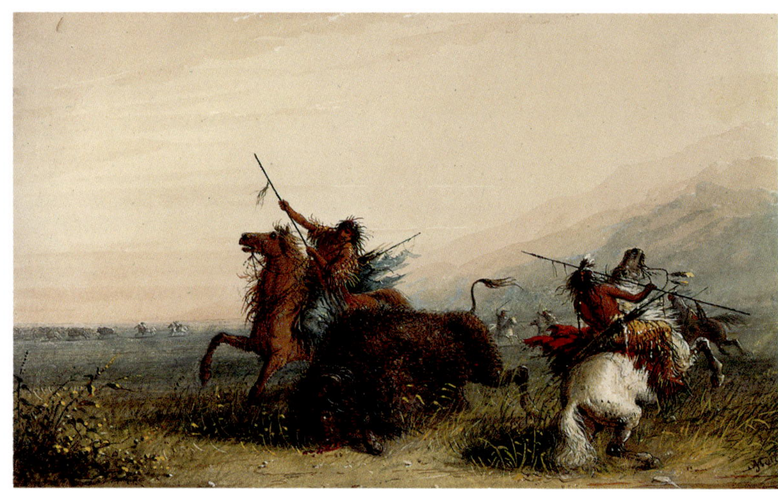

Figure 14. Alfred Jacob Miller, *Hunting the Buffalo, Attack with Lances*, 1867. Watercolor on paper, 8 × 13¼ in. (20.3 × 33.7 cm). Library and Archives Canada, Ottawa, Ontario, Acc. No. 1946-108-1, Gift of Mrs. J. B. Jardine

split among its merchant elite, many of whom ardently supported one side or the other.[38] Miller could count among his patrons both active supporters of the Union and Southern sympathizers.[39] The Baltimore partners of Alexander Brown and Sons were well-known Southern sympathizers, but the New York branch supported the Union. William T. Walters was a Southern sympathizer as well.[40] He was so ostracized for his views among his immediate circle of mercantile elite friends that he moved to Europe for the duration of the war. The sketches Miller made for Walters and Miller's accompanying text abound in references to the freedom and liberty of western life, suggesting the possibility that the West offered Walters not only the promise of future business but a place free of sectional strife. Although the West had been a site of contention leading up to the war, the Rocky Mountain region Miller painted lacked a clear Northern or Southern identity. The region therefore may have represented a kind of imaginary safe zone for the fractured Baltimore elite. Moreover, Northern- and Southern-sympathizing merchants alike were united in their ambitions for western markets. Paintings of the West may thus have offered a promise of reconciliation among the merchant class for those who purchased them. Indeed, the purchase of Miller's *A Reconnoitre* (c. 1865; location unknown) in 1865 by Isaac Bell, an employee of the Brown and Sons' New York branch, may have been connected to Bell's innovative campaign to integrate the firm's Northern and Southern offices by cementing his personal, if not political, ties to Baltimore.[41]

As was the case with his earlier commissions, Miller's last major commission for Alexander Hargreaves Brown also appears to have been motivated at least in part by the business interests of the firm. Although Alexander Brown and Sons had offices in Liverpool, New York, and Philadelphia, the company had been founded in Baltimore, and the Baltimore branch remained its flagship. Thirty-six of the forty images Graham selected for Brown were among the two hundred in the Walters commission.[42] It is more than likely that Graham, himself an art collector, was familiar with many of the works Miller painted for Baltimore patrons. He served with some of Miller's other patrons on the boards of banks and would later be treasurer of the Maryland Academy of Art.[43]

Despite the overlap with the Walters sketches, Graham's particular selection of images differs markedly in tone from those in the Walters collection. While Walters's watercolors depict many trappers and specific incidents from Miller and Stewart's trip, Graham chose more generic, stereotypical scenes of Indian life that resembled images in Catlin's or Karl Bodmer's published portfolios of Indian sketches.[44] Compared with the works in the Walters's or bank's collection (cat. 14), Miller's *Hunting the Buffalo, Attack with Lances* (fig. 14), for instance, shows much more detail in clothing and accoutrements, particularly in the German silver hair plates worn by the figure at right, which were popular on the Plains in the 1830s. On a number of levels, commissioning a series of Indian sketches from Alfred Jacob Miller made sense for Alexander Hargreaves

Brown. Paintings by Miller would remind Brown and his Liverpool office of their Baltimore roots. Alexander Brown and Sons began as a mercantile firm and bank but after the 1850s increasingly directed its focus to the sale of credit information. The firm rated American companies and backed their loans to British merchants and creditors.[45] Paintings of American Indians displayed either in the corporate offices or in the homes of its directors could attest to the company's intimate American ties. The authoritative, quasi-ethnographic flavor of the sketches Graham selected may have reassured Brown's English clients of their owner's objective and therefore reliable knowledge of America as a whole and, by extension, of American credit.

The Bank of America Collection and Miller's Studio Practice

The Bank of America collection of Miller's art offers examples that illuminate the artist's working method over the course of his career. Several of the works in the collection appear to be studies for popular compositions that Miller produced in multiple versions. It is important to note that Miller's decision to paint and repaint versions of particular scenes would not have been regarded at the time as a creative compromise or a blot on his career. It was common for nineteenth-century European painters to produce several versions of successful compositions. For instance, Jacques-Louis David produced multiple canvases of his *Death of Marat* (1793; Royal Museum of Fine Arts, Brussels), Jean-Antoine-Dominique Ingres reproduced his *Oedipus and the Sphinx* (1808; Musée du Louvre, Paris), and Jean-Léon Gérôme produced a smaller version of his award-winning *Duel after the Masquerade* (1857; Musée Condé, Chantilly), which was purchased by William T. Walters in 1859.[46] Before the 1870s, when Impressionism raised the value of depicting a unique vision and a specific moment, the ability to copy an artwork accurately and convincingly was regarded as a sign of artistic skill. Miller was especially

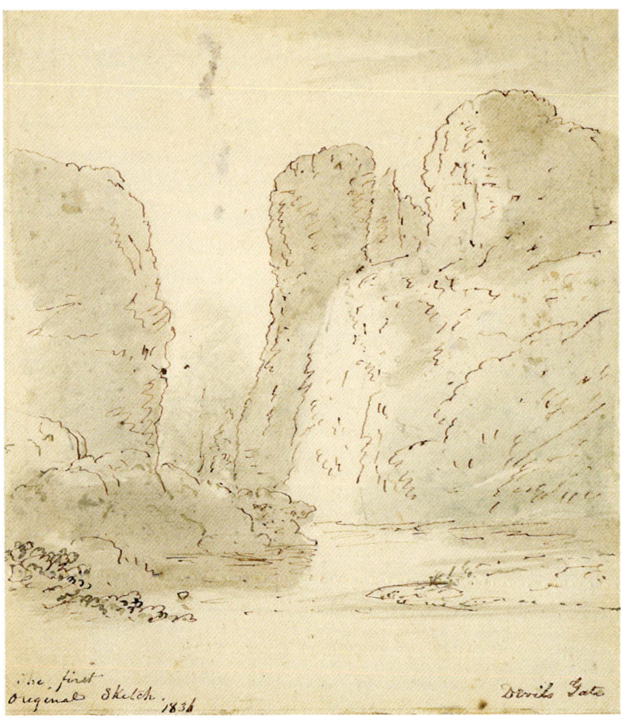

FIGURE 15. Alfred Jacob Miller, *Devil's Gate*, c. 1837. Watercolor, pen and ink, and graphite on paper, 7⅜ × 6¹¹⁄₁₆ in. (18.7 × 17 cm). Gilcrease Museum, Tulsa, Oklahoma

proud of his abilities as a copyist, telling friends in Baltimore that in Paris he was known as the "American Raphael."[47]

One image that appears, in fact, to be unique in Miller's oeuvre is *Indian Fort* (cat. 7). It has the hallmarks of a work Miller created in the field during his journey with Stewart. If we compare it with one of the few sketches that Miller attributed to his time in the field, *Devil's Gate* (fig. 15), which bears the inscription "the first./original sketch/1836," we see that it has the characteristics of what Miller scholars refer to as a field sketch. Both images are simple in execution and composition. Like *Indian Fort*, *Devil's Gate* is sketched in pencil with thin contour wash and

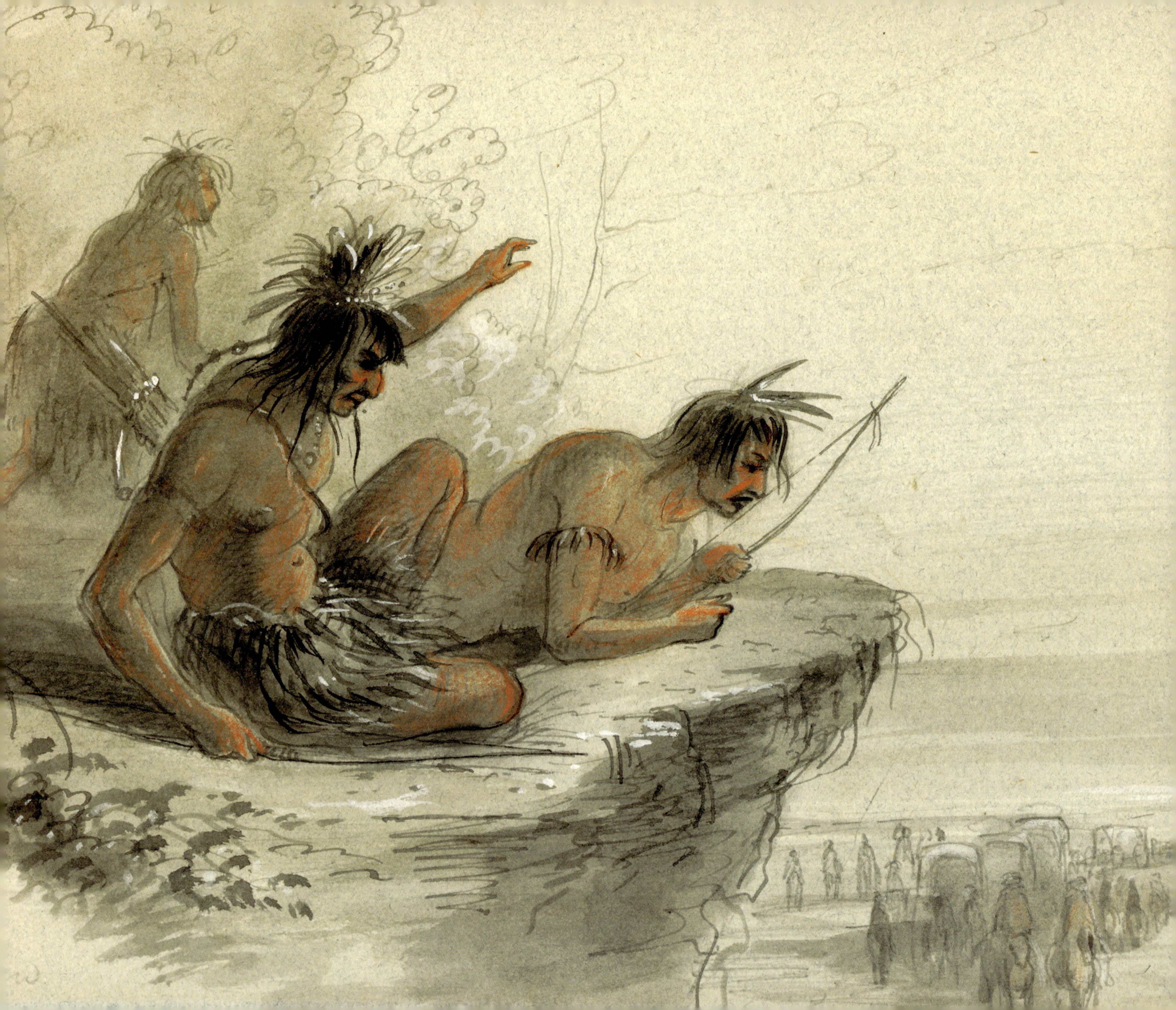

ink laid over it on a small sheet of thin paper probably cut from a sketchbook. Devil's Gate, an important landmark along the route west, was a 350-foot-deep gorge through which the Sweetwater River traveled. Miller captures its essential forms. *Indian Fort* takes a similarly documentary approach, excluding narrative elements or descriptive flourishes. As is the case with some other works that appear to be field sketches, there are no finished works relating to *Indian Fort*. It appears that Miller drew the fort because it was an interesting Indian artifact. Based on the subject matter contained in Stewart's album, however, Miller's patron was principally interested in his own adventures and was not attracted to aspects of Indian life that did not involve interactions with him.

Some of the paintings in the Bank of America collection appear similar enough in style and execution to works in the Stewart album that they may, in fact, be either studies for works in that album or finished works that the patron did not want included. In *Watching the Caravan* (cat. 2) Miller seems to be exploring a satisfactory arrangement for the composition he finally arrived at in *Indians Surprised at the Appearance of the Caravan* (fig. 16). *Watching the Caravan* is executed on a moderately thick paper that a technical examination has revealed was once blue. Several of the works in Stewart's album, including *Indians Surprised at the Appearance of the Caravan*, which is on a gray-green tinted card, also were done on tinted papers or cards. Miller's use of broad washes over a sharp pencil line and his handling of the fur trade caravan in the distance in *Watching the Caravan* are also characteristic of his early work for Stewart. In *Indians Surprised at the Appearance of the Caravan*, the composition is better balanced by a dark wash, perhaps representing a tree trunk or outcropping between the second and third figure from the right, and a dark shrub between the first and fourth. Miller has also placed the caravan at a greater distance, making the surprise and apparent concealment of the Indians both more plausible and more dramatic. Additionally, he replaced the fiber skirts, articles worn by West Coast or South Seas indigenous peoples in the Bank of America sketch, with

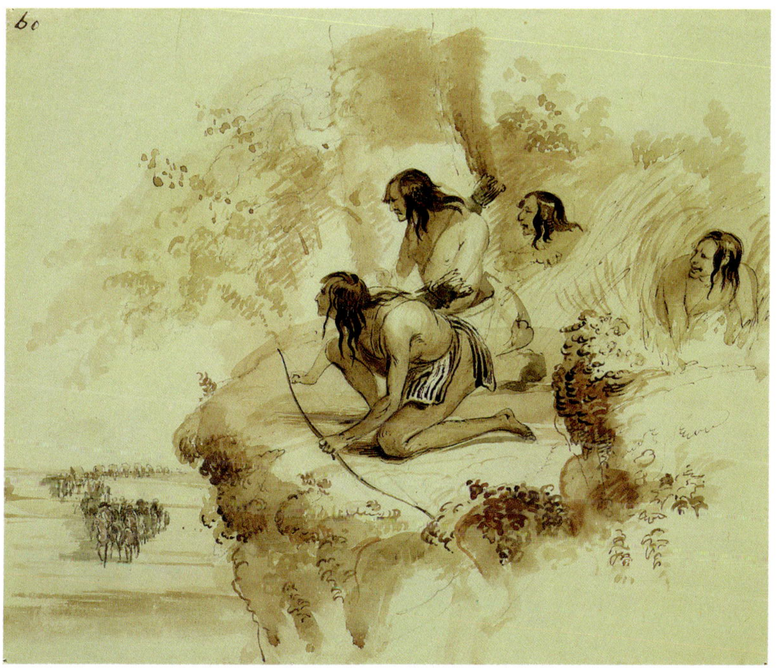

FIGURE 16. Alfred Jacob Miller, *Indians Surprised at the Appearance of the Caravan*, c. 1837. Pen and ink with brown and touches of green and white wash on paper, 6⅞ × 8⅜ in. (17.5 × 21.3 cm). Buffalo Bill Historical Center, Cody, Wyoming; Bequest of Joseph M. Roebling, 11.80

more plausible loincloths in *Indians Surprised at the Appearance of the Caravan*.

Antelope (cat. 6), which Miller may have intended for Stewart's album, is a beautifully painted sketch, cleanly executed in a crisp, light pencil line with confidently applied, transparent layers of gold, green, gray, and blue. The even paint application, neatly trimmed edges, and relatively large size suggest that it was done in the studio and meant for sale or display as a finished watercolor. Its draftsmanship and paint application similarly show it to be an early work, in the style of Stewart's album sketches.[48] If it was indeed painted for the album but not included, either

Alfred Jacob Miller, *Watching the Caravan*, detail (cat. 2)

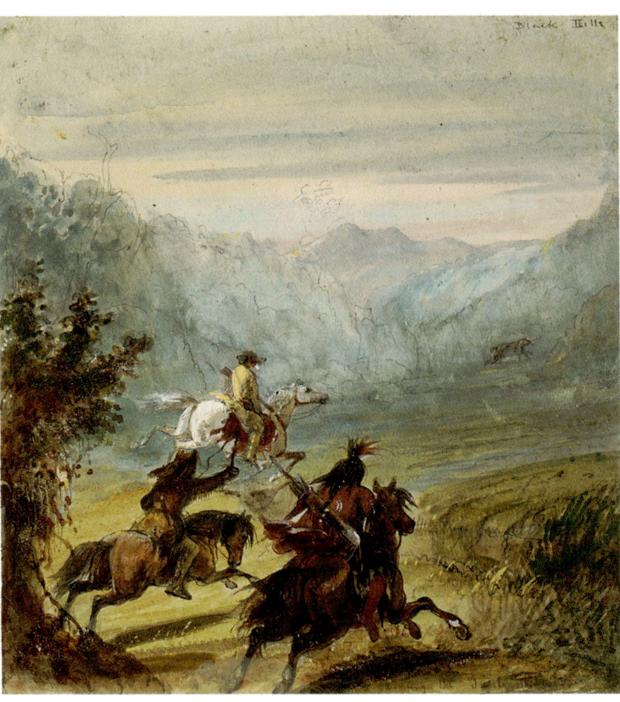

Alfred Jacob Miller, *Chase of the Grizzly Bear, Black Hills* (cat. 11)

Stewart or Miller could have left it out. According to Miller, during their journey, Stewart pointed out the scenes or incidents he wanted Miller to sketch.[49] He also checked on the progress of the sketches while Miller was in New Orleans, and the artist indicated that his patron selected which of the sketches he wanted reproduced in oil.[50]

If *Antelope* has no directly related image among Stewart's sheets, many of Miller's later watercolors and oils do. This raises the question how Miller was able to model so many of his works on those in Stewart's album when the album remained in Scotland. The answer may lie with three examples in the Bank of America collection that are painted on tissue paper and then glued to a thicker paper: *Chase of the Grizzly Bear, Black Hills* (cat. 11), *Grizzly Bear Hunt* (cat. 12), and *Visit to an Indian Camp on the Border of a Lake* (cat. 9). Two of them conform closely in size and almost exactly in composition with those Miller prepared for Stewart's album. As such, they may be tracings Miller made before leaving Scotland in order to retain his valuable compositions. *Chase of the Grizzly Bear, Black Hills*, for instance, almost exactly replicates the composition of *Pursuit of a Grisly Bear in the Black Hills near Fort Larrimier* (fig. 17). It also bears evidence of the earlier Stewart sketch in the pencil tracing of the chasm and the distant tree. In addition, infrared reflectography reveals that the bear was originally the larger size portrayed in the earlier sketch made for Stewart. *Grizzly Bear Hunt* includes all the main compositional elements of the Stewart sketch, *Starting a Grizzly Bear from Covert* (see fig. 27), including the tiny but masterfully drawn figure on horseback at the horizon. *Visit to an Indian Camp on the Border of a Lake* departs most substantially from its possible model, *Visit to the Lodge of an Indian Chief* (c. 1837; Fred Jones Jr. Museum of Art, University of Oklahoma, Norman), but the three main figures beneath an awning, flanked by a standing figure on the bank of a stream, have been maintained in roughly the same positions relative to the page.

Some of the works in the Bank of America collection may also have been studies for a second major commission Miller received in 1858–60 for two hundred watercolor sketches for the prominent Baltimore collector William T. Walters. The commission also included a request for one-page notes to accompany each image. The images and notes were bound facing one another in four plain, leather volumes.[51] *Indian Women, Snake Tribe, Oregon* (cat. 22), for instance, appears to have been a preliminary sketch for the final version, *Indian Encampment on the Eau Sucre River* in the Walters album. Miller has pushed toward the middle ground the central pair of women to include more of the river and the canoe that are just suggested in the initial sketch.

About one-third of the works Miller made for Walters in 1858–60 were based on sketches he had originally made for Stewart, and several of the Bank of America images seem to have been attempts to rework compositions originally devised for the earlier commission to suit the later one.[52] *Elk Taking the Water* (cat. 10), for instance, is likely based on a sketch for Stewart, *A Wounded Stag Taking Soil, on a Tributary of the Yellow Stone* (location unknown). The former is so close in composition to the Walters sheet, *Hunting the Elk* (1858–60), as to confirm a direct relationship between the two. *Visit to an Indian Camp on the Border of a Lake* (cat. 9) shows Miller experimenting with a tree lightly sketched in pencil on a far bank, which he omitted from the Walters version, *Visit to an Indian Camp* (see fig. 31), but the Walters watercolor otherwise includes the main compositional elements of the earlier work.

Of course, by necessity because of the large number of watercolors, Walters's commission contained a number of unique compositions that Miller surely devised for the project but did not, in the end, include. *Indian Lodges near the Missouri* (cat. 18) appears to be one such picture. The work is neatly executed on fine paper and appears to have been completed in a single effort, without evidence of extensive reworking or drying between successive layers of paint. It also bears the inscription "76" in the upper right corner, a number that corresponds to the number of the accompanying note in Miller's "Rough Draughts for Notes to Indian Sketches," the first draft of the text Miller wrote to accompany Walters's sketches.[53] Miller's text discusses at length the round structure in the foreground in words that fairly closely follow the main points of a lengthier discussion of Mandan lodges on the Upper Missouri by George Catlin in his widely read *Letters and Notes*.[54] In 1832 Catlin traveled up the Missouri River to the villages of the Mandan and Hidatsa, where he painted numerous sketches and collected artifacts. Miller likely saw Catlin's work in an Indian museum compiled by William H. Clark during a visit he made to Clark's St. Louis home about a week before he and Stewart left for the rendezvous. Stewart, who admired Catlin's work, introduced Miller to Catlin, and Miller's correspondence mentions that Catlin visited him often in his London studio.[55] We might consider Catlin's and Miller's overlapping accounts accurate and mutually reinforcing, if there were any evidence that Miller visited the Mandan, but there is not. Miller's party traveled no farther north on the Missouri than St. Louis or, perhaps, Bellevue. In *Indian Lodges near the Missouri* he appears to rely on Catlin's *Bird's Eye View of Mandan Village* (fig. 18), which shows the round lodges with people sitting on the roofs, although, as the catalogue entry points out, Miller must have had a further source beyond Catlin, since his version is more detailed and accurately rendered.

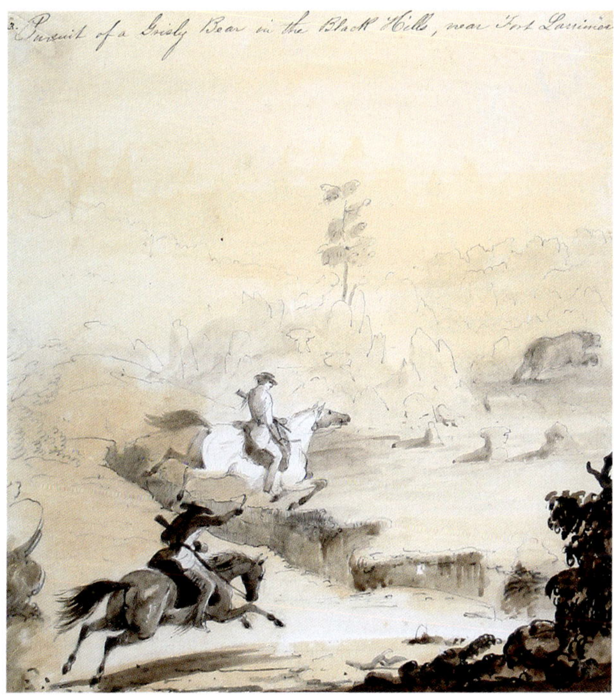

FIGURE 17. Alfred Jacob Miller, *Pursuit of a Grisly Bear in the Black Hills near Fort Larrimier*, c. 1837. Pencil with brown and yellow wash on paper, 7¾ × 7⅛ in. (19.7 × 18.1 cm). Sheldon Museum of Art, University of Nebraska–Lincoln, U.N.L.; Gift of Olga N. Sheldon

The similarity between Miller's and Catlin's texts makes Catlin the likely source for *Indian Lodges near the Missouri*, but living near

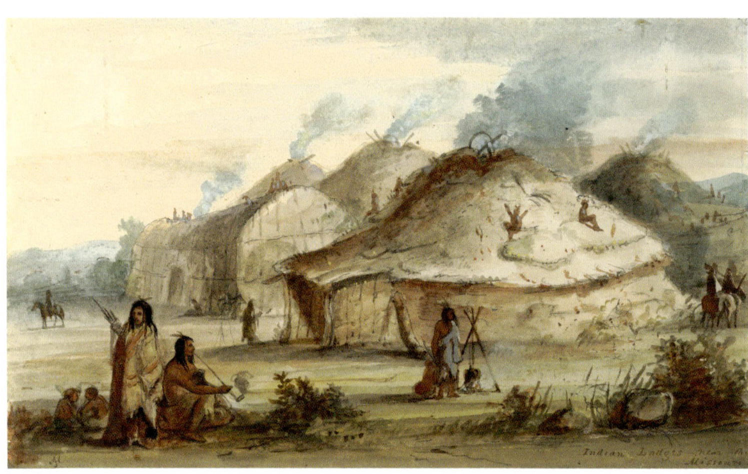

Alfred Jacob Miller, *Indian Lodges near the Missouri* (cat. 18)

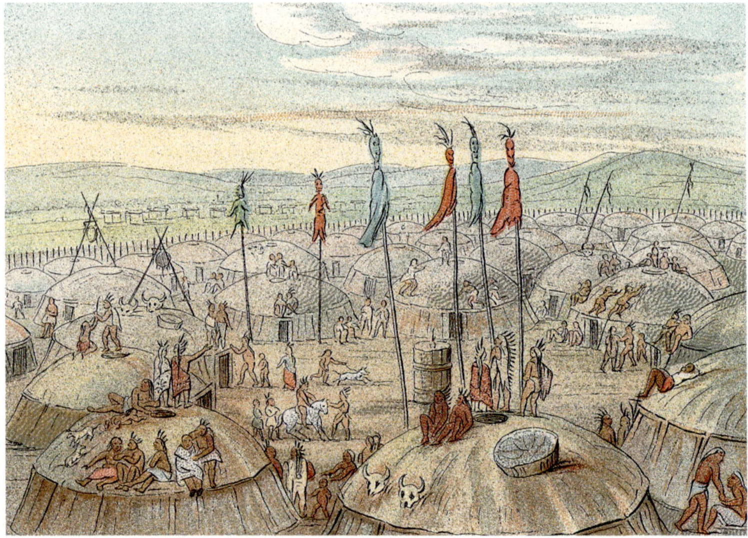

FIGURE 18. George Catlin, *Bird's Eye View of Mandan Village*, from *The Manners, Customs, and Condition of the North American Indians* (London: the author, 1841), 1: pl. 47. Courtesy The Nelson-Atkins Museum of Art, Kansas City, Mo., Spencer Art Reference Library

Washington, D.C., from 1857 to 1860, Miller had several other possible sources of information on the Mandan or other Native American people, including the paintings and collections of fellow artists Charles Bird King, John Mix Stanley, and Seth Eastman. In addition, the visiting delegations of Indians who came from the western territories to negotiate treaties with the United States government or rival groups offered new subjects for the artist.

Finally, several of the Bank of America watercolors relate closely to Alexander Hargreaves Brown's 1867 commission as either studies in preparation for that commission or studio watercolors that Graham selected for reworking as finished pieces. *Departure of the Caravan at Sunrise* (cat. 1) is closer to the composition of *Breaking up Camp at Sunrise* (fig. 19) than to any other version of the subject. The two works share all the same principal compositional elements, from the trapper climbing into the saddle of the white horse at center to the standing figure in the foreground holding the lance. More important, the relative size of the sheets and the proportions of the figures are closest between these two works, as compared with the version painted for Walters (*Breaking up Camp at Sunrise*, 1858–60; The Walters Art Museum) and a sepia version, perhaps a compositional sketch (*Starting the Caravan at Sunrise*, n.d.; Yale Collection of Western Americana, Beinecke Rare Book and Manuscript Library). *Departure of the Caravan*, however, has the number "132" inscribed at the upper right, which corresponds to the number on the rough draft of the text accompanying this image.[56] This suggests that Miller used *Departure of the Caravan* as the preparatory sketch for the Walters version as well as for Brown's, which, ironically, hewed more closely to the composition of the Bank of America sketch than did the earlier Walters version.

For decades, Miller's work has been understood as a record of the American West. Consequently, it has been situated within the context of such phenomena as the fur trade, Indian-white relations, and expansionism. But Miller's works, particularly those in the Bank of America collection, were created in Baltimore and resonated within the milieu of that city. The collection demonstrates the extent to which Miller's western scenes were meaningful within a specific local, rather than a broader, national, context. Though in Baltimore as throughout America, there was a nationalist rhetoric concerning the arts, Miller's images served and promoted a distinct class and civic culture. By placing these works within the locality of Baltimore, we enrich our understanding not only of the works themselves but of American patronage and art making in both the West and the East.

Notes

1. Inventory of Property, Alfred Jacob Miller Estate Papers, 1842–75, MS 1624, Special Collections, Maryland Historical Society, Baltimore. On William H. Graham and the firm Alexander Brown and Sons, see J. Thomas Scharf, *History of Baltimore City and County*, 2 vols. (Baltimore: Regional Publishing Company, 1971), 1:474–75; and Edwin J. Perkins, "Brown, Alexander," in *American National Biography* (New York: Oxford University Press, 2000).

2. The contract for the commission appears among the loose papers in one of Miller's scrapbooks, private collection, Baltimore.

3. William R. Johnston, "Back to Baltimore," in *Alfred Jacob Miller: Artist on the Oregon Trail*, with catalogue raisonné by Karen Dewees Reynolds and William R. Johnston, ed. Ron Tyler (Fort Worth: Amon Carter Museum, 1982), 7n3.

4. For a list of Miller's paintings, see Tyler, *Miller: Artist on the Oregon Trail*. Tyler's book provides the definitive biography of Miller as well as the history of the Stewart commission.

5. This list is extrapolated from Miller's Inventory of Property, the catalogue raisonné of his works in ibid., and examination of collections of watercolors at the Joslyn Museum of Art, Omaha, the Gilcrease Museum of Art, Tulsa, Oklahoma, and the Bank of America collection.

6. Miller Estate Papers.

7. Decatur H. Miller III, conversation, 10 September 2008; and Miller Family Tree, William R. Johnston Files, The Walters Art Museum, Baltimore.

8. The intermediary was the Old Print Shop in New York. See Harry Shaw Newman to Tom K. Smith, New York, 14 May 1947, copy in Alfred Jacob Miller Exhibition Files, The Nelson-Atkins Museum of Art.

9. Lisa Strong, *Sentimental Journey: The Art of Alfred Jacob Miller*, exh. cat. (Fort Worth: Amon Carter Museum, 2008), 15.

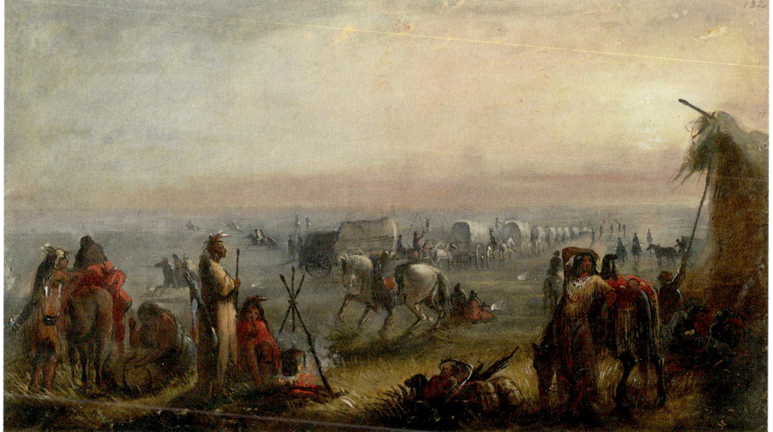

Alfred Jacob Miller, *Departure of the Caravan at Sunrise* (cat. 1)

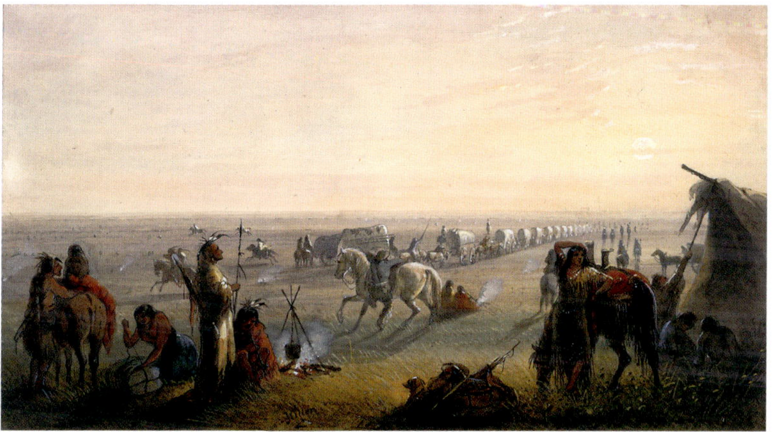

FIGURE 19. Alfred Jacob Miller, *Breaking up Camp at Sunrise*, 1867. Watercolor, gouache, and pen and ink over pencil on paper, 8 × 13⅛16 in. (20.3 × 33.4 cm). Library and Archives Canada, Ottawa, Ontario, Acc. No. 1946-134-1, Gift of Mrs. J. B. Jardine

10. Alfred Jacob Miller, Journal, 15, Archives, The Walters Art Museum, Baltimore. Miller's journal is a series of vignettes probably written in later life (for instance, they record the death of William Drummond Stewart in 1871).

11. Carol Clark, "A Romantic Painter in the American West," in Tyler, *Miller: Artist on the Oregon Trail*, 49; Joan Carpenter Troccoli, *Alfred Jacob Miller: Watercolors of the American West from the Collection of the Gilcrease Museum, Tulsa, Oklahoma,* exh. cat. (Tulsa, Okla.: Thomas Gilcrease Museum Association, 1990), 12–16; and Dawn Glanz, *How the West Was Drawn: American Art and the Settling of the Frontier* (Ann Arbor: UMI Research Press, 1982), 32.

12. Clark, "Romantic Painter," 50; and Miller, Journal, 34.

13. Gretchen M. Cooke, "On the Trail of Alfred Jacob Miller," *Maryland Historical Magazine* 97, no. 3 (Fall 2002): 333.

14. Miller, Journal, 61–64. Miller arrived in New Orleans on 7 December 1836 on the *Platina*. Johnston, "Back to Baltimore," 18n53.

15. Miller, Journal, 53.

16. For a biography of Stewart and a description of the 1837 trek, see Mae Reed Porter and Odessa Davenport, *Scotsman in Buckskin: Sir William Drummond Stewart and the Rocky Mountain Fur Trade* (New York: Hastings House, 1963).

17. Fred R. Gowans, *Rocky Mountain Rendezvous: A History of the Fur Trade Rendezvous, 1825–1840* (Provo, Utah: Brigham Young University Press, 1975), 191.

18. Bernard DeVoto, *Across the Wide Missouri* (Boston: Houghton Mifflin Company, 1964), 309–10; and William H. Goetzmann and William N. Goetzmann, *The West of the Imagination* (New York: W. W. Norton & Company, 1986), 61–63 and 66.

19. Parke-Bernet Galleries, New York, *A Series of Watercolour Drawings by Alfred Jacob Miller, of Baltimore: Artist to Captain Stewart's Expedition to the Rockies in 1837*, 6 May 1966; and Marvin Ross, ed., *The West of Alfred Jacob Miller* (Norman: University of Oklahoma Press, 1968), xxxi–xxxvi.

20. Ron Tyler, "Alfred Jacob Miller and Sir William Drummond Stewart," in Tyler, *Miller: Artist on the Oregon Trail*, 40; and Alfred Jacob Miller to Decatur H. Miller, Murthly Castle, 16 October 1840, Mae Reed Porter and Clyde H. Porter Papers, American Heritage Center, University of Wyoming, Laramie, Box 45.

21. Tyler, *Miller: Artist on the Oregon Trail*, 35–41. Some of the sketches may have been exhibited at this time. A review in the *New York Weekly Herald*, 11 May 1839, 149, describes the works exhibited as "a number of original sketches and views" and later says Miller's sketchings and paintings are on view in the gallery.

22. Alfred Jacob Miller to Decatur H. Miller, Murthly Castle, 16 October 1840, Porter Papers, Box 45; Alfred Jacob Miller to Brantz Mayer, Murthly Castle, 18 October 1840, Mayer-Roszel Papers, Maryland Historical Society; and J. Watson Webb, introduction to William Drummond Stewart, *Altowan: or, Incidents of Life and Adventure in the Rocky Mountains, by an Amateur Traveler*, ed. J. Watson Webb, 2 vols. (New York: Harper & Brothers, 1846), 1:x.

23. Strong, *Sentimental Journey*, 87–88.

24. Stewart, *Altowan*, 1:228.

25. Harry Liebersohn, *Aristocratic Encounters: European Travelers and North American Indians* (Cambridge: Cambridge University Press, 1985), 10; and Strong, *Sentimental Journey*, 103–6.

26. This paragraph summarizes the argument in Strong, *Sentimental Journey*, 85–120.

27. Alfred Jacob Miller to Decatur H. Miller, Murthly Castle, 31 October 1840, 25 December 1840, and 1 November 1841, Porter Papers; and Miller, Journal, 44–45. Tyler, "Alfred Jacob Miller and Sir William Drummond Stewart," 40–43.

28. Anna Wells Rutledge, "Robert Gilmor, Jr.: Baltimore Collector," *Journal of the Walters Art Gallery* 12 (1949): 19–39.

29. *A Century of Baltimore Collecting: 1840–1940,* exh. cat. (Baltimore: Baltimore Museum of Art, 1941); J. Hall Pleasants, *Two Hundred and Fifty Years of Painting in Maryland* (Baltimore: Baltimore Museum of Art, 1945); and *The Taste of Maryland: Art Collecting in Maryland, 1800–1934,* exh. cat. (Baltimore: Walters Art Gallery, 1984).

30. William R. Johnston, *William and Henry Walters: The Reticent Collectors* (Baltimore: Johns Hopkins University Press, in association with the Walters Art Gallery, 1999), 1–85.

31. *Matchett's Baltimore Directory* (Baltimore: R. J. Matchett, 1845).

32. Account Book, The Walters Art Museum, Baltimore. A complete transcript of the book can be found in the J. Hall Pleasants files, Maryland Historical Society. Excerpts from the account book have been published. Miller's western works are listed in Ross, *The West of Miller*, lv–lix.

33. Complete names, addresses, professions, and work addresses for Miller's patrons can be found in *Baltimore Business Directory* (Baltimore: John Murphy); *Matchett's Baltimore Directory*; *Woods Baltimore City Directory* (Baltimore: John W. Woods) for the years 1845–72; and the Dielman-Hayward card file, Maryland Historical Society.

34. Gary Lawson Browne, *Baltimore in the Nation, 1789–1861* (Chapel Hill: University of North Carolina Press, 1980), part 2, esp. 84–85; Scharf, *History of Baltimore*, 1:315–42; Miller, Inventory of Property; and "Baltimore and Ohio Railroad," in *Encyclopedia Britannica* (Chicago: Encyclopedia Britannica, 2003).

35. Glanz, *How the West Was Drawn*, 37–41.

36. Ross, *The West of Miller*, opp. pl. 12.

37. Miller, Account Book.

38. Robert J. Brugger, *Maryland: A Middle Temperament, 1634–1980* (Baltimore: Johns Hopkins University Press, 1988), esp. chap. 6; and Robert I. Cottom Jr. and Mary Ellen Hayward, *Maryland in the Civil War: A House Divided* (Baltimore: Maryland Historical Society, 1994).

39. Among Miller's patrons, Jacob Brandt Jr. was president of the Baltimore–Richmond Steamboat line, a major supplier for the Union troops. "Jacob Brandt, Jr.," *Baltimore Sun*, 14 January 1882, 4; and "Funeral of Mr. Jacob Brandt," *Baltimore Sun*, 16 January 1882, 4. Other ardent supporters of the Union included Heinrich Oelrichs, the merchant-philanthropist Johns Hopkins, and the hardware merchant Augustus Albert. "Henry Ferdinand Oelrichs," Dielman-Hayward card file; Helen Hopkins Thom, *Johns Hopkins: A Silhouette* (Baltimore: Johns Hopkins University Press, 1929), 66–67; and "Death of Augustus James Albert," *Baltimore Sun*, 10 September 1886, 4. In contrast, the banker Thomas Harris and the merchant Patrick Henry Sullivan were supporters of the South and members of the Maryland Club, an organization for Southern sympathizers. "Patrick Henry Sullivan," *Baltimore Sun*, 30 November 1874, 4; and "Thomas Harris," Dielman-Hayward card file.

40. Johnston, *Reticent Collectors*, 22–33.

41. "Isaac Bell," *Dictionary of American Biography* (New York: C. Scribner's Sons, 1943), 155.

42. *Braves and Buffalo: Plains Indian Life in 1837*, intro. Michael Bell (Toronto: University of Toronto Press, 1973) includes all the plates and text from the Brown collection.

43. Strong, *Sentimental Journey*, 216–17; and Edwin J. Perkins, "William H. Graham: Branch Manager and Foreign-Exchange Dealer in Baltimore in the 1850s," *Maryland Historical Magazine* 87, no. 1 (Spring 1992): 10–11.

44. Prinz Maximilian von Wied-Neuwied, *Reise in das innere Nord-America in den Jahren 1832 bis 1834* (Coblenz: J. Hoelscher, 1839–41), with illustrations by Karl Bodmer.

45. Edwin J. Perkins, *Financing the Anglo-American Trade: The House of Brown, 1800–1880* (Cambridge, Mass.: Harvard University Press, 1975).

46. Eik Kahng, ed., *The Repeating Image: Multiples in French Painting from David to Matisse*, exh. cat. (Baltimore: Walters Art Museum, 2007).

47. Maud Early, *Alfred J. Miller, Artist* (Baltimore: privately published, 1894), 2.

48. This sketch may have been omitted from the album because the subject was otherwise amply treated. Stewart's album contained another image of an antelope, *Head of an Antelope* (1837–39; location unknown), illustrated in Parke-Bernet Galleries, New York, 6 May 1966, lot 69, as well as two sketches of an elk fleeing hunters, both titled *Death of the Elk* (1837–39; Earl C. Adams Collection, San Marino, Calif., and National Wildlife Museum, Jackson Hole, Wyo.).

49. Ross, *The West of Miller*, opp. pl. 139.

50. John Crawford to William Drummond Stewart, New Orleans, 11 October 1838, Sublette Papers, Missouri Historical Society, St. Louis. Alfred Jacob Miller to Brantz Mayer, Murthly Castle, 18 October 1840, Mayer-Roszel Papers: "He is delighted with the last pictures I sent him & from the sketches has already selected subjects that will occupy me all the winter in transferring to Canvass."

51. The original albums are in the Walters Art Museum. On the inside cover of each volume are the number of sketches included in each: forty-seven in volume one; fifty-three in volume two; and fifty each in volumes three and four.

52. See also *Departure of the Caravan at Sunrise* (cat. 1), *Watching the Caravan* (cat. 2), *Chase of the Grizzly Bear, Black Hills* (cat. 11), *Grizzly Bear Hunt* (cat. 12), *Taking the Hump Rib* (cat. 15), *Chimney Rock near Scott's Bluff* (cat. 24), and *Stampede of Wild Horses* (cat. 26), of which there were versions in both the Stewart and the Walters commissions.

53. Alfred Jacob Miller, "Rough Draught for Notes to Indian Sketches," Archives of American Art, roll 3280.

54. Ross, *The West of Miller*, opp. pl. 94. Catlin's text appears in *Letters and Notes on the Manners, Customs, and Condition of the North American Indians* (London, 1841; reprint, New York: Dover Publications, 1973), 1:82.

55. Alfred Jacob Miller to Brantz Mayer, Esq., St. Louis, 23 April 1837, Mayer-Roszel Papers; Alfred Jacob Miller to Decatur Howard Miller, 10 February 1842, Porter Papers, Box 46; Sir William Drummond Stewart to George Catlin, New York, May 1839, Catlin Papers, Bureau of Ethnology, Smithsonian Institution, Archives of American Art, roll 2136, frames 513–15.

56. "Rough Draughts," which relates to Ross, *The West of Miller*, opp. pl. 142.

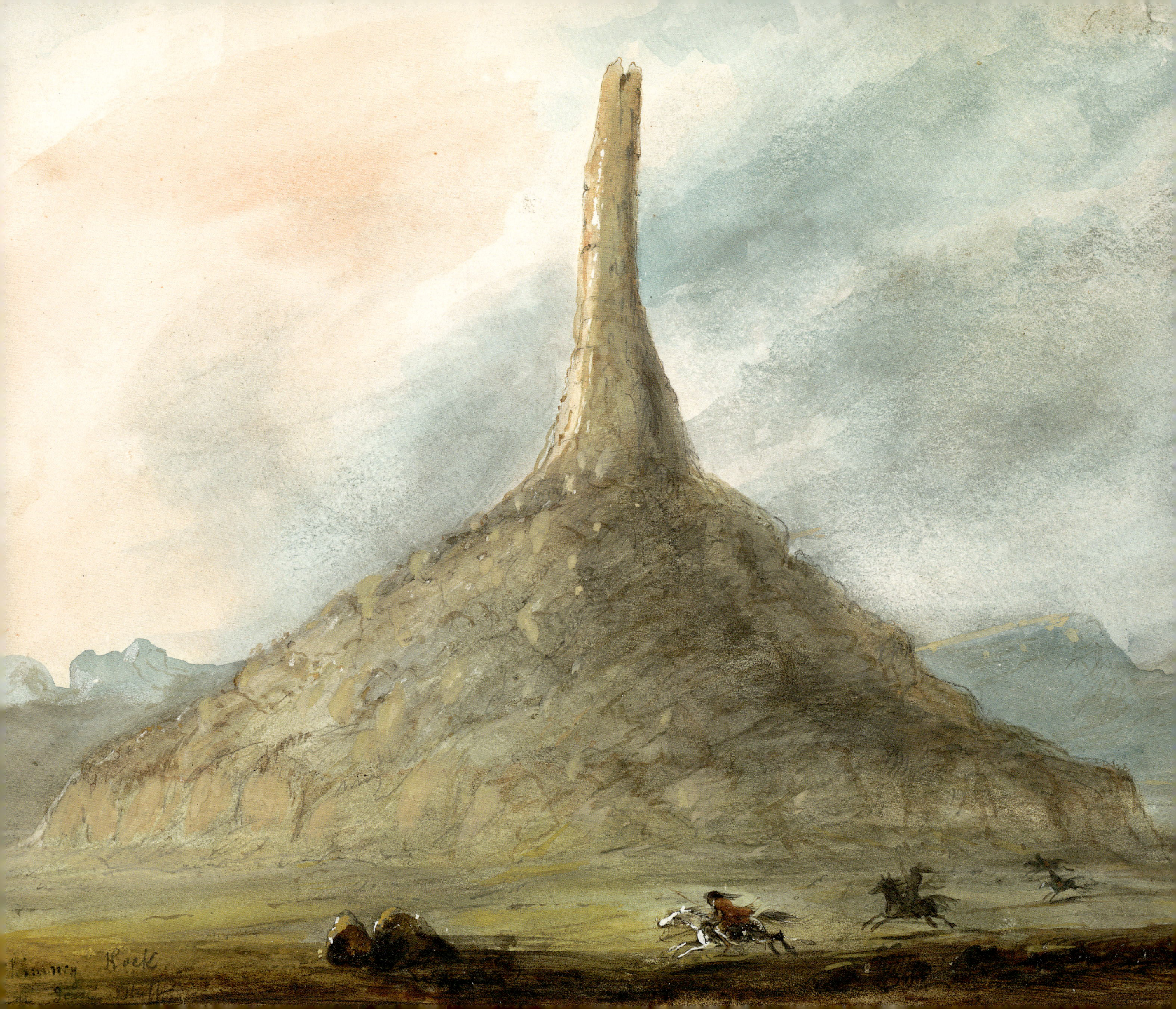
Rock

Alfred Jacob Miller, the Sketch, and the Album

The Place of Watercolor in Mid-Nineteenth-Century American Art

Kathleen A. Foster

When Captain William Drummond Stewart invited Alfred Jacob Miller to join his adventure to the foothills of the Rockies in the spring of 1837, the Scottish adventurer transformed Miller's career and, in the process, turned him into a serious watercolor painter. Miller never set out to be a watercolorist, but by the end of his career his output in this medium far surpassed his work in oil, and today he is most admired for lively, delicate, and masterful works on paper.[1] Like Karl Bodmer, his colleague in western subjects who was also rediscovered in the twentieth century, Miller won a place in American art history for work in a medium that, in his own day, was seen as the province of amateurs or specialists: miniature painters, naturalists, printmakers, and a few British émigrés. His path as a watercolorist, exploring many traditions to discover a personal method and style, maps the development of the medium in nineteenth-century America; the course of his reputation a hundred years later traces a transformation in his audience. Initially prized for their relationship to the intimate, old-fashioned experience of the album, his watercolors rose to fame with the triumph of the modern sketch aesthetic.

Miller's choice to work in watercolors on the trail was a natural one. The materials were simple and portable, and generations of explorer-artists had sanctioned their use. The expedition records that Miller and Stewart might have known—those of Lewis and Clark, Samuel Seymour and Titian Peale (figs. 20, 21) with the Long expedition, Karl Bodmer and his patron, Prince Maximilian von Wied-Neuwied—used pocket-size bound sketchbooks as small as five by four inches, with graphite pencil, pen, and ink and watercolor washes.[2] With the notable exception of the eccentric (and largely self-taught) George Catlin, few artists before about 1850 and the invention of collapsible paint tubes worked *en plein air* with anything but sketchbooks, and even professional watercolor artists usually completed their work in the studio. Watercolor equipment was speedily set up and just as quickly stashed away, perfect for sketching in awkward spots or on the fly. And, more than convenient, watercolor signaled the field experience. It represented authenticity, original work done from nature, on the spot. Miller packed watercolor for practical reasons in 1837, but he would invoke the power of the word *sketch*—and its inference of truthful, eyewitness validity—for the rest of his life.

Fortunately, Miller had been working in wash and watercolor for more than a decade before he set off with Stewart's party. Although little is known about his training, his earliest schoolboy drawings illustrate the habits of the largest class of watercolor painters in the United States, even today: middle-class amateurs and children, who picked up watercolors at home or at school. As he grew older and began to watch the practice of professional artists in Baltimore and Philadelphia, he would have encountered the principal uses of watercolor painting in this period,

Alfred Jacob Miller, *Chimney Rock near Scott's Bluff*, detail (cat. 24)

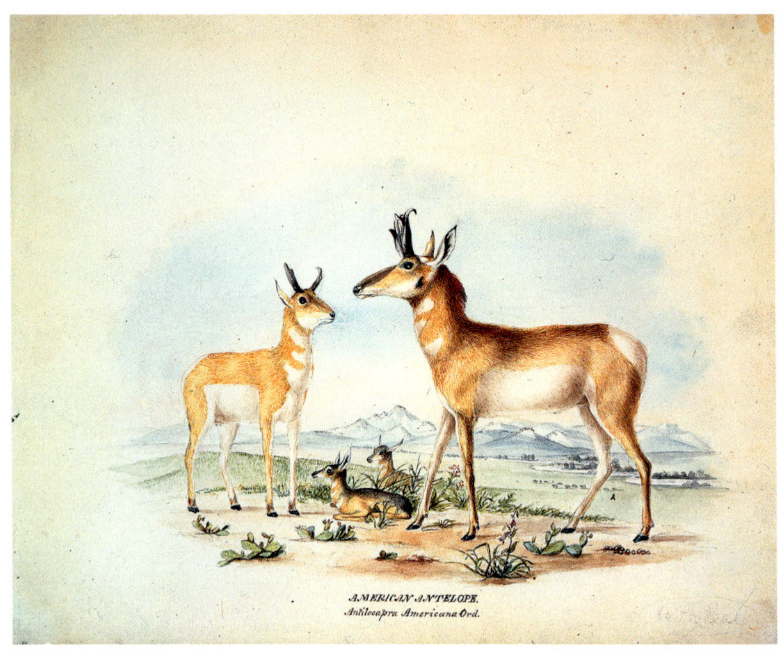

FIGURE 20. Titian Ramsay Peale, *Antelope (Gazelle)*, c. 1821–22. Watercolor over graphite on paper, 11 1/16 × 13 7/16 in. (28.1 × 34.1 cm). American Philosophical Society, Philadelphia

all on view at the Peale family's two museums in these cities, or at the Pennsylvania Academy of the Fine Arts in Philadelphia. Peale's Baltimore Museum, founded by Rembrandt Peale in 1814 near the Miller family home, held four annual exhibitions between 1822 and 1825 and retained a standing collection that, by 1831, included three of Miller's old master copies.[3] All three venues would have made obvious the prestige and priority of oil painting, but miniature paintings, the occasional watercolor landscape, and architectural drawings, usually tinted with washes, were on view.

More important, both of the Peale museums integrated art and natural history, associating watercolor with the realms of science and exploration. Titian Ramsay Peale exhibited at the academy in 1822 four finished watercolors prepared after his return from the Long expedition, such as *Antelope (Gazelle)* (fig. 20), which expressed his role on the trip as a naturalist. In watercolor, Peale united his authority as a witness to new topography and animal life with his expertise as a scientific illustrator. Titian's more action-packed field sketches in pencil and ink, such as figure 21, augmented the large exhibition watercolors prepared back at home, demonstrating the two modes of the explorer-naturalist-illustrator: dashing memoranda in simple materials, painted on the spot; and refined, delicately detailed and colored images prepared in the studio, perhaps years later, intended for public display and subsequent publication as engravings or lithographs. Briefly on view at the academy's exhibitions, Titian Peale's images were apparently shared later with visitors to Peale's Museum in Philadelphia, along with the specimens returned by Lewis and Clark and the records of the Long expedition, including hundreds of sketches and finished views by Titian and his fellow artist on the trip, Samuel Seymour. Prince Maximilian and Bodmer made a special visit to examine these pictures before their own trip west. With the same understanding of the role of watercolor in such an undertaking, Bodmer produced similar bold field sketches and fine finished views, followed by printed reproductions that might, in turn, be hand tinted with watercolors to better resemble the original model (see fig. 3). Miller surely knew about this major trove at Peale's Museum and understood watercolor's alliance with science, fieldwork, and publication. His western watercolors fall into the same two types, recognizing the dual utility of the medium. Embracing the excitement of encounter as well as the discipline of documentation, and closely affiliated with printmaking, watercolor was the explorer's and the illustrator's choice.[4]

This association, long noted in practice, was a source of symbolic power. Although Charles Willson Peale would make oil versions of the Long expedition watercolors for long-term display in his museum, and other artists—including Miller—would prepare larger oil paintings from their field sketches, watercolor remained a viable medium for the more elaborate studio rendition, even though it was less tractable than oils and had less impact on exhibition. Why? For some, its precision and delicacy offered truth. Titian Peale, like John James Audubon, surely valued the delicacy of watercolor tints when he described butterflies and birds for exacting new natural history texts. Others, like Bodmer and Seymour, were trained with the professional habits of printmakers, who worked principally in line and wash, or from the watercolors of others. But for Miller, with no interest in science and only a peripheral involvement in printmaking, the appeal of watercolor would have been mainly in the more subliminal message of immediacy and authenticity palpable in the field sketch. His mandate, to record the colorful people and adventures of the trip as Stewart's personal journalist, made his assignment more dramatic than scientific, and, as many scholars have noted, his version of the experience was profoundly shaped by Romantic attitudes. Even so, Miller was eager to adopt the stance of the field-worker and gain credibility from his medium as well as his method.[5]

This Romantic impulse to express a personal encounter with nature was fed by another source, the modern use of watercolor as an outdoor sketching medium by landscape artists in search of the picturesque. Recently developed by British artists raised in the topographic tradition, this new genre of watercolor was seen rarely at the Pennsylvania Academy or the Baltimore Museum before 1840. The Philadelphia-based painter Thomas Sully, born in England, owned a text by John Varley, an artist often cited as the father of modern landscape painting in watercolor; Sully's student John Neagle conscientiously transcribed "Sully's copy of Varley" and owned work by Samuel Prout.[6] Neagle's earnest notes and exercises demonstrate that such work was so little known and watercolor instruction manuals were so scarce, that John H. B. Latrobe could feel justified in appropriating much of Varley's advice, verbatim, in his *Progressive Drawing Book*, published in Baltimore in 1827.[7] Latrobe's text summarizes the standard English watercolor method of an already formulaic and somewhat old-fashioned order, with layered transparent

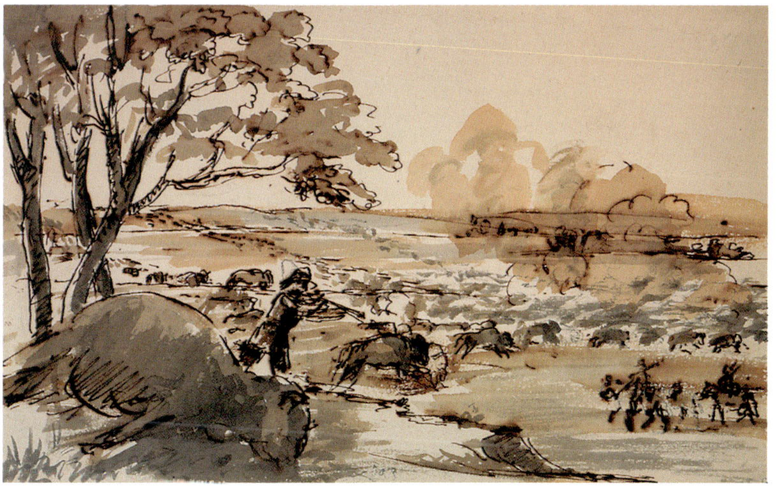

FIGURE 21. Titian Ramsay Peale, *Bison Hunt*, 1820. Watercolor and wash over ink on paper, 11 1/16 × 13 7/16 in. (28.1 × 34.1 cm). American Philosophical Society, Philadelphia

washes building to a soft and generalized atmospheric effect. Miller may have known this text, and perhaps he studied examples of this exotic new work, but his technique in Europe from 1833–34, when he was sketching Swiss scenery and Italian architecture, shows a less patient and systematic approach to landscape as well as a mixed transparent and opaque technique that seems to have come from more modern English sources, such as Prout and James Duffield Harding. However, the Romantic rhetoric that fueled the enthusiasm for watercolor in Britain—the notion of working in nature, responding spontaneously to fleeting effects—only enhanced the practical and scientific arguments for its use as a field medium. In the United States, the beauties of the national landscape inspired work by British-born watercolorists in this new picturesque tradition, such as Joshua Shaw, William Guy Wall, John Hill, William J. Bennett, George Harvey, and William H. Bartlett, who worked up field sketches into studio compositions and then successful print portfolios between about 1820 and 1840. Miller's awareness of this work would show up in his western

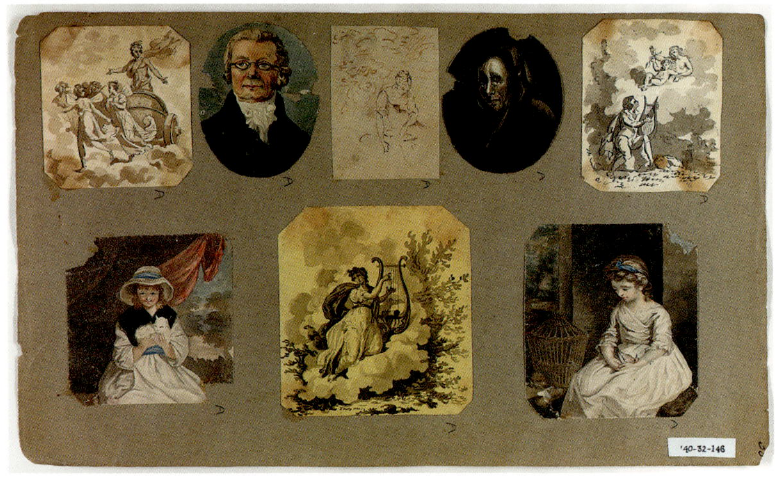

FIGURE 22. Thomas Sully, scrapbook page, assembled by 1849. Philadelphia Museum of Art, Gift of E. A. Belmont, 1940

landscapes, such as *Chimney Rock near Scott's Bluff* (cat. 24), with its soft layers of color and complex lifting, scratching, and blotting techniques.[8]

But Miller's long suit was never landscape painting, and his early focus on portraits and figure subjects entailed a different set of watercolor conventions. Miniature painters, who would thrive until the onset of the photographic age in the 1840s, learned a dainty, mostly transparent technique of stippling and hatching that appears in looser form in Miller's Indian portrait studies in watercolor. He could have learned this from many artists, including the Peale family, whose works abounded in Baltimore and Philadelphia, but he seems to have had no interest in such work early in his career. Miniature painters tended to specialize in watercolor; not so portrait artists and figure painters in oil, who used watercolor and wash in more open-ended ways. Miller, clearly set on this latter path, followed the example of the most famous American portraitist in his neighborhood, Thomas Sully.

The earliest accounts of Miller's training record that he studied with Sully in 1831–32, although an examination of Sully's journal reveals that "Miller of Baltimore, student of painting, brought me letters of introduction" on 13 April 1830.[9] Evidently, Miller traveled to Philadelphia seeking advice and had a chance to visit Sully's studio, where he could have seen many books, portfolios of prints and drawings, and a wide range of paintings. Miller's 1831 copy of Sully's 1809 portrait *Miss Mary Coale* (Maryland Historical Society) suggests he continued to absorb lessons from the master beyond this first visit, and their many mutual friends in Baltimore hint at a more extended contact.[10]

Some of Sully's studio material, kept in albums and portfolios, has survived en bloc to demonstrate the varied use of watercolors that Miller might have witnessed. First employed as a miniature painter, Sully was a master at this small scale before 1804, and, like many painters trained in the medium who shifted over to oils, he continued to use it for more informal, backstage purposes. Ink wash and watercolor served as study media, to note memorable compositions seen in other artists' work. Pen and wash drawings taken from engravings and paintings appear in Sully's scrapbook (fig. 22), just as they occur in Miller's European sketchbooks, filled with memoranda of paintings by Rembrandt and Turner.[11] Sully used wash and watercolor for sketching, to record first impressions, or to block out compositional ideas. He suggested to his students that they make a quick study of their portrait subject before launching into work on the final canvas. Some of Sully's surviving watercolors may be such preliminary forays, to confirm his intended composition and perhaps share it with the client for his or her approval. Miller, in the 1840s, was preparing watercolor studies for exactly this purpose, to be shown to one patron or saved in a scrapbook to pique the imagination of the next.[12]

Either made at the outset of work or summarily recording a picture after the fact, such small, personal drawings have an abstracted, shorthand style, often based entirely on light and dark washes, with emphatic pen detailing. Superimposing several ink washes of graduated density to a scaffold of pen line (frequently reinforcing an initial graphite sketch), this technique was widely practiced by European artists in the eighteenth century for many kinds of study drawings. Sully could have learned this kind of pen, ink, and wash handling in the studio of Benjamin West, who was a master of this shorthand, but it was widely practiced by such American artists as Thomas Cole.

Miller's fondness for pen line and ink washes also suggests the inspiration of prints, which functioned as models for so many generations of American artists. Book illustrations or single plates in gift books, images from plays and novels, or genre subjects and caricatures surely shaped the visual conventions as well as the humor that drive the dozens of wash figure drawings that were found in Miller's studio after his death. His sense of the human comedy emerges in drawings such as *Now! Come on Butcher if You Want to Fight* (fig. 23), evidently made for his personal delight and the entertainment of his friends. Some record characters and scenes from his earliest years as an artist, but they may have been done retrospectively, like his journal, or reworked decades later. Usually based on a graphite underdrawing, sometimes very loose and scribbled, the sketches are typically reinforced with a warm brownish black pen line and then built up with overlaid washes in brown and a cooler black. Often, he added opaque white watercolor for highlights and occasionally a single tint of transparent color.[13]

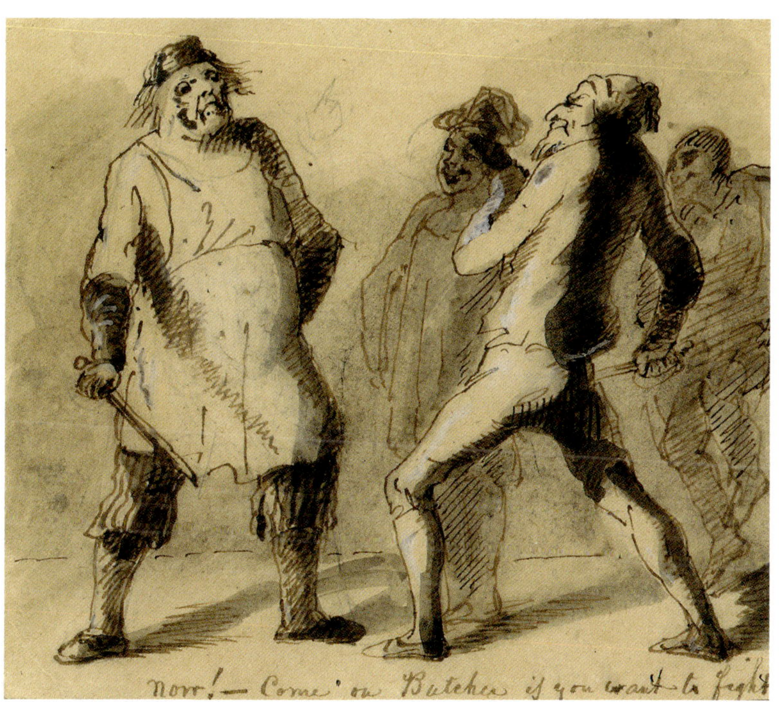

FIGURE 23. Alfred Jacob Miller, *Now! Come on Butcher if You Want to Fight*, n.d. Black and brown inks, pen and brush, with gouache highlights on paper, 4 × 4⅝ in. (10.2 × 11.8 cm). Courtesy of The Maryland Historical Society, Baltimore

Miller could have developed a taste for this kind of figure drawing from American humorists, such as David Claypoole Johnston, but it is more likely that he absorbed it from French and English prints, seen in the United States or Europe. Numerous scholars have noted his attention to Eugène Delacroix, whose work he copied and whose bold wash and watercolor technique may have been inspirational. However, it remains most likely that Miller, who produced various lithographic projects in the 1830s, looked keenly at the prints of Delacroix and other French Romantics such as Théodore Géricault, or those who specialized in modern bourgeois life, such as Eugène Lami, Nicolas Charlet, Alphonse Devéria, Paul Gavarni, Honoré Daumier, and Constantin Guys. Likewise, the English tradition of Thomas Rowlandson and George Cruikshank could have supplied a language of animated line and strong dark and light forms, conveying humorous topics. Usually framed with conversational captions, jokes, puns, or exclamatory titles, such prints served as a basis for Miller's caricatures back in Baltimore, again demonstrating the intersecting worlds of watercolor, book illustration, and printmaking. His love of the theater—shared with Sully and many of these printmakers—emerged in a mode perfectly adapted to storytelling.[14]

Armed with two nascent watercolor modes—a full-color, more deliberate technique and a speedy pen, ink, and wash manner—Miller set forth with Captain Stewart in the summer of 1837. Probably he saw little of the work of his immediate predecessors on the same trail. Some of Catlin's oils were inspected in St. Louis, but Bodmer had returned to Germany with his sketchbooks.[15] So Miller had to learn on the job, goaded by Stewart, who was full of ideas about what was interesting to record. Given the rapid pace of their travels, most of Miller's actual field sketches depict moments in camp, at daybreak, siesta, or sunset. Assuming many risks to his materials during the trip as well as the time available for sketching, probably no more than about one hundred items from the journey survive.[16] His view of an abandoned Indian fort was made on cream-colored paper that may represent the size of one of his pocket sketchbooks (see cat. 7), similar to those he had carried in the Musée du Louvre in Paris to make thumbnail sketches of Rembrandt's paintings.[17] Working fast, Miller used his high-speed system: brown and black ink washes and pen line over a quick graphite underdrawing, with a few white highlights. Watercolor paints seem to have been pulled out in camp and for portrait sessions.[18] *Old Bill Burrows, a Free Trapper* (cat. 5), also on a small sketchbook-size page, may be the straightforward record of a pose taken on the prairies. To his basic materials of graphite and ink, Miller added a very few pigments—transparent blue and opaque ocher and red (possibly vermilion)—to produce a very fresh and aerial effect. Clean, simple bands of wash create a sense of distance, while fine touches construct the picturesque trapper and his mule.

Miller returned to New Orleans in the fall of 1837, charged with producing a portfolio of sketches and paintings focusing on Stewart's adventures. From this moment, until eighteen oil paintings were shown in New York in May 1839 and the whole lot was shipped to Scotland, Miller developed a new, more fluent language of watercolor painting. It was based on the field sketches (most of which, following Sully's advice, he held back for his own later use) but enlarged by the opportunity for improvements based on memory, imagination, and more stable studio conditions. This campaign produced eighty-seven watercolor and wash sketches that Stewart promptly bound in an album. Wrote Miller to his brother, "The Sketches which I sent with the pictures and some prepared while in New Orleans which you have not seen, are all placed in a richly bound port-folio and form one of the Chief Attractions of the drawing room to his [Stewart's] distinguished visitors who are profuse in their compliments to me."[19]

The vision of Miller's "Sketches . . . neatly arranged in a richly bound Scrap book"[20] in the parlor at Murthly Castle introduces the special viewing context of the watercolor in this era, which drove the scale and the affect of Miller's work in this medium. Understanding the appeal of the album, allied to the themes of scientific documentation and Romantic sketching, helps explain the special charm of Miller's work and unites it with the work on paper of many printmakers and watercolorists of this period. Most prints, drawings, and smaller watercolors were kept in portfolios or bound albums, to keep them clean and safe, and for ease of viewing.[21] Miller himself was an inveterate keeper of scrapbooks. Some fifteen were found in his studio after his death, showing signs of revision and reuse over time (as in fig. 25), and almost all of the watercolors in the Bank of America collection show signs of such mounting.[22] Sully's album (see fig. 22) from the same era demonstrates the informal use of such scrapbooks by artists, to preserve travel sketches, *modelli*, memoranda, engravings held for reference or inspiration, and, in the tradition of the *liber amicorum*, gifts from friends.[23]

The purposes of such albums—to enshrine precious engravings, souvenirs of travel and friendship, or images to be mined for future work—take us in one direction; in another direction lies the special viewing experience they supplied. The antipode of the collective, public, and often dazzling viewing arena of the gallery exhibition, the panorama, and the increasingly spectacular theater arts of this period, albums offered the intimacy and privacy of the book. With Stewart's guests in his drawing room or among Miller's cronies in his studio, the album was perused in small, conversational groups, seated knee to knee. Their experience was close-range, without intervening glass or frame, allowing a very direct sense of participation in the making of the surface, and hence a close sense of communication with the artist. With the sketch on your lap, you are effectively in the place of the artist when the drawing was made, and the experience of making and perhaps the reality of the scene depicted become palpably immediate. As appreciation for an artist's "signature" handling grew and the collecting of artists' sketches increased in the nineteenth century, so, too, did the viewing of albums and portfolios become an invitation to share the creative moment.

Those less engaged by the technique and style of the artist might be entertained by the book-like narrative or documentary pleasure of such albums. Although some were randomly organized, many—like Stewart's—united a series of related subjects that told a story of travel or society. The idea of the voyage or the record of colorful people—trappers, Sioux, or the Parisian bourgeoisie—animates many an album of prints or drawings from this period. Miller's handwritten texts, which accompanied each of Stewart's watercolors, follow the conventions of printed portfolios and illustrated books, bringing the image to life with personal anecdote. His remarks reinforce the credibility of the pictures and redouble the power of the album as a vicarious experience.

Artists and publishers fed this popular taste in the middle of the nineteenth century with a flood of illustrated books and portfolios, mostly based in watercolor and wash technique. Some created unique watercolor albums, such as the lavish set of sixty-one watercolors painted by Eugène Lami for Prince Anatoly Demidoff in the 1830s (and published in 1848 as a print portfolio) recording contemporary Parisian society. Others, including Pavel Svinin, Shaw, Hill, Wall, Bennett, Harvey, and Bartlett in the United States, or Turner, Prout, Harding, and a legion of British artist-travelers abroad, produced watercolors expressly intended for engraved portfolios, while artists such as Seymour, Peale, Lesueur, Bodmer, Audubon, and Eastman translated watercolor field sketches into prints that, however beautiful, served a largely documentary or illustrative mission. Working between these poles, Catlin produced his album *Souvenir of the North American Indian* in 1849, with fifty watercolors summarizing the imagery of his Indian Gallery of oil paintings, followed by his series of *Albums Unique* in the 1850s, containing "sketch" replicas of his earlier oils that were vended as original fieldwork.[24] Representing the same phenomenon in figure studies, Nicolino Calyo painted in gouache several sets of his *Cries of New York* in the 1840s, then published them as a print portfolio.[25] In 1842, spurred by this general idea if not the parallel publication projects of Bodmer and Catlin, Captain Stewart invited Miller to develop his album sketches into lithographs to illustrate a planned book on his travels.[26] Although Miller was unable to comply, such projects, from the high-end princely commission to the mass-market publication of Bartlett's *American Scenery*, demonstrate how watercolor stood at the intersection of scientific documentation, Romantic sketching, printmaking, and the culture of the album.

Better than Miller, perhaps, Stewart understood the place of the album and its multiple uses—as a trophy record of his exploits, a conversation piece in his drawing room, a set of proposals for larger oils, and a visual draft of his illustrated memoir. For Miller, driven by Stewart's agenda and growing as an artist, the Murthly album and the related sketches and copies from 1837–42 would be a mine of inspiration for three decades. Although no examples in the Bank of America collection are from Stewart's album, many (such as cats. 9, 12) were derived from it, and the clean dating of the album makes it the benchmark for Miller's early style in watercolor. It was a style based on his field method, certainly because this was the system—with graphite and two inks—that Miller knew best. To this palette of brown and gray, he added a few tints of watercolor—most often yellow, sometimes blue, green, and brown—and occasionally touches of opaque white on the highlights and gum glazes on the darks (see figs. 24, 27). Of different sizes (perhaps because they were trimmed for mounting in the album) and on different papers, they suggest work done over time, in different locations. The handling is spirited, with a lively pen line and dashing washes, giving a feeling of

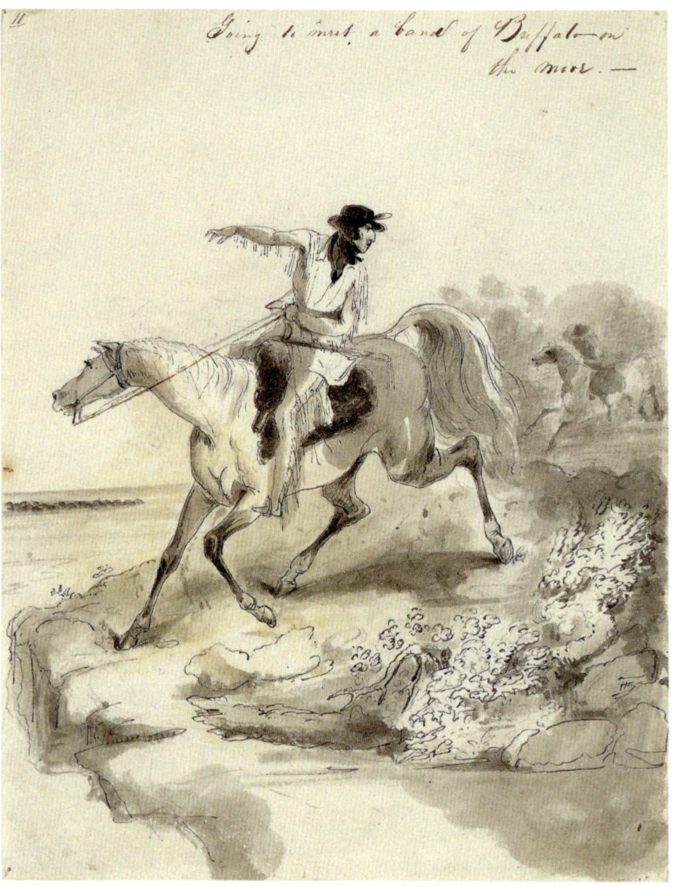

FIGURE 24. Alfred Jacob Miller, *Going to Meet a Band of Buffalo on the Move*, c. 1837. Ink and wash over graphite underdrawing on paper, 8½ × 6⅝ in. (21.6 × 16.8 cm). Amon Carter Museum, Fort Worth, Texas, 1966.25

spontaneity and freshness. Some of these images may have been done on the trail, and others may have been colored later, over pencil sketches done on the spot, but the majority were probably created in the studio, if only because of their size, the difficulty of the action depicted, and the nicety of the composition.[27]

The scenes showing horses, in particular, suggest reference to prints, such as the many lithographs by Victor Adam found in one of Miller's personal scrapbooks (fig. 25).[28] Adam specialized in prints like these of animals, carriages, wagons, and picturesque figures—the staffage of many a landscape or urban view. Made for the instruction of students and the convenience of artists, these prints were commonplace in Paris, where Miller may have acquired them. Prancing and elegantly posturing or galloping at full tilt in a rocking-horse pose never seen in nature, Miller's horses could not have been drawn from life with such confidence; certainly nothing in his earlier work shows such proficiency. Miller taught himself to draw horses at this moment, just as he may have consulted the natural history studies of Peale or John D. Godman, to inform his depictions of antelopes and elk.[29]

Although he prepared these images with deliberation and research, Miller nonetheless referred to them as his "sketches," intentionally blurring the distinction between the actual field drawings and those made later in the studio and downplaying the role of memory and artifice. His term categorizes them as spontaneous and unfinished—"rough draughts," as he titled his first set of accompanying texts. Labeled as such, they claim the virtue of first inspiration and the authenticity of an original encounter with the subject. The style and medium, so like the field sketches of Titian Peale (see fig. 21), signify on-the-spot observation, and so they served as illustrations to many an after-dinner story at Murthly Castle. Captain Stewart and his contemporaries did not care that they were not actually painted in the field; to say that a work was "from nature" or done "on the spot"—as frequently noted in print portfolios—simply professed that the artist of the original image really witnessed the subject.[30] Holding true to the memories these sketches represented, Miller enlarged them into oils that, like Catlin's early field oils, carry the same sketch aesthetic, inflated with varying degrees of success. In this sense, the Murthly watercolors were also "sketches" in that they were proposed paintings, as Sully taught, while the subsequent oil paintings sometimes intentionally remained sketchlike, to capture the "wonderful power and spirit" of work done in the field.[31]

Miller returned to Baltimore in 1842, bought a farm, and only slowly turned to his western subjects as a sidebar to his principal work as a portrait artist. The western subjects that he sent to exhibition in New York, Philadelphia, and Baltimore were evidently in oil; sketches saved from the journey or early drafts made not long after and tracings from the Stewart album remained a treasured lode of ideas for ninety-four oils he produced over the next three decades.[32] For Miller, watercolor continued to be the arena of "the sketch"—including compositional planning, outdoor sketching, and imaginative invention. In this period he adopted a new dark manner on tan or brown paper, which required more gouache to build all tones lighter than the paper. The works in the Bank of America collection from the 1840s and 1850s also show that he was looking at prints by Catlin (see fig. 36) and Bodmer to enlarge his own repertoire of Indian subjects. He was also preparing "drawings" for publishers who would develop his images as prints, perhaps hoping to partially fulfill Stewart's concept, although he was never able to muster the investment of energy and funds required for a portfolio like Bodmer's or Catlin's.[33]

The concept of the portfolio returned, however, to propel Miller's mature style in watercolor: a commission in June 1858 for "15 sketches of Indian scenes at $12 each" from his friend the forty-one-year-old Baltimore businessman William C. Wait. Eight months later another local patron and new collector, the thirty-nine-year-old liquor merchant William T. Walters, ordered forty "drawings in watercolors at $12." In June 1859, shortly before his tragic death, Wait asked for another group of "22 drawings (cold.) [colored] Indian scenes" at the same price.[34] Walters continued the pace, building to a total of two hundred images, and the last batch of fifty "Indian sketches" was delivered in August 1860.[35] Walters placed his watercolors in four "richly bound" albums embossed with the title *Original Sketches*, which joined a similar portfolio of French drawings. At the same time, demonstrating his enthusiasm for

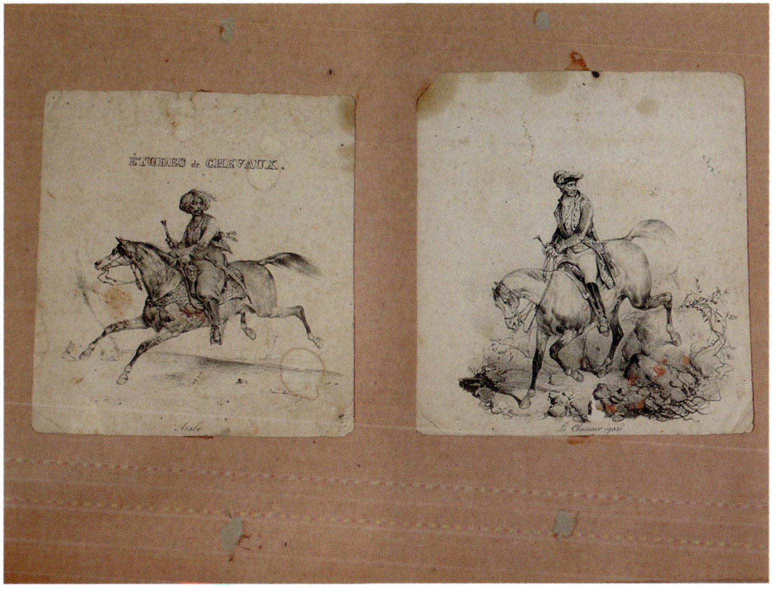

FIGURE 25. Alfred Jacob Miller, scrapbook page with two *Études de Chevaux* by Victor Adam, c. 1833. Private collection

this kind of intimate material, he acquired an album in the fall of 1859 also designated *Original Sketches*, containing more than one hundred drawings and paintings on paper by American artists.[36]

For Miller, the Walters commission, like the Murthly album, inspired steady work under pressure that consolidated a new style in watercolor. Tightly dated to 1858–60, the Walters albums establish the second benchmark for Miller's work in the medium. Although done with speed, these images are more detailed and elaborate, and more colorful—with a recurrent use of red, blue, and gold—using naturally opaque pigments or white gouache mixed liberally into the tints. With sparkling gum glazes to give depth to the darks, the Walters images have the impact of small paintings. Although it has been argued that this more detailed style catered to the taste of Miller's unsophisticated merchant patrons, this manner followed the Continental taste of the 1830s

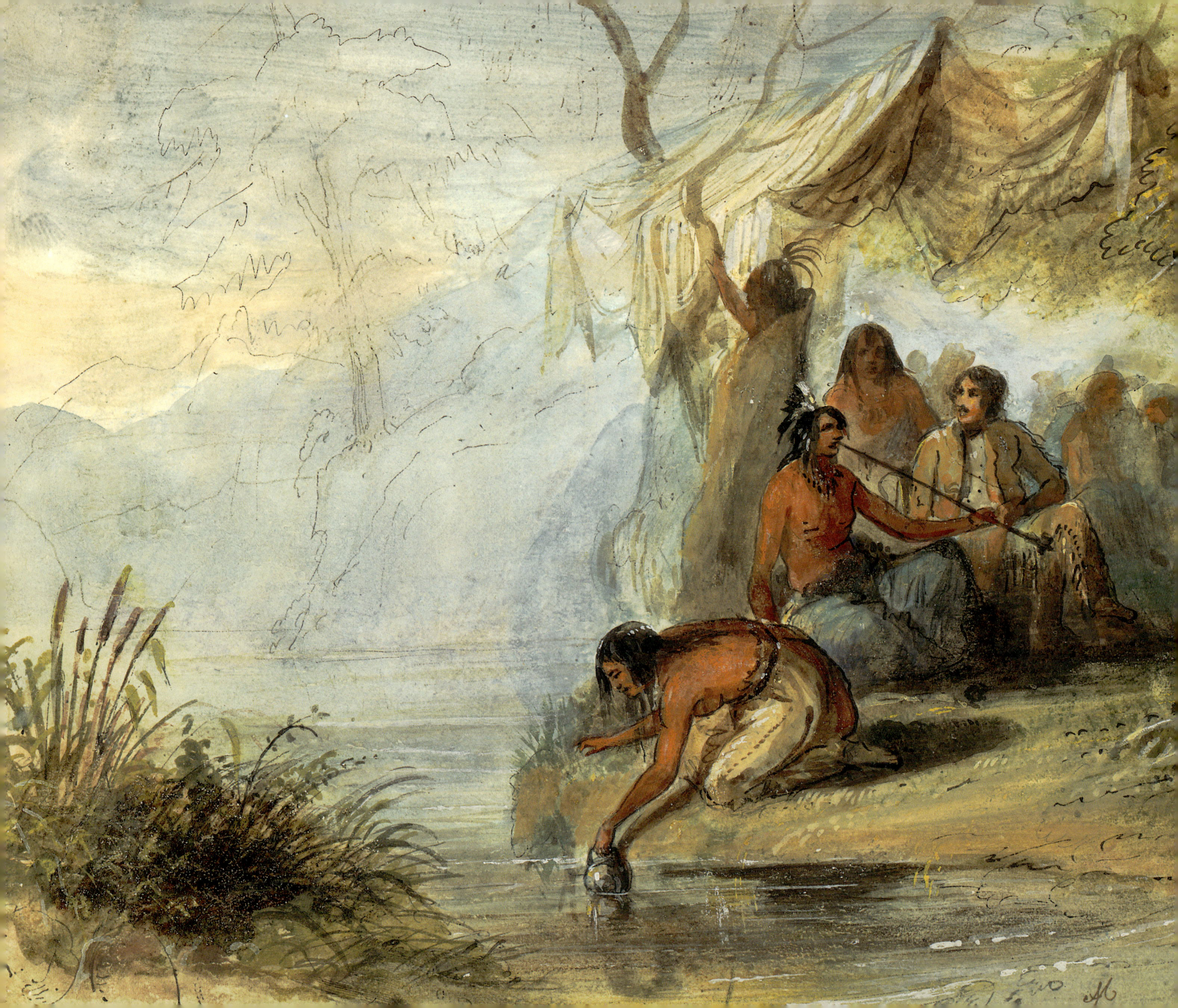

for mixed gouache technique, seen in popular illustrations, the stylish French genre subjects of Lami, or the gouaches of the Italian-born Calyo, whose work remained in Baltimore collections.[37] As the experience of the trail receded, Miller's work grew finer and sweeter, in keeping with the taste of the 1850s, but the "sketch" identity held fast.

To construct two hundred images for Walters, Miller ransacked his earlier work for ideas. His process may be visible in *Visit to an Indian Camp on the Border of a Lake* (cat. 9), which is on tissue evidently used to trace some of the Stewart sketches for his own record. Using a jagged, bouncing graphite line characteristic of his early work, Miller added curly pen detailing that appears in other drawings in the Murthly album. Made sometime before 1842, this drawing may have been colored then and revisited many years later. The splashy, milky washes at the left, akin to the heavier gouache mixtures in Miller's late style, override the pencil trees and landscape outlines in the drawing, finding new mountain contours that correlate better to a third solution in the version painted for Walters in 1858–60 (fig. 26). Testing this older sketch for possibilities, Miller moved to a new sheet to redraw the subject completely for Walters, making the poses more graceful and convincing and shifting the light source.

Miller's growth as a watercolorist, and the value of the Bank of America portfolio, can be measured in a comparison of a sketch from the Murthly album, *Starting a Grizzly Bear from Covert* (fig. 27), a later version of the same subject painted for Walters (fig. 28), and an interim image (cat. 12), which bridges the gap. The first, showing Captain Stewart and the half-breed hunter Antoine, has the fantastic energy of many of the Murthly album compositions, with the doglike bear, in a rocking-horse gallop that mirrors that of the horses, bursting out of his lair in an explosion of brushmarks. On gray card, the image uses no gouache but relies on gum glazes to reinforce the dark, foreground form of the bear. *Grizzly Bear Hunt* (cat. 12), on tissue mounted on heavier paper, seems to have been traced from the Stewart sketch. Miller subtly improved the composition by placing the tissue sheet so that the figure of the bear

Alfred Jacob Miller, *Visit to an Indian Camp on the Border of a Lake*, detail (cat. 9)

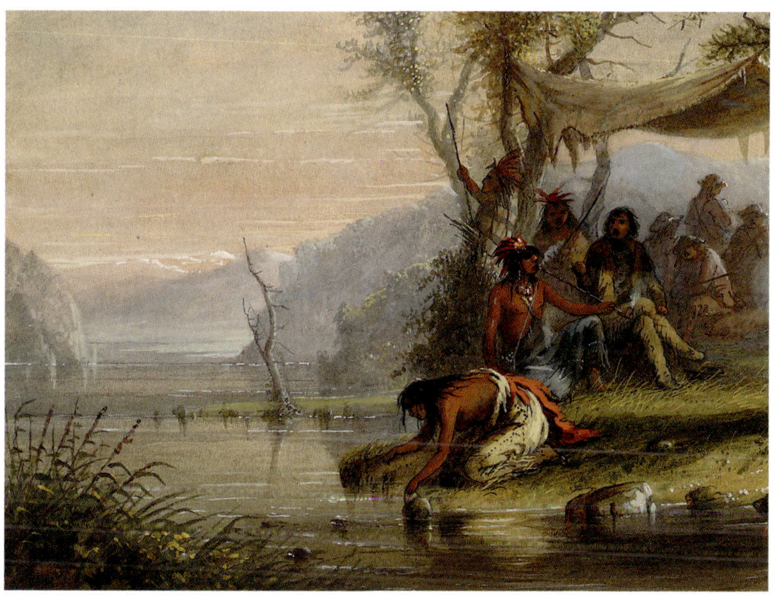

FIGURE 26. Alfred Jacob Miller, *Visit to an Indian Camp* (detail), c. 1858–60. Watercolor on paper, 8 15/16 × 13 3/16 in. (22.7 × 33.5 cm). The Walters Art Museum, Baltimore

comes closer to the lower edge, allowing more room for the sky. Once his figures were in place, he revised the principals—replacing Stewart and his company with Indians and elaborating the trees at left and right to give more drama to the bear's hideaway. These revisions could have been done any time after 1842, but the stronger color, lavish use of gum glazes, and denser washes signal the taste of the 1850s. The image done for Walters, *The Grizzly Bear* (fig. 28), like all the "sketches" in the commission, was on a larger sheet of good watercolor paper that gave the figures more room and clean margins free of annotations. With the removal of the barricade of trees on the left, the total effect is more spacious, but the figures seem farther away, and the bear—in his thicket of dainty berry bushes—seems less surprising and threatening. This general curve, often noted, holds throughout Miller's career, which moves from the spontaneity of the

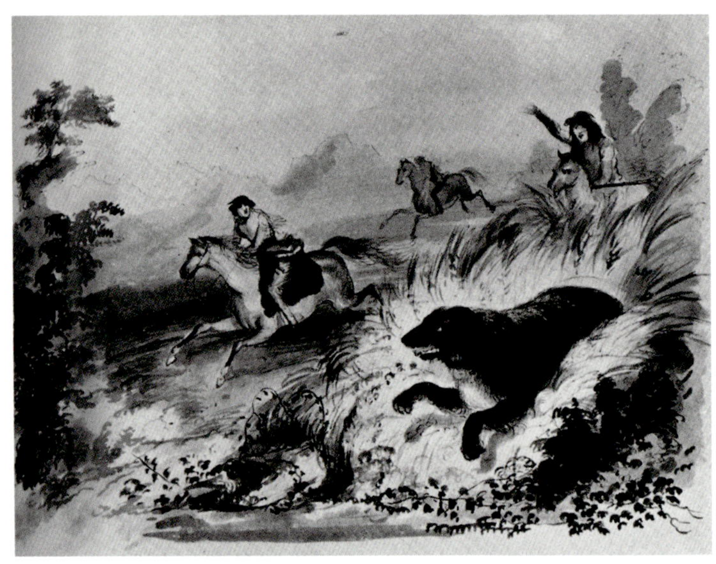

Figure 27. Alfred Jacob Miller, *Starting a Grizzly Bear from Covert*, c. 1837. Pen and ink with gray wash and gum glazes on gray card, 8¾ × 11 in. (22.2 × 27.9 cm). Location unknown

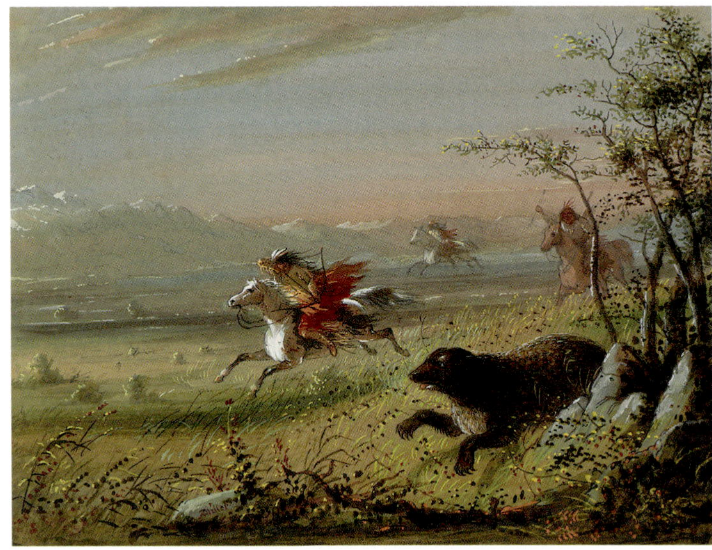

Figure 28. Alfred Jacob Miller, *The Grizzly Bear*, c. 1858–60. Watercolor heightened with white, on paper, 10¹⁄₁₆ × 9⁵⁄₁₆ in. (25.6 × 23.7 cm). The Walters Art Museum, Baltimore

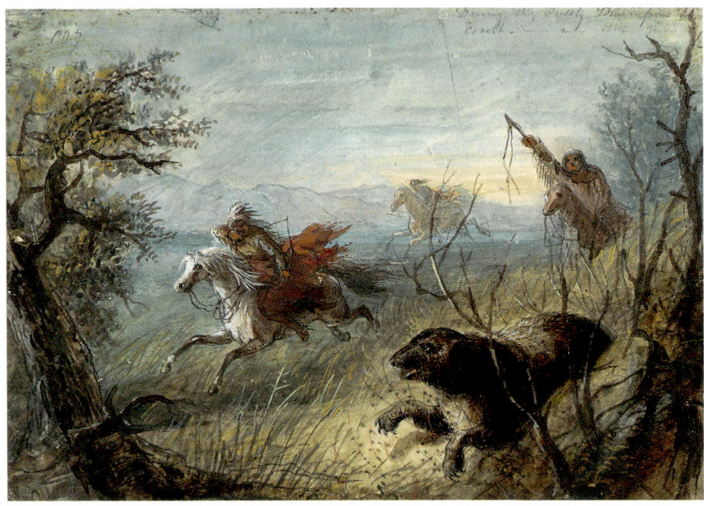

Alfred Jacob Miller, *Grizzly Bear Hunt* (cat. 12)

work done close to the time of his trip west to the more finished and distant versions of the Walters commission. Ten years later, in a final rendition of *The Grizzly Bear* made for a final album commission of forty "sketches" for the Liverpool (England) collector Sir Alexander Hargreaves Brown, the bear has been more carefully studied anatomically, but the effect is far less mysterious and ferocious than the first two versions.[38]

Nonetheless, Miller insisted in his prefatory notes to the Walters portfolio that he "made the following sketches, in every case from life, and nature, on the spot,"[39] and his commentaries stress the personal, field experience. His patrons clearly valued that authenticity and accepted these watercolors as the closest possible recapitulation of the spirit of the expedition twenty years earlier. However, his "sketches" were becoming almost indistinguishable from his smaller work in oils. Close inspection by conservators has been required to identify the materials in work such as *Taking the Hump Rib* (cat. 15). Both oil and watercolor may be present in some of these late works, demonstrating how much the scale and finish of his two media had begun to interpenetrate. This tendency followed the midcentury emergence of the exhibition watercolor, which aimed to rival in brilliance, finish, and scale the gallery impact of oils, but—as many watercolor painters were to discover—it was artistically confusing and economically unsound, since an oil and a watercolor of the same size and finish were not comparably priced.[40] And for Miller, the trend perversely undermined the album culture, which valued the window into creativity and personal expression held in the spontaneous sketch.

As it happened, the album experience and the sketch aesthetic would soon go public. Within a few years of Miller's death, special exhibitions for watercolors and sketches would be held in New York and Philadelphia to celebrate in gallery spaces the intimate qualities that connoisseurs had treasured in their parlors and libraries.[41] Miller's financial security, which made it unnecessary for him to hustle ambitiously for new clients, his poor health, and his retiring personality, all conspired to diminish his participation in this next, liberating phase in the history of American watercolor painting. His two most prestigious commissions, for Stewart and Walters, were held in private hands and fell out of sight, demonstrating the vulnerability of work held in such albums. The last of his album commissions, in 1867, coincided with the organization of the American Water Color Society in New York, but this new forum was too late for Miller, who had ceased exhibiting work by this time. His younger colleague in Baltimore, Hugh Newell, became a member of the society and exhibited genre subjects there regularly, enjoying the surge in popularity for the medium in the 1870s.[42] A better successor in both subject matter and style was F. Hopkinson Smith, the Baltimore-born engineer, artist, and writer whose semi-autobiographical novel, *The Fortunes of Oliver Horn*, memorialized Miller as the wise and kindly, bohemian artist "Mr. Crocker."[43] Smith was a mainstay of the Water Color Society and, in the diversity of his travel sketches, became an outgoing, Gilded Age version of Miller as artist-explorer.

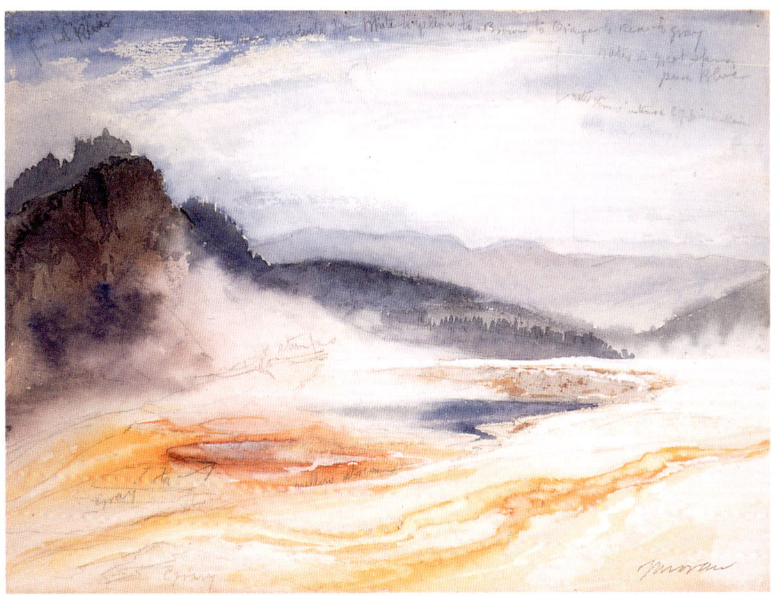

FIGURE 29. Thomas Moran, *Great Springs of the Firehole River*, c. 1871. Watercolor, graphite, and gouache on paper, 8⅛ × 11⅛ in. (20.6 × 28.3 cm). Courtesy National Park Service, Yellowstone National Park, YELL 8536

Miller's most brilliant heir, however, was another neighbor, briefly in Baltimore in 1844 before moving on to Philadelphia, Thomas Moran (fig. 29). Trained to work in watercolor for printmakers, Moran matured in the 1850s with a dense technique of gouache and glazes and a similarly late Romantic spirit. In the year before Miller's death, Moran went west with the Hayden expedition, returning to compose in his studio a series of spectacular watercolor landscapes for exhibition and glorious chromolithographic reproductions that took the American art world—and the U.S. Congress—by storm. With strong color and an animated style of pen detail, Moran carried forward Miller's technique and purposes, using the medium for plein air sketching and travel records, linking painting, illustration, and printmaking, and enjoying the moment in American art that the watercolor, and the sketch, leapt from the album to the wall.[44]

Notes

First, thanks to my colleagues on this project, Margaret C. Conrads, Stephanie Fox Knappe, Lisa Strong, and William Truettner, who supplied much good conversation and—from Lisa—a generous helping of primary research documents. Thanks to Mr. and Mrs. Decatur Miller, for generously sharing the Miller material in their collection. Special thanks to Carol Soltis for advice on Sully, the Peales, Neagle, and the Baltimore context, and to other colleagues at the Philadelphia Museum of Art, Mark Mitchell, Nan Goff, Shelley Langdale, and Ann Percy. At the Walters Art Museum, thanks to William Johnston, Betsy Dahl, Liz Flood, Joy Peterson Heyrman, and Elissa O'Loughlin; and likewise to Louise Brownell and the library staff at the Maryland Historical Society.

1. The best focused study of the medium in relation to the artist's work is Joan Carpenter Troccoli, *Alfred Jacob Miller: Watercolors of the American West from the Collection of the Gilcrease Museum, Tulsa, Oklahoma,* exh. cat. (Tulsa, Okla.: Thomas Gilcrease Museum Association, 1990). The seventy-seven watercolors in the Gilcrease Museum, like the work in the Bank of America collection, are all western subjects, mostly descended from the artist's studio, and so represent a wide-ranging survey of his practice in the medium. Troccoli notes (1) the modern preference for Miller's watercolors, echoing Wilbur Hunter, who remarked that the watercolors are "artistically more successful than the oils on the whole, being fresher and brighter, while the oils are too often muddy and indistinct by comparison"; see Hunter, "Alfred Jacob Miller, Artist of Baltimore and the West," in *The Paintings of Alfred Jacob Miller, Artist of Baltimore and the West* (Baltimore: Peale Museum, 1950), [12]. Marvin C. Ross, *Artist Explorers of the 1830's: George Catlin, Karl Bodmer, Alfred Jacob Miller, also Drawing by Plains Indians,* exh. cat. (Omaha, Nebr.: Joslyn Art Museum, 1963), 27, asserted that "for most connoisseurs there seems to be no hesitation in ranking the watercolours above the oil paintings of the Far West."

2. An overview of these different expeditions and the ties uniting them can be found in Martha A. Sandweiss, *Pictures from an Expedition: Early Views of the American West,* exh. cat. (New Haven: Yale Center for American Art and Material Culture and the Yale University Art Gallery, 1978). Stewart, who had been to the West several times before 1837, met Bodmer and Maximilian in St. Louis in 1833 and brought naturalists with him on a later trip, so his sense of conventional practice was well developed. Troccoli, *Miller: Watercolors,* 13. Ron Tyler, "Alfred Jacob Miller and Sir William Drummond Stewart," in *Alfred Jacob Miller: Artist on the Oregon Trail,* ed. Tyler (Fort Worth: Amon Carter Museum, 1982), 19.

3. William R. Johnston, "The Early Years in Baltimore and Abroad," in Tyler, *Miller: Artist on the Oregon Trail,* 9–10 and 17; on these early exhibitions, see Wilbur H. Hunter Jr., *Rendezvous for Taste: Peale's Baltimore Museum, 1814–1830,* exh. cat. (Baltimore: Peale Museum, 1956), 13–31. Rembrandt and then his brother Rubens Peale gave up on the museum and departed for Philadelphia and New York in 1825, but some of the Peale displays remained in Baltimore. Miller evidently stayed in Philadelphia long enough to copy two "Vandyck" portraits of Isabella and Ferdinand of Spain, exhibited at the Pennsylvania Academy in 1829, 1830, and 1831; Anna Wells Rutledge, *The Annual Exhibition Record of the Pennsylvania Academy of the Fine Arts, 1807–1870,* ed. Peter Hastings Falk (Madison, Conn.: Sound View Press, 1988), 234. By the fall of 1831 these paintings (previously unrecorded and recently identified at the Maryland Historical Society) were on view at Peale's Museum in Baltimore, the earliest documented record of Miller's exhibition work and an early display of his accomplishment as a copyist. "Baltimore Museum Exhibition of Paintings," *Baltimore Patriot,* 5 November 1831, 2.

4. On Titian Peale, see Sandweiss, *Pictures from an Expedition,* 16–21; and Kenneth Haltman, *Looking Close and Seeing Far: Samuel Seymour, Titian Ramsay Peale, and the Art of the Long Expedition, 1818–1823* (University Park: Pennsylvania State University Press, 2008). Miller probably knew the prints after animal subjects by Peale and C.-A. Lesueur in John D. Godman, *American Natural History* (Philadelphia, 1826 and 1831). Miller's study with Thomas Sully in about 1830 indicates that he was in Philadelphia from time to time; his lithographic drawing *Skeleton of the Mastodon Forming a Part of the Baltimore Museum,* for the cover of the museum's brochure in 1836, indicates his continuing association with the later manifestation of the Peales' museum. Johnston, "The Early Years," 17. On Charles Willson Peale's copies in oil of Titian Peale's watercolors, see Haltman, 178; and David R. Brigham, *Public Culture in the Early Republic: Peale's Museum and Its Audience* (Washington, D.C.: Smithsonian Institution Press, 1995), 142. Brigham describes the donor-based collection of Peale's Museum in chap. 6, 107–21.

5. Mid-twentieth-century scholars appreciated Miller's record of Plains Indians and trappers at face value, but more recent scholarship has emphasized the Romantic refashioning of his experience in the West; see Sandweiss, *Pictures from an Expedition,* 8–9; Troccoli, *Miller: Watercolors,* 1–2 and ff.; and Lisa Strong, *Sentimental Journey: The Art of Alfred Jacob Miller,* exh. cat. (Fort Worth: Amon Carter Museum, 2008).

6. See Neagle's notebooks at the American Philosophical Society, including citations from Varley in notebook 1, and "Lessons on Landscape Painting" in notebook 5, with extracts from the text and watercolor copies of the plates from "Sully's copy of Varley." In notebook 5, Neagle noted Joshua Shaw's arrival from London in 1834 with a group of contemporary English watercolors by Clarkson Stanfield, J. M. W. Turner, James Pyne, and James Duffield Harding; Neagle bought the Harding and also owned a watercolor by Samuel Prout, which he lent to the Pennsylvania Academy exhibition of 1835. Fascinated by the novelty of Prout's technique, Neagle asked the artist and drawing teacher Hugh Bridport (also a collector of English watercolors) to copy Prout's image while he recorded the different phases of the technique. Likewise, Rembrandt Peale owned "7 sheets of Varley's drawings," sold at auction 15–18 November 1862. Smithsonian American Art Museum, Pre-1877 Art Exhibition Catalogue Index, at www.siris.si.edu.

7. On American drawing books in this period, see Peter C. Marzio, *The Art Crusade: An Analysis of American Drawing Manuals, 1820–1860* (Washington, D.C.: Smithsonian Institution Press, 1976). Miller surely knew the publisher of this book, Fielding Lucas, as well as the author of the text; both men were pillars of the Baltimore cultural community.

8. Lithographs by Harding and Turner appear in Miller's scrapbook, one page of which is reproduced as fig. 25.

9. Clara Erskine Clement Waters and Laurence Hutton, *Artists of the Nineteenth Century and Their Works,* rev. ed. (1879; Boston and New York: Houghton Mifflin, 1884), 117; Maud G. [Mrs. John D.] Early, *Alfred Jacob Miller, Artist* (Baltimore: privately printed, 1894), 1; Marvin C. Ross, *The West of Alfred Jacob Miller,* rev. ed. (1951; Norman: University of Oklahoma Press, 1968), xiii. Thomas Sully, Journal, typescript, American Philosophical Society, Archives of American Art, roll 75.

10. I have not found other references to Miller in Sully's journal. Sully's Coale portrait was exhibited at the fourth annual exhibition at Peale's Museum in Baltimore in 1825, lent by "Mrs. M. Proud," probably a relative of the sitter, later Mrs. William Proud, so Miller probably copied it in Baltimore after establishing a studio there in 1831. Students made such copies to learn, but they were also a routine part of the portrait business; Sully himself made many copies of his own as well as other artists' work. *Fourth Annual Exhibition in Peale's Baltimore Museum, of the Works of American Artists* (Baltimore, 1825), 1. Sully's residence in Baltimore in 1822–23 established friendships with influential citizens, such as Fielding Lucas, Robert Gilmor Jr., and Brantz Mayer, all well known to Miller.

11. For a discussion and examples of Miller's European sketching, see Johnston, "The Early Years," 12–16, and Album II, cat. 889 (Maryland Historical Society), and Album III, cat. 890 (private collection), 413–24. Sully also may have taught Miller the use of the camera lucida for copying; see Sully's journal, 1 August 1830, for a reference to his sale of such a device; and Miller's description of the British traveler (and artist) Basil Hall, who used a camera lucida to sketch old master subjects in Italy; Miller, Journal, The Walters Art Museum, 12. Miller may have used this device to replicate his own sketches.

12. See Thomas Sully, *Hints to Young Painters, and the Process of Portrait-Painting* (Philadelphia: J. M. Stoddart and Co., 1873), cited in Carrie Rebora Barratt, "Thomas Sully," in Kevin Avery, *American Drawings and Watercolors in the Metropolitan Museum of Art*, vol. 1, *A Catalogue of Works by Artists Born before 1835* (New York: Metropolitan Museum of Art, 2002), 122–26, which includes several examples of Sully's pen and wash sketches and portrait studies. Sully also prepared compositional studies in charcoal, in oil on canvas, in a very thinly washed oil on paper (much resembling watercolor), and in unconventional mixtures of pen and ink, charcoal, and oil wash, seen in examples in the Philadelphia Museum of Art. Many watercolors of this type by Miller, in a very similar style and often in mixed media, are in the collection of the Maryland Historical Society. Those that can be dated are from the late 1840s, when his portrait business was booming. Some are in graphite and pen with brown and black ink washes and gouache highlights, whereas others employ watercolor and strong gouache tints over an initial sketch in graphite and pen, showing the emergence of the technique displayed in the Walters album, discussed below.

13. These drawings, mostly now in the Maryland Historical Society or the Walters Art Museum, show signs of revision. Many have been trimmed, repaired, and remounted, some have been re-signed and the inscriptions erased and rewritten, suggesting a campaign to place them in scrapbooks, perhaps late in Miller's life. A recurrent brownish pen line may be Miller's later addition, although this ink (perhaps iron gall) seems to have been used throughout his career for both outline and washes. The system of graphite, pen, and warm and cool ink washes persists in landscape sketches made as late as 1866 in Virginia. See Tyler, *Miller: Artist on the Oregon Trail*, no. 891-28.

14. The impact of Delacroix has been noted by Carol Clark, in "A Romantic Painter in the American West," in Tyler, *Miller: Artist on the Oregon Trail*, 49–50; Troccoli, *Miller: Watercolors*, 13 and 16; and Strong, *Sentimental Journey*, 20 and 24. On Miller's genre studies, see William R. Johnston, "Alfred Jacob Miller—Would-be Illustrator," *Walters Art Gallery Bulletin* 30, no. 3 (December 1977): 2–3. On his watercolors of the Ravel family's theatrical troupe, see William R. Johnston, "Sketches by Alfred Jacob Miller," *Walters Art Gallery Bulletin* 21, no. 7 (April 1969): 3–4; and William R. Johnston, "Back to Baltimore," in Tyler, *Miller: Artist on the Oregon Trail*, 69 and 72.

15. On Miller and Catlin, see Troccoli, *Miller: Watercolors*, 6–7; Tyler, "Alfred Jacob Miller and Sir William Drummond Stewart," 19; and Clark, "A Romantic Painter," 62. Miller was in New Orleans when Catlin's Indian Gallery was first exhibited in New York, but Catlin's lecture tour took him to New Orleans in 1837, Baltimore in 1838, and Philadelphia in 1839.

16. Revising earlier estimates of about two hundred field sketches, Lisa Strong, *Sentimental Journey*, 13, has concluded that many fewer were done. Miller's accounts attest to being soaked by rain, and the expedition left him "a martyr to rheumatism" for the rest of his life, so some materials may have been lost or damaged on the trip. However, it has been noted that Stewart traveled with many delicacies and Oriental carpets, so the baggage train for the company could have carried larger portfolios, plausibly including sheets as large as 8 by 13 inches; for example, see Strong, 168. Ross, *The West of Miller*, opp. pl. 147, and xxi on the characteristics of the field sketches. Henry T. Tuckerman comments on Miller's health in *Book of the Artist* (New York: G. P. Putnam & Sons, 1867), 496. Miller's "Rough Draughts" describe Stewart urging him on to the next subject; Robert Combs Warner, *The Fort Laramie of Alfred Jacob Miller*, vol. 43, no. 2 (Laramie: University of Wyoming, 1979), 56.

17. Many of Miller's European sketches after the work of other artists are on small sheets about 4 by 6 inches or less, although very few are the same size, perhaps because they were cut from the book and trimmed (as with cat. 7, on three sides) for mounting in an album. Miller also used a wide range of papers; the paper of the sketch of the log fort is unlike that of any other drawings in the Bank of America group. On sketchbook sizes, see Clark, "A Romantic Painter," 55.

18. For examples of portrait studies that may have been done on the trip, see items from the Gilcrease collection in Troccoli, *Miller: Watercolors*, 23–31. Strong, *Sentimental Journey*, 55, speculates that few portraits were done in the field. For other examples of field sketches, see Strong, 167, 175, and 179.

19. Alfred Jacob Miller to Decatur H. Miller, 16 October 1840, transcript from the Bernard DeVoto Papers, Stanford University Libraries, quoted in Warner, *Fort Laramie*, 154. See also Strong, *Sentimental Journey*, 89. Following Sully's advice to Neagle, Miller evidently agreed that "the sketches and studies made from nature are the most valuable materials for future compositions, which a painter can collect and should never be parted from." John Neagle Papers, Book 5 (1827), 4, American Philosophical Society.

20. Miller to Brantz Mayer, 18 October 1840, in Warner, *Fort Laramie*, 157.

21. Miller records his pleasure in viewing the "large folios of the old masters works (engraved)" at the Library of Congress in the 1830s and the portfolios in the library at Murthly Castle as well as those at Taymouth Castle, home of the Marquis of Breadalbane in Scotland; Miller, Journal, 28 and 52; and Miller to Dr. Cockey, 15 November 1840, DeVoto Papers. The largest collection of prints in the United States, more than 40,000 amassed by John S. Phillips in the 1850s and bequeathed to the Pennsylvania Academy of the Fine Arts in 1876, was entirely housed in albums with ring bindings. Deemed to be state-of-the-art, this system allowed for the insertion of new items and easy rearrangement. Artists and connoisseurs preferred unbound portfolios, presuming

that the sheets would be handled by knowledgeable viewers. The participation of less sophisticated viewers in the parlor or the library made mounting the pictures on album pages preferable, for it preserved items from handling and theft and allowed space for written commentary.

22. Strong, *Sentimental Journey*, 154–55, notes that fifteen albums were listed in Miller's will. Johnston, "Back in Baltimore," 69, mentions these scrapbooks, each containing about 120 drawings. Most have been disbound now, although the contents of six (in the Walters Art Museum and the Maryland Historical Society) are catalogued in album groupings by Johnston, "The Early Years," 404–44. Glue residues on the versos of many Miller drawings, often with traces of paper of another color and texture, like the softer pages of a scrapbook, can be compared with the ghost traces of drawings once pasted in Miller's own scrapbooks and then removed, as seen in fig. 25. The typical trimming of his sketches close to the image also implies album mounting, rather than overmatting and framing. The random order of material in these albums, with work of different periods intermixed, and the battered condition of some of the drawings, suggests that these albums were composed at a retrospective moment in Miller's career.

23. Neagle's notebooks (American Philosophical Society) would be another instance from Sully's circle, as well as the scrapbook of Dr. Stedman R. Tilghman, which included clippings, engravings, and drawings by his friend Richard Caton Woodville (Maryland Historical Society). Other examples include the *album amicorum* (friendship album) of the artist John Ludlow Morton compiled in the 1830s (The New-York Historical Society), and the Hosack album and the McGuire scrapbook from the same era at the Metropolitan Museum of Art. See Roberta J. M. Olson, *Drawn by New York: Six Centuries of Watercolors and Drawings at the New-York Historical Society* (New York: New-York Historical Society in association with D. Giles, 2008), cats. 40, 62, and 86; and Avery, *American Drawings and Watercolors in the Metropolitan Museum of Art*, checklist nos. 98, 129, 226, 425–39, and 480–86.

24. William H. Truettner, *George Catlin's Souvenir of the North American Indians: A Facsimile of the Original Album* (Tulsa, Okla.: Gilcrease Museum, 2003) reproduces all the plates of the album. He describes the dozen-odd *Albums Unique* produced between 1849 and 1863 on xvi–xvii, and in Truettner, *The Natural Man Observed: A Study of Catlin's Indian Gallery* (Washington, D.C.: Smithsonian Institution Press, 1979), 53, 134. Passing off watercolor copies of his oils as field drawings, Catlin claimed, "I painted thus many of my pictures in water colours during my eight years travel, and most, though not all of them I enlarged onto canvass." However, as Truettner notes (*The Natural Man Observed*, 131–32), "he did no such thing." Catlin began to produce these watercolor copies in the 1830s, sold a group of twenty-five to the American Art-Union in 1847, and received commissions for portfolios from collectors in 1845 and 1855. To enhance the "sketch" authority of his compilations of tracings, Catlin (like Miller) handwrote the introductory text that insisted on the authenticity of the work done on the spot.

25. Calyo's portfolio borrows from a European tradition of such imagery of street figures, represented by Hogarth, Rowlandson, and the multivolume compilation with work after Gavarni, Lami, Charlet, and others, *Les Français Peints par Eux-Mêmes* of 1839–42. Like Miller, Calyo also painted single images from this portfolio on demand, leading to many duplicates of certain popular subjects. See Olson, *Drawn by New York*, 192–99.

26. Ill and dispirited at the time, Miller deferred; see Tyler, *Miller: Artist on the Oregon Trail*, 44. Stewart's first novelized memoir appeared without illustrations as *Altowan: or, Incidents of Life and Adventure in the Rocky Mountains, by an Amateur Traveler*, ed. J. Watson Webb, 2 vols. (New York: Harper & Brothers, 1846). See Strong, *Sentimental Journey*, 89–90.

27. The materials in the album, which were the property of Major G. H. Power, are described in Parke-Bernet Galleries, New York, *A Series of Watercolour Drawings by Alfred Jacob Miller, of Baltimore: Artist to Captain Stewart's Expedition to the Rockies in 1837*, 6 May 1966, 8–9. These drawings are three or four times larger than the field sketches and also very irregular, showing the use of different papers and the cropping of the paper to odd dimensions, for mounting in the album. For a comparison between the field sketches and the Murthly (also known as the Power) album, see Ross, *The West of Miller*, xxxii–xxxv. Troccoli, *Miller: Watercolors*, 1, comments on the technical and iconographic complexity of his watercolors, which appear to be "fresher, freer, and more spontaneous" than his oils and seem truer to his experience, although based on "memory, hearsay, and imagination" (2–3). Regarding *Approach of a Band of Sioux* from the Murthly album, Sandweiss, *Pictures from an Expedition*, 47, comments, "It is doubtful that Miller ever witnessed such a scene." Strong, *Sentimental Journey*, 88–116, gives extended discussion to the content of the Murthly album.

28. Miller's scrapbook, a faux-leather album with pages 16 by 12 inches, contains about thirty-eight different horse studies by Adam, evidently from several different portfolios, none dated, although some with Parisian publishers noted. The torrent of work produced by Adam beginning in 1823, including many "études d'animaux," "souvenirs de chasse," and military subjects, makes it difficult to identify these prints precisely, although the title page seen in fig. 25 may indicate a portfolio of this title published in Paris by Christy in 1833, exactly when Miller was in the city. The album contains many other etchings and engravings of animals, landscapes, and portraits of figures such as Turner and Byron, as well as a newspaper clipping from 1870. Many pages show signs of earlier mountings, also as seen in fig. 25.

29. The introduction to the catalogue for the sale of the Murthly album sketches (Parke-Bernet Galleries, 6 May 1966, 8) noted the "French influence" on Miller's "somewhat mannered" drawings of horses. Clark, "A Romantic Painter," 49–50, remarks on the impact of French painters on Miller's work and comments (59–60) on the Arabian stallions in place of the sturdy Indian ponies. The Miller scrapbook illustrated in fig. 25 also includes lithographs of elk and deer by Elias Ridinger, similar to the image by Titian Peale, fig. 20.

30. Ross, *The West of Miller*, xxv, notes the confusion created by Miller's insistent use of the term *sketches* for all his watercolors. Clark, "A Romantic Painter," 55, remarks that Miller added his monogram and the note "after nature" to his own field sketches, perhaps much later.

31. A newspaper review of Miller's work exhibited in New York in 1839 before it was shipped to Scotland praised the "wonderful power and spirit of though by no means *finished* productions." An itemized review of the exhibition in the *New York Herald* mentions only oils (Ross, *The West of Miller*, xxiii–xxiv), but other reviews describe "sketchings" and "paintings" on view, raising the possibility that watercolors were shown; see Strong, *Sentimental Journey*, 117n10.

32. Ross, *The West of Miller*, xxvi. Period exhibition records rarely describe medium, except to remark items that are not oil. Watercolors, prints, and drawings were frequently segregated in the galleries and publications. By these indications, as well as title and provenance records, it seems that, apart from a possible display in 1839, Miller never sent his watercolors to a public exhibition.

33. These "drawings" for the publishers Webber and Putnam mentioned in his Account Book (The Walters Art Museum, Baltimore) have not been precisely identified; following period terminology, they could have been either crayon or wash "drawings." Tyler, *Miller: Artist on the Oregon Trail*, 44, suggests that Miller's poor health as well as the competition of other publications may have discouraged him. Certainly the history of all the print portfolios of this era indicates many years of work and substantial capital outlay, daunting for even the most ambitious entrepreneurs.

34. See Miller's Account Book. Lisa Strong has shared with me the story of Wait, a Baltimore merchant who joined the Artist's Association and lent paintings to the exhibitions of the Maryland Historical Society. A small oil portrait of "Wm C Waite Esq. an old friend" is in Miller Album I; see Tyler, *Miller: Artist on the Oregon Trail*, 393, no. 786. Wait died before the sketches were delivered; the executor of his estate paid for the work, and they have since disappeared. Some scholars have identified a group of watercolors in the Beinecke Rare Book and Manuscript Library at Yale University as part of Wait's commission, but Strong has commented to me in conversation that the Beinecke items seem to be random studio work, not a set of consistently handled images, like the Walters watercolors from the same moment. Perhaps Miller sold Wait a selection of informal studio sketches, but that seems unlikely, since Miller was mining this material for the enormous Walters commission at the same time. The simultaneous interest by these two young merchants, both wishing to own a group of sketches, suggests the network of taste and friendships among Baltimore patrons that Strong analyzes in *Sentimental Journey*, 123–61.

35. See Miller's Account Book. The Walters collection would become the core of the Walters Art Museum. On "the commission of a lifetime" for Miller, see William R. Johnston, *William and Henry Walters: The Reticent Collectors* (Baltimore: Johns Hopkins University Press, in association with the Walters Art Gallery, 1999), 13.

36. All the Walters albums were dismantled in the mid-twentieth century, although the bindings were retained. Nineteen and a half by 15½ inches in size, they are not marked to indicate where they were made, but they are significantly less ornate than the albums prepared for Walters's acquisitions in France. On the American album, gathered for Walters by the New York dealer Samuel P. Avery, see Johnston, *Walters*, 16.

37. Ross, *Catlin, Bodmer, Miller*, 28, argues that Miller's patrons were pleased by more finished work and would not have appreciated his rougher sketches. On Calyo, see Sona K. Johnston, discussing work from the collection of Dr. Thomas Edmondson, one of Miller's patrons, in *American Paintings, 1750–1900, from the Collection of the Baltimore Museum of Art* (Baltimore: Baltimore Museum of Art, 1983), 25–31. British artists, including Turner, also moved from the canonical transparent technique of the early nineteenth century, taught by Varley, to more dense and detailed effects at midcentury.

38. Miller's account book recorded forty drawings sold; he added a facsimile of an Indian drawing, to bring the total to forty-one as published in *Braves and Buffalo, Plains Indian Life in 1837, Watercolours of Alfred J. Miller*, intro. Michael Bell (Toronto: Public Archives of Canada, University of Toronto Press, 1973). Bell comments (8) on the "Rousseauian" spirit of Miller's work that increased with the distance from his experience. In a parallel development, Catlin moved from the sketchy freedom of his field oils to later, smaller, "better behaved" replicas that lose the edgy "wildness" of the earlier work. See Truettner, *Souvenir of the North American Indians*, xx–xxi.

39. From Miller's preface to the Walters's sketches, in Ross, *The West of Miller*, not paginated.

40. Miller's price to Wait and Walters in 1858 of $12 per "sketch" was increased to $25 for Brown's commission in 1867, but this was about one-third to one-quarter the price of his smallest oils, as noted in his account book. Nonetheless, work ordered in large groups at this rate made a handsome income for Miller, whose portrait work dropped off dramatically after 1858. In chronically poor health, he may have preferred the scale of the watercolors as less tiring. He also complained as early as 1842 that the smell and "deleterious ingredients" of oil painting made him ill. Alfred Jacob Miller to Decatur H. Miller, 10 February 1842, DeVoto Papers.

41. See Jane Bayard, *Works of Splendor and Imagination: The Exhibition Watercolor, 1770–1870* (New Haven: Yale Center for British Art, 1981). Miller's move toward greater finish and stronger color may have been encouraged by inspection of the major loan exhibition of British art that appeared in several American cities, including Philadelphia, in 1857–58. See Susan Casteras, "The 1857–58 Exhibition of English Art in America: Critical Responses to Pre-Raphaelitism," in Linda S. Ferber and William H. Gerdts, *The New Path: Ruskin and the American Pre-Raphaelites*, exh. cat. (Brooklyn: Brooklyn Museum, 1985), 109–33.

42. On Newell, see Johnston, *American Paintings, 1750–1900*, 111–12.

43. F. Hopkinson Smith, *The Fortunes of Oliver Horn* (New York: Scribner's, 1902). Smith revealed Miller as the model for the character of his unsung but worldly Baltimore mentor in W. H. Shelton, "Artist Life in New York in the Days of Oliver Horn," *Critic* 43 (July–December 1903): 31–40. Miller's student Francis (Frank) B. Mayer also followed his teacher's precedent in filling sketchbooks and albums with Indian subjects encountered on a trip west in 1851.

44. Moran's watercolors of the Yellowstone, exhibited in Washington, D.C., have been cited as the impetus for the national parks legislation of 1872. Nancy K. Anderson, *Thomas Moran*, exh. cat. (Washington, D.C.: National Gallery of Art, 1997), 53. Moran grew up in Philadelphia, but it is impossible to know if he knew Miller or his work. His watercolor style was shaped by the close study of Turner's work, and it may be that Turner's mixed gouache method and pen detailing in the 1830s offers the link between Moran and Miller, whose respect for Turner is cited in Ross, *The West of Miller*, opp. pl. 69. On the link between sketching, illustration, printmaking, and watercolor that produced the American watercolor movement, see Kathleen A. Foster, "Makers of the American Watercolor Movement, 1860–1890" (Ph.D. diss., Yale University, 1982; University Microfilms International, 1983).

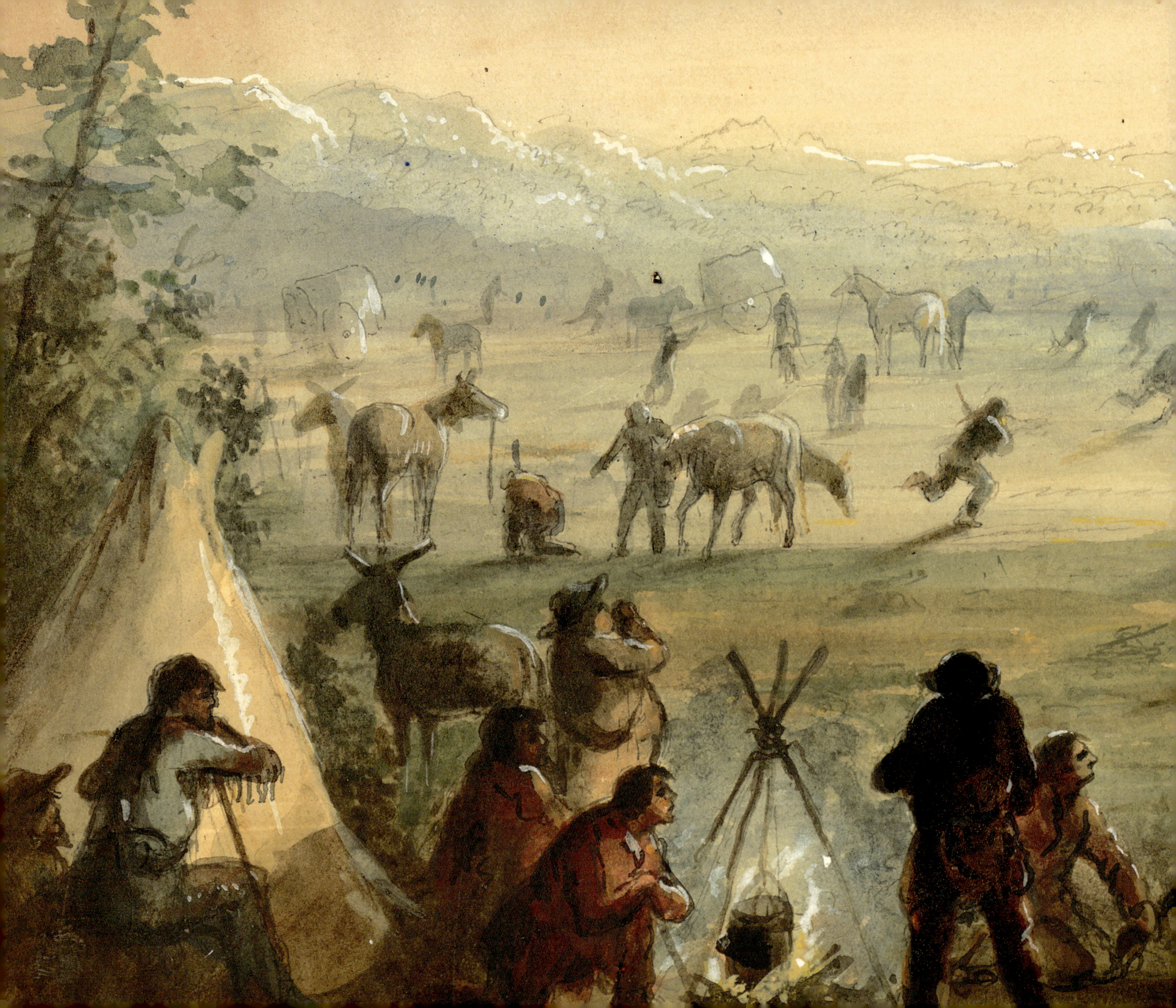

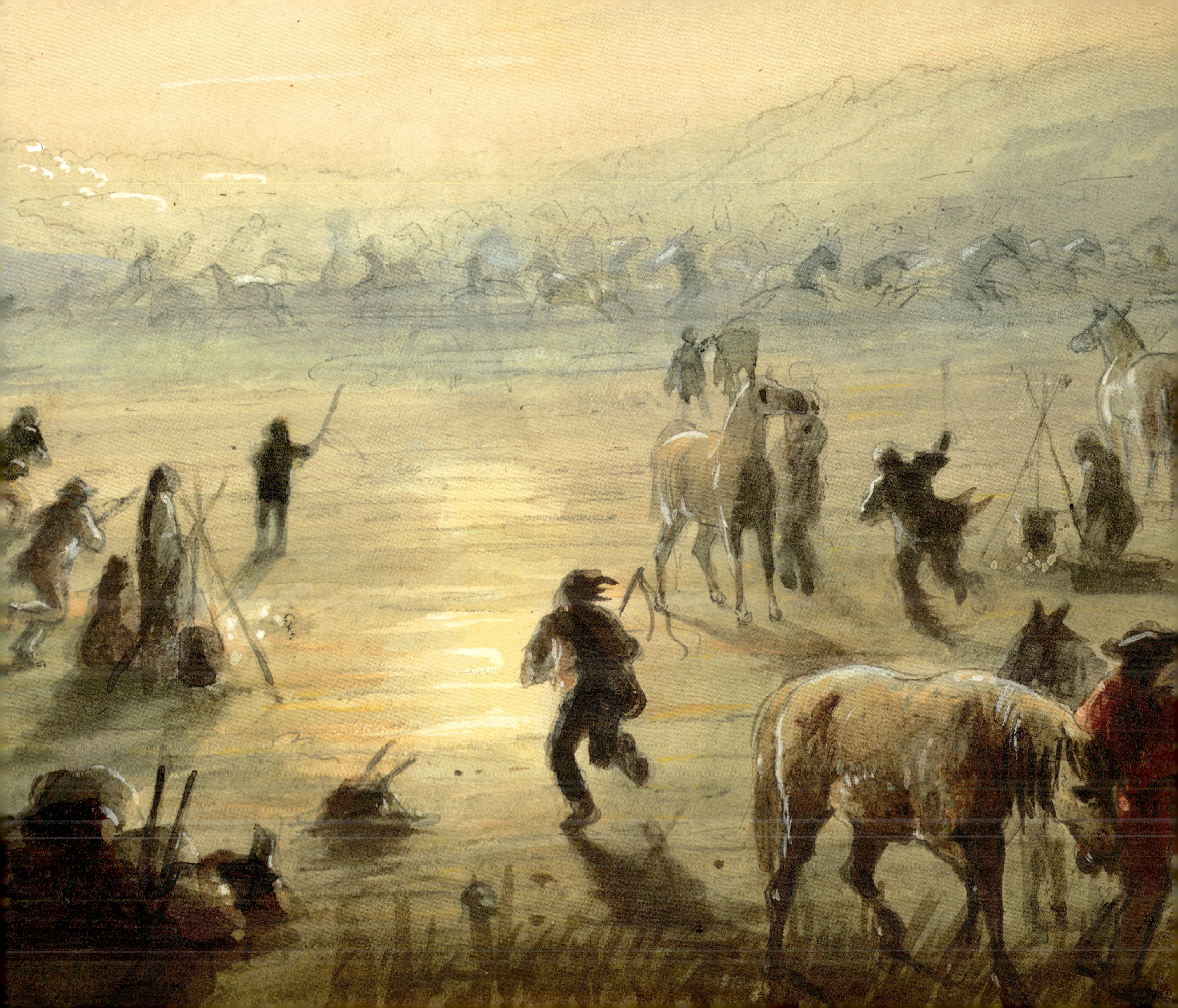

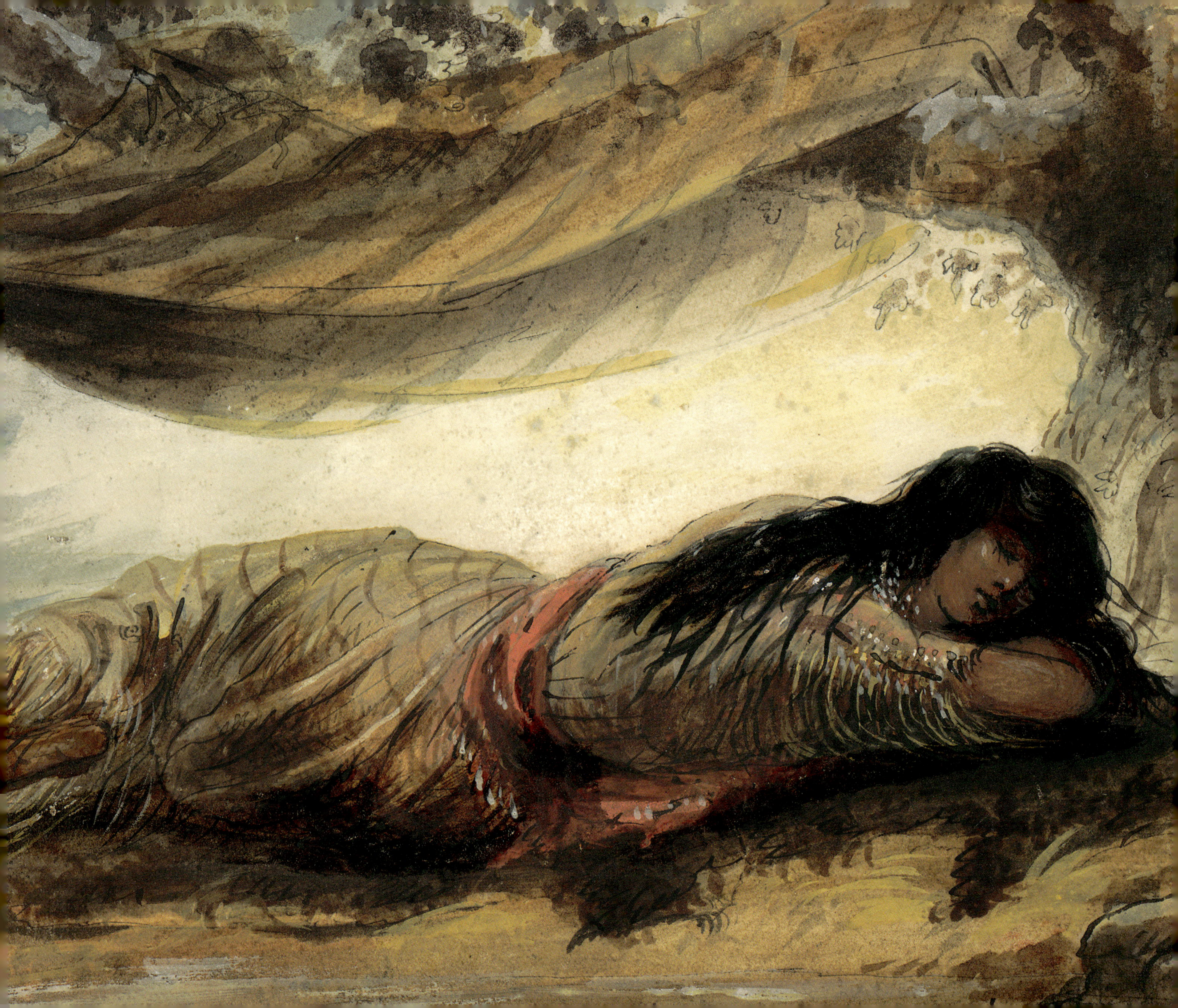

Note to the Reader

Catalogue entries by
MARGARET C. CONRADS (MCC)
STEPHANIE FOX KNAPPE (SFK)

All technical and condition remarks are based on examinations and reports by Nancy Heugh, Heugh-Edmondson Conservation Services, Kansas City, Missouri.

All of the works by Alfred Jacob Miller in the Bank of America collection are undated. Each sheet is identified by a Bank of America inventory number (BAC).

Frequently cited sources in the notes for the entries use the following short forms.

DeVoto, *Across the Wide Missouri*
DeVoto, Bernard. *Across the Wide Missouri.* Boston: Houghton Mifflin, 1947.

Miller, Journal
Miller, Alfred Jacob. Journal. The Walters Art Museum, Baltimore.

Miller, "Rough Draughts"
Miller, Alfred Jacob. "Rough Draughts for Notes to Indian Sketches." MS. Library, Thomas Gilcrease Institute of History and Art, Tulsa, Okla. Microfilm, Archives of American Art, Smithsonian Institution, Washington, D.C., roll 3280.

Ross, *The West of Miller*
Ross, Marvin E., ed. *The West of Alfred Jacob Miller.* 1951. Rev. ed. Norman: University of Oklahoma Press, 1968.

Strong, "Images of Indian-White Contact"
Strong, Lisa. "Images of Indian-White Contact in the Watercolors of Alfred Jacob Miller, 1837–1860." Ph.D. diss., Columbia University, 1998.

Strong, *Sentimental Journey*
Strong, Lisa. *Sentimental Journey: The Art of Alfred Jacob Miller.* Exh. cat. Fort Worth: Amon Carter Museum, 2008.

Troccoli, *Miller: Watercolors*
Troccoli, Joan Carpenter. *Alfred Jacob Miller: Watercolors of the American West from the Collection of the Gilcrease Museum, Tulsa, Oklahoma.* Exh. cat. Tulsa, Okla.: Thomas Gilcrease Museum Association, 1990.

Tyler, *Miller: Artist on the Oregon Trail*
Tyler, Ron, ed. *Alfred Jacob Miller: Artist on the Oregon Trail.* Catalogue raisonné by Karen Dewees Reynolds and William R. Johnston. Fort Worth: Amon Carter Museum, 1982.

Alfred Jacob Miller, *Snake Female Reposing,* detail (cat. 23); overleaf: Alfred Jacob Miller, *Attrapez des Chevaux,* detail (cat. 3)

1 *Departure of the Caravan at Sunrise*

Oil and glazes over ink, pencil, and watercolor on cream wove paper mounted to gray paperboard, 8 1/16 × 14 1/4 in. (20.5 × 36.3 cm). Inscribed upper right: 132. BAC 10308

EVERY MORNING THE MEMBERS OF THE 1837 CARAVAN TO THE FUR TRADERS' rendezvous had to break up and pack the previous night's encampment before returning to the trail. Under a glowing sky of pastel colors that suggests the sun burning off an early morning mist, Miller reflected on the contrast of cultures he perceived between white and Indian travelers, most notably the eagerness of the former and the more relaxed approach of the latter.[1] Indians leisurely pack their gear while others still mill around the campfire. At center, a baby in a cradleboard rests against belongings waiting to be loaded, while a woman to the right poses provocatively, arm flung over her head, leaning against a saddled horse. Miller set these foreground figures against the bustle of tents being dismantled and a trapper or guide mounting his prancing horse as the convoy moves toward the horizon. Such details in the center as the raised whip held by the driver in the last wagon and the seated Indians to the immediate right of the prancing horse add to Miller's comparison of the demeanor of Indians and whites. Even though Miller witnessed many such departures during the six-month trek west and back, the picture betrays his debt to European painting, especially in the pose of the woman, who looks more like a Moroccan from the brush of Eugène Delacroix than one of the Delaware women who accompanied the group.[2]

Although Miller employed pencil and watercolor as he began *Departure of the Caravan at Sunrise*, he covered the entire surface with opaque oil. More than any other sheet in the Bank of America collection, it has the feel of a small oil painting. Indeed, the image closely relates to *Breaking up the Camp* (n.d.; Anschutz Collection). Miller successfully translated the complex composition, colorful palette, and thick paint application from the large oil to a more intimate scale, a move that seems to have aided the artist as he converted the image into watercolors for William T. Walters and Alexander Hargreaves Brown (see fig. 19). MCC

1. Miller's thoughts are recorded in the "Rough Draught" for *Breaking up Camp at Sunrise* (1858–60), a closely related image in the Walters Art Museum. See Ross, *The West of Miller*, opp. pl. 142. For safe travel, small groups of Indians frequently joined larger convoys.

2. On the impact of Delacroix and other French artists, see Troccoli, *Miller: Watercolors*, 11–12; Lisa Strong's essay in this volume; and cats. 4, 10, 12, 20, 22, and 23. Miller in his "Rough Draught" noted that twenty-five or thirty Delaware Indians accompanied the convoy, yet the figures depicted wear generic Plains Indian clothing, and the woman poses in a manner counter to Delaware behavior. Wesley Dunn, Museum of Indian Culture, Allentown, Pennsylvania, kindly answered inquiries regarding Delaware dress and comportment. Telephone conversation, 20 October 2009.

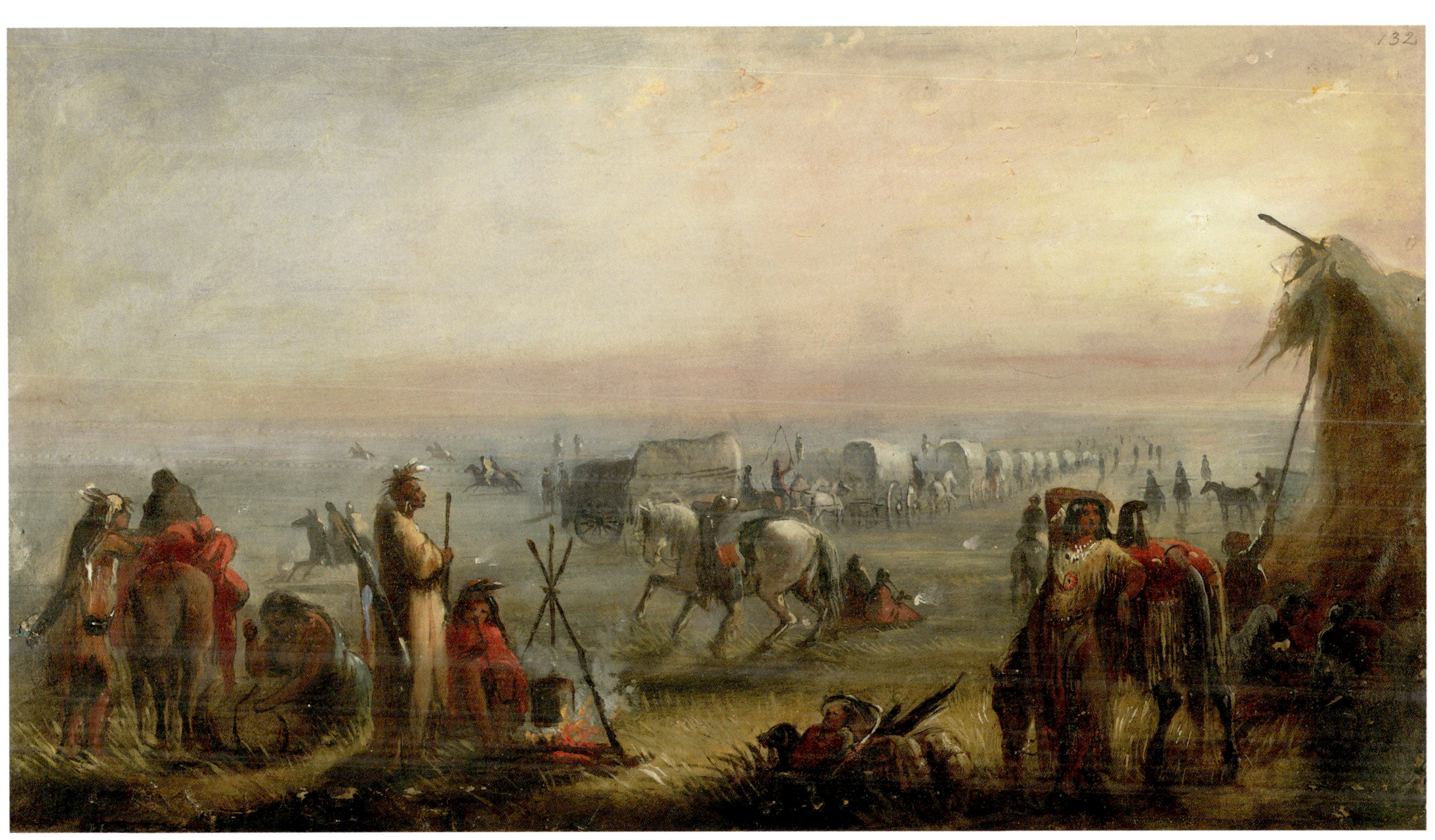
132

2 *Watching the Caravan*

Watercolor, wash, and pencil with white gouache highlights on mid-tone blue paper, 7¾ × 10⅝ in. (19.7 × 27 cm). Signed with monogram, lower left: AJM; inscribed lower left: Watching the Caravan. BAC 10315

As Stewart and his entourage made their way to the annual fur trappers' and traders' rendezvous early in the summer of 1837, Miller was keenly aware that their progress was monitored by members of the Indian tribes across whose lands they journeyed. Throughout his "Rough Draughts for Notes to Indian Sketches," Miller acknowledged surveillance by Indians concealed in tall grasses, behind rocks, and, especially, atop bluffs. He likened the practiced visual acuity of native sentinels occupying prime vantage points from which to scan expanses of prairie to that of sailors at watch at sea.[1]

American Indians surreptitiously scrutinizing the arrival of interlopers – be they Columbus; the Pilgrims; or western explorers, entrepreneurs, and settlers – were a popular subject in both art and literature during the nineteenth century. To describe this vignette of watching and being watched, Miller assumed attributes that are the unique purview of an artist: omniscience and omnipresence. These traits allowed him to depict not only the caravan with which he traveled but also the three Indians who observe it from the rocky promontory, a bit of scenery that frequently recurs in Miller's western oeuvre. This sketch appears to be an early effort in the lineage of the five sketches Miller composed on this theme.[2] For example, the faintly and summarily evoked foliage and clouds and the broad areas of wash suggest a trial effort.[3]

At the final stage of creating *Watching the Caravan*, Miller employed a crumbly red-orange pigment that colors the skin of the vigilant Indians. It sets the figures off from the remainder of the monochromatic composition and also distinguishes this sketch from the other four to which it is related.[4] Technical analysis was unable to determine whether the color is watercolor applied with a very dry brush or pigment in stick form. In either case, it runs over the brush-applied black outlines that define the Indians' forms and the white highlights on the musculature of the figure closest to the picture plane.

SFK

1. Miller, "Rough Draughts," nos. 57, 59, and 147, which relate to Ross, *The West of Miller*, opp. pls. 75, 5, and 44.

2. The other sketches are listed in Tyler, *Miller: Artist on the Oregon Trail*, nos. 397, 397A (see fig. 16), 397B, and 397C. In nos. 397, 397B, and 397C, Miller identified the Indians specifically as Pawnee.

3. For a further discussion of the position of *Watching the Caravan* in Miller's work, see Lisa Strong's essay in this volume.

4. This pigment is also found, albeit fainter, on the lead horses and riders of the distant caravan. Miller selected this same pigment for other sketches in the Bank of America collection, including *Old Bill Burrows, a Free Trapper* and *Antelope* (see cats. 5, 6).

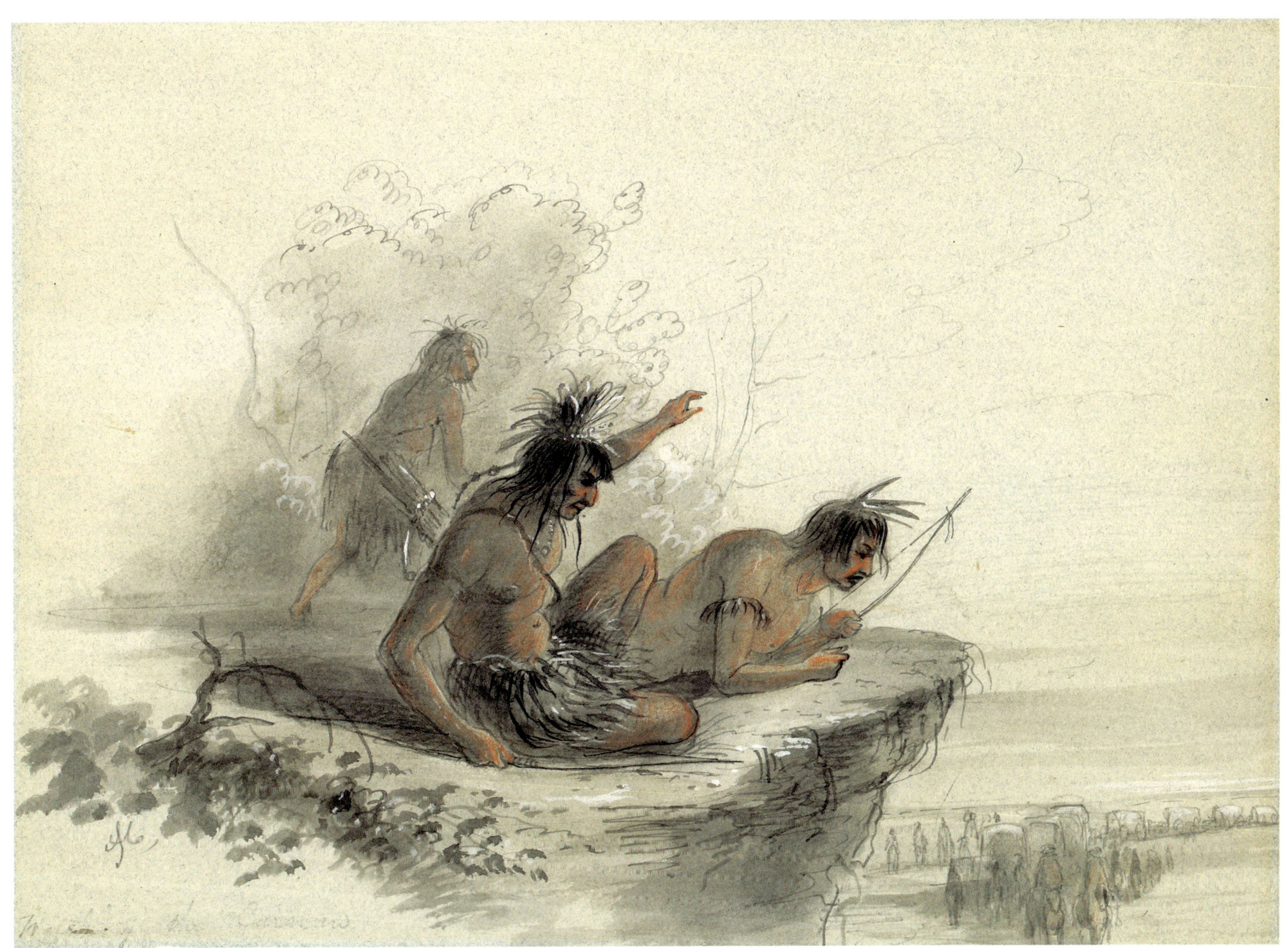

3 *Attrapez des Chevaux*

Watercolor, gouache, and pencil, with ink and gum glazes on beige wove paper, 8¾⁄16 × 12⅜ in. (20.8 × 31.4 cm). Inscribed upper right: (loquitur) Monsieur Proveau / Attrappez [*sic*] des Chevaux. BAC 10306

"CATCH THE HORSES!" THIS ORDER, BELLOWED BY ETIENNE PROVOST, THE Canadian trapper and guide who escorted the American Fur Company and Stewart to the annual Green River rendezvous, jolts the men clustered around their smoky cooking fires out of their twilight reverie.[1] Provost, whom Miller vividly described as "adipose & rotonde" with a "corpus round as a porpoise," raises his hands to his mouth to amplify the command, while the men, brandishing quirts (riding whips), race toward a cloud of dust rising in the distance.[2] The caravan's horses are being driven toward camp. They must be collected and tethered to pickets, where they will graze securely until morning.[3]

Miller cleverly selected a beige paper on which to compose this evening scene. Beneath the transparent washes of watercolor, the beige color contributes a warm glow, evocative of the quality of light at sunset. The freshness of the details of this ritual gives the impression that they were directly observed and committed to paper on the spot. However, the layers of media that compose *Attrapez des Chevaux* refute the notion that this sketch was made while Miller was in the West. Pencil appears both as underdrawing and on top of pigment. Ink reinforces pencil lines and defines painted elements, while rich washes flow beneath and also cover gouache highlights. Gum glazes, atop which ink lines are discernible, saturate areas of color in the foreground. This complexity of technique, combined with the requisite drying time between applications of wet media, makes it improbable that Miller created this sketch while on the trail, but the quality of line and overall tonality suggest that it was completed not long after the artist's western sojourn.

The lack of a monogram or signature indicates that Miller may not have expected this aspect of his adventure to garner much interest from his clients. The quotidian scene did not appear in the album he compiled for Stewart. However, two decades after Miller experienced this daily routine on the western plains, he revisited this sketch in *Catching Up* (1858–60) for his Baltimore patron William T. Walters.

SFK

1. Miller misspelled the name of the manager of the caravan in the inscription and throughout his "Rough Draughts." For additional information on Etienne Provost, see Jack B. Tykal, *Etienne Provost: Man of the Mountains* (Liberty, Utah: Eagles View Publishing, 1989).

2. Ross, *The West of Miller*, opp. pl. 197; and Miller, "Rough Draughts," no. 56. Miller also quoted Shakespeare's *Henry IV* to emphasize Provost's girth, likening him to Falstaff "larding the lean earth as he walks along." Ross, *The West of Miller*, opp. pl. 197. Falstaff seems to have held great interest for the artist. He painted two oils of the American actor James Hackett in that role. See Tyler, *Miller: Artist on the Oregon Trail*, nos. 43 and 43A.

3. The procedure for picketing horses is described by the artist in Ross, *The West of Miller*, opp. pl. 178.

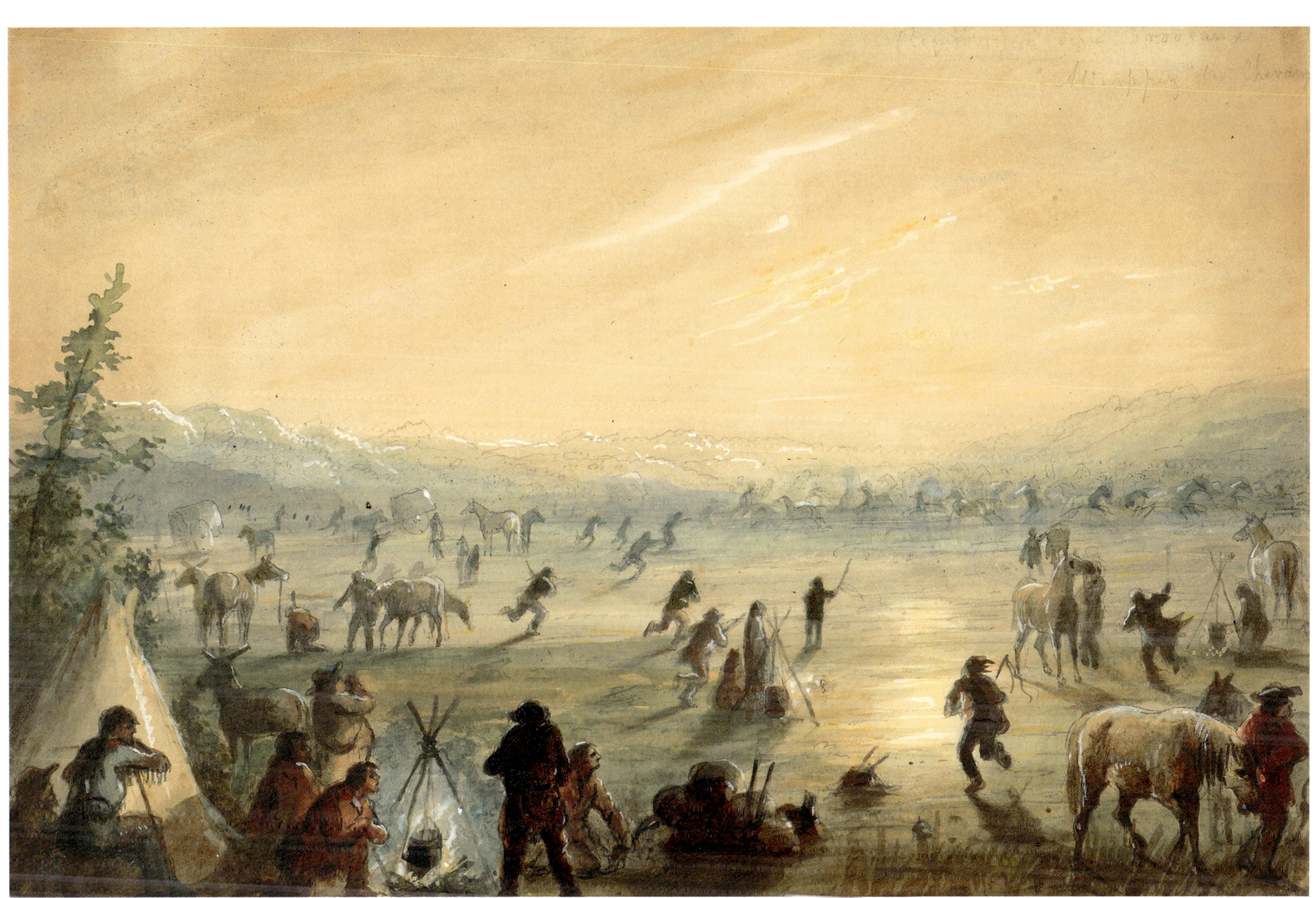

4 *Trappers, Auguste and Louis*

Black, gray, and brown ink and wash, white and yellow gouache, and graphite on brown laid paper, 9 15/16 × 7 13/16 in. (25.2 × 19.8 cm). Inscribed lower left: Trappers; lower right [H]alf [illegible, possibly Half Breeds]. Verso: *Portrait of a Young Man.* Black chalk with traces of red. BAC 10313.A; 10313.B

THE TWO MEN PORTRAYED ON THE FRONT OF THIS DRAWING ARE MOUNTAIN MEN, known today as Auguste and Louis, whom Stewart employed during his 1837 journey west.[1] Even though they likely were camp laborers, they are pictured here as trappers, the backbone of the fur trade. As either free agents or employees, trappers provided the key product for fur companies, like the American Fur Company with which Miller and Stewart traveled.

Miller pictured the trappers relaxing in a barely suggested landscape. The artist described Auguste's face, on the left, with a portraitist's specificity. Using the paper, which has darkened over time, for skin mid-tones, Miller shaped the French Canadian's facial features with gray wash over an initial pencil sketch. The ragged texture of his hair, intensity of his eyes, and bristle of his beard and mustache are amplified with short strokes of black ink and white highlights. Auguste's formal upright pose with his hands on his knee and outward gaze, reminiscent of European portraits of genteel men and Salvator Rosa's *banditti* etchings, contrasts with the calligraphic lines of ink, wash, gouache, and graphite that describe his fringed buckskin clothing.[2] Unlike Auguste, Louis lies on his stomach, giving the impression of nonchalance. Surrounded by hastily sketched blades of grass, his figure, conjured mainly in muted gray tones, melds with the ground, suggesting the man's complete comfort in the natural environment.

A mostly obliterated inscription at the lower right may have read "Half Breeds." If accurate, this not only indicates the heritage of both men but aligns with Miller's belief that trappers occupied that space in between primitive and civilized culture. Miller admired the hardy and self-reliant men, whom he credited with leading "the march of civilization." The buckskin clothing and feather-adorned hats, typical trapper garb, remind us of Auguste and Louis's close bonds with Indian culture, which Miller and his patrons associated with a greater closeness to nature and primitive masculinity.[3] The *gage d'amour*, a love token Auguste wears around his neck, signals a relationship with an Indian woman and perhaps trade relations with Indians more broadly. All these attributes point to the intricate weave between whites and Indians in the West.[4] Additionally, a puff of smoke from Louis's pipe adds a pungent suggestion of the earthiness of the duo and the artist's witness to such an experience and the feelings it engendered.

The portrait on the verso lacks firm attribution of sitter or artist. A comparison of the young man with a sketch likely from 1837 (Joslyn Art Museum, Omaha) and a later self-portrait in oil (frontispiece) strongly suggests Miller himself is the subject. Yet the confident and fluid line augmented by accomplished shading present a Byronic figure with a depth of expression that would have been extraordinary if an early self-portrait. Whoever the subject and artist, Miller had the sheet on hand when he turned it over to picture the trappers. MCC

1. The attribution of the figure of Louis, on the right, is based on a portrait drawing of him and the longtime titling of the Bank of America sheet. DeVoto, *Across the Wide Missouri*, 309–10 and pl. 72; and Tyler, *Miller: Artist on the Oregon Trail*, cat. 55. In his note for the Walters version of this image, Miller refers to a trapper known as Black Harris but does not imply that Harris is pictured. Ross, *The West of Miller*, opp. pl. 29.

2. See, for example, *Figurine*, in Richard W. Wallace, *The Etchings of Salvator Rosa* (Princeton: Princeton University Press, 1979), 203, cat. 66. I am grateful to Ian Kennedy, Louis L. and Adelaide C. Ward Curator of European Painting and Sculpture, The Nelson-Atkins Museum of Art, for the possible connection to Rosa, whose prints Miller could have seen in Europe or Baltimore.

3. For quote, see Ross, *The West of Miller*, opp. pl. 29; on notions of primitive masculinity, Strong, "Images of Indian-White Contact," 17ff., 93–97, and 108–19.

4. Strong, *Sentimental Journey*, 187.

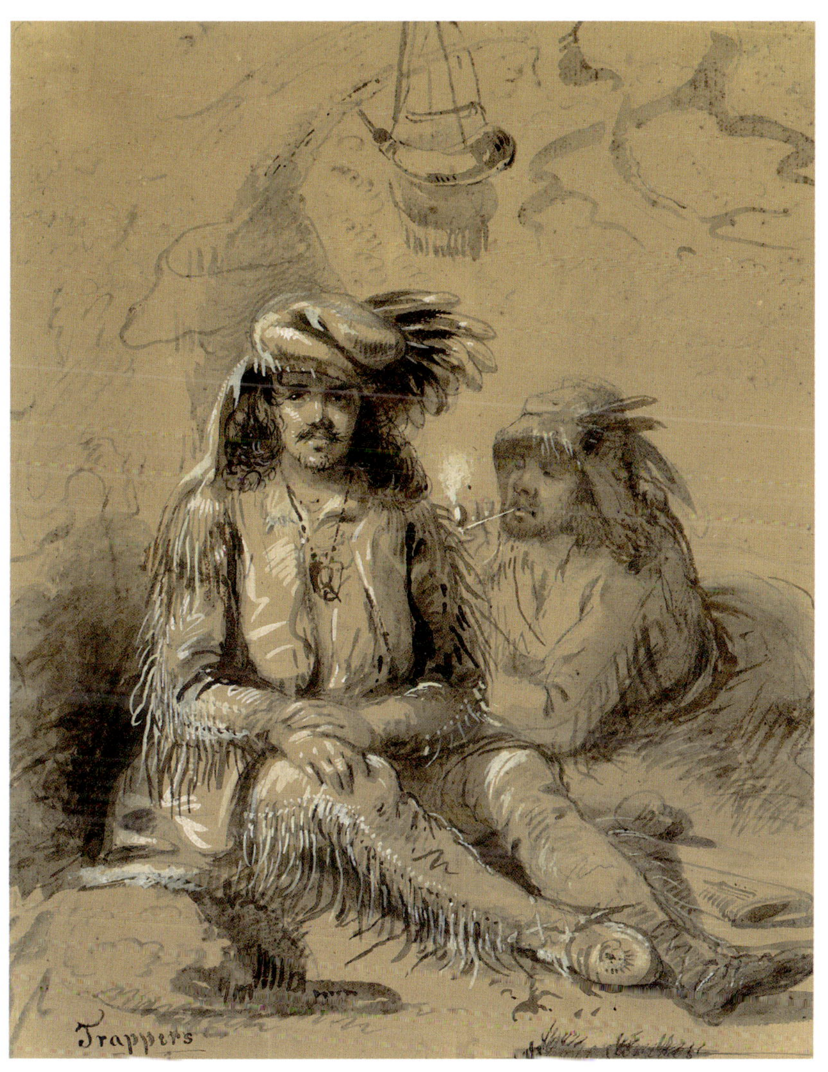
Trappers

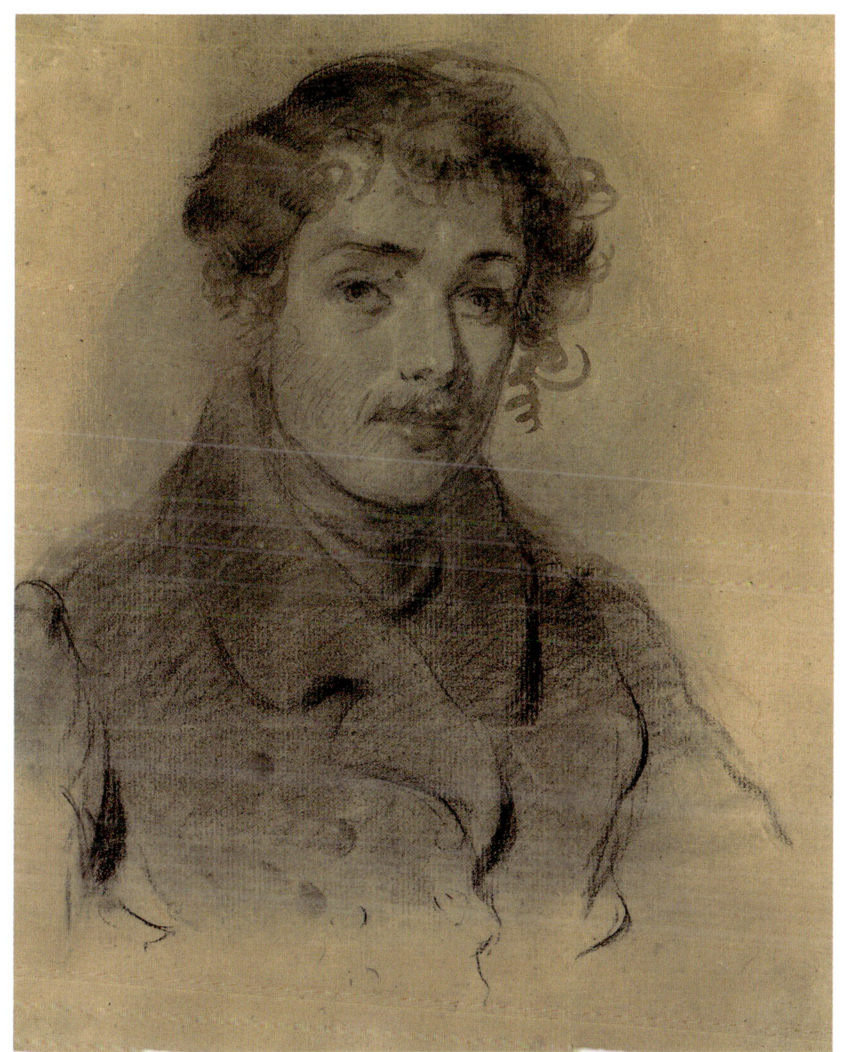

5 *Old Bill Burrows, a Free Trapper*

Watercolor, gouache, ink, pencil, and gum glazes on wove rag paper, $4\frac{3}{16} \times 6\frac{1}{4}$ in. (10.6 × 15.9 cm). BAC 10289

MILLER WAS NOT THE FIRST AMERICAN ARTIST TO VENTURE WEST AND CAPITALize on the experience to further or, in Miller's case, launch an artistic career. Of the early artist-explorers who shaped an enduring vision of the West, only Miller traveled overland with the American Fur Company, rather than aboard a company steamboat, as George Catlin, Karl Bodmer, and John James Audubon all had done.[1] Those six months on the trail allowed Miller to meet men who worked in the fur trade such as Auguste and Louis (see cat. 4). He also became acquainted with other players in that enterprise both during and after the annual assembly of trappers, traders, and Indians in Wyoming. Miller encountered the Rocky Mountain free trapper Bill Burrows in the Oregon Territory once Stewart's party left the rendezvous for a few weeks of hunting.[2]

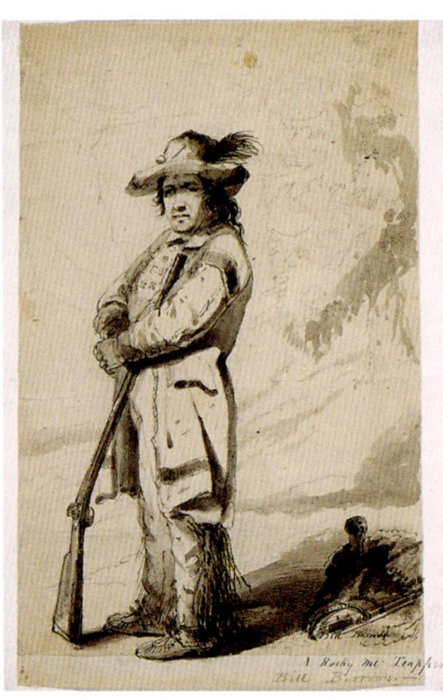

FIGURE 30. Alfred Jacob Miller, *A Rocky Mountain Trapper, Bill Burrows*, n.d. Pencil, pen and ink, and wash on paper, $13 \times 8\frac{1}{8}$ in. (33 × 20.6 cm). Joslyn Art Museum, Omaha, Nebraska, InterNorth Art Foundation Collection

This diminutive portrait of the seasoned mountain man was likely based on a sketch believed to have been made in the field (fig. 30).[3] Although Miller faithfully transcribed Burrows's confident pose from the earlier sketch, for this version he exchanged the trapper's overcoat for a fringed buckskin jacket and paired him with a trusty mule bearing a deer carcass slung across its back. He added an expansive landscape backdrop—two-thirds of which is given over to a sweeping sky—and enhanced the tableau with color. Transparent blue, brown, yellow-ocher, and gray washes are enlivened with touches of opaque red-orange and yellow gouache atop which white highlights and gum glazes were judiciously applied.

Artists such as Miller, Charles Deas, and William Ranney, along with authors including Washington Irving and James Fenimore Cooper, helped position men like Burrows as embodiments of the Romantic natural man. In this sketch, Burrows exemplifies attributes synonymous with this ideal. Miller highlighted the trapper's self-reliance by depicting him after a successful hunt that will provide him with both meat and a hide. He intimated Burrows's dissociation from society and its norms by setting him back from the picture plane and, therefore, the viewer. He also took care to render Burrows's attire, which was appropriated from Indian culture and appeared suitably exotic to eastern audiences. Finally, Miller situated Burrows within a vast landscape that recedes for miles, implying the trapper's access to untrammeled freedom.[4]

SFK

1. For additional information, see Dawn Glanz, *How the West Was Drawn: American Art and the Settling of the Frontier* (Ann Arbor, Mich.: UMI Research Press, 1982), 31.

2. Although there was a dearth of trapper imagery in the album of sketches Miller made for Stewart, a character named Old Bill Burroughs [*sic*] appears in Stewart's thinly veiled autobiography *Edward Warren*. William Drummond Stewart, *Edward Warren* (1854), ed. Bart Barbour (Missoula, Mont.: Mountain Press Publishing Company, 1986), 187.

3. Strong, *Sentimental Journey*, 168 and 209n8.

4. For more on Miller's estimation of trappers, see Miller, "Rough Draughts," no. 135, which relates to Ross, *The West of Miller*, opp. pl. 29.

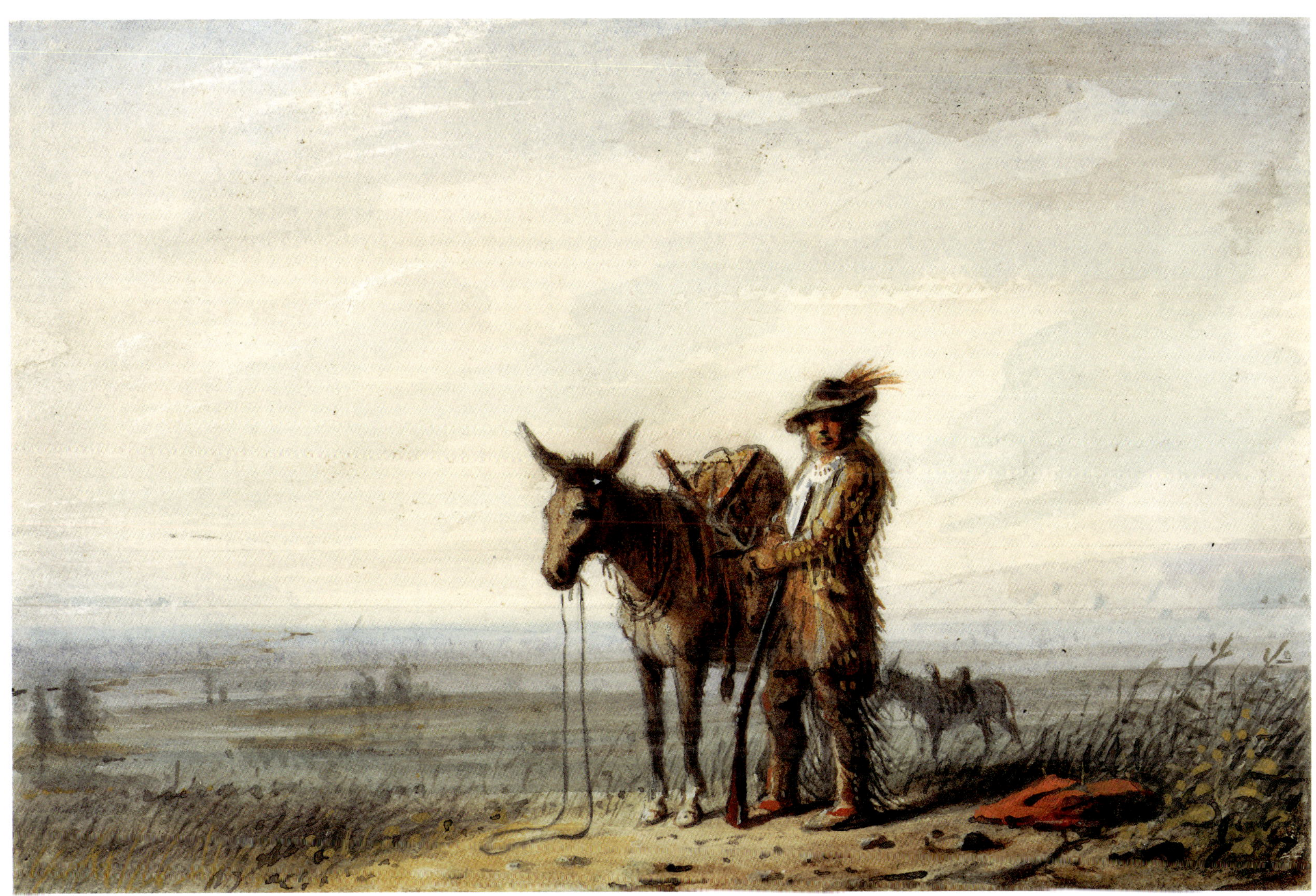

6 *Antelope*

Watercolor, ink, touches of gouache, and pencil on cream wove paper, 6⅞ × 10⅝ in. (17.5 × 27 cm). Inscribed lower left: Antelope. BAC 10287

An estimated forty million antelope inhabited the West during the early nineteenth century. Vast herds roamed the Plains and rivaled the bison in their abundance. A prized quarry, *Antiolocapra americana* was valued by American Indians and Euro-Americans for its meat, hide, and distinctive horns. This species, indigenous to the American West, was also renowned for its tremendous speed and keen eyesight, especially useful traits in its flat grasslands habitat that offered few places to hide from predators.[1]

Miller conveyed both the celebrated agility and sharp-eyed nature of the antelope in this lovely sketch, a composition that he seems never to have repeated. At its center, a gravity-defying specimen bounds gracefully across the prairie. It is described in pen-applied black, gray, and brown ink with gouache and now-discolored lead white highlights. The light areas of its muzzle, chest, underbelly, and rear leg are the cream tone of the paper. While this particularly plucky antelope fixes its gaze on the viewer from beneath its long lashes, its more timid, less fully described cohorts dash nimbly in the distance.[2]

Miller's own artistic dexterity and critical eye are also on display in this sketch. One can see the light pencil underdrawing that delineates the foreground antelope. The animal's proper right front leg was initially longer and its proper right eye lower than when they were later drawn with the pen. Additional changes from the artist's original intention to the finished composition are visible as well. Miller faintly sketched foliage, mountains, and clouds in pencil, elements that are noticeable in the thin blue and gray wash that colors the sky, but opted not to define them further with watercolor, ink, or gouache. These details reveal Miller's working method. Like the partial inky fingerprint on the belly of the foreground antelope and the loose brush hairs caught in the shrubbery at the left, these features make Miller's presence felt in a more intimate manner than an encounter with his more highly finished works may provide.[3]

SFK

1. See Colin F. Taylor, *The American Indian* (London: Salamander Books, 2002), 64; and Howard Ensign Evans, *The Natural History of the Long Expedition to the Rocky Mountains, 1819–1820* (New York: Oxford University Press, 1997), 103–4.

2. Miller developed a sort of shorthand for rendering four-legged creatures in the distance by reducing their forms to the most simplified elements. Like the horses in *Attrapez des Chevaux* (cat. 3), the five summarily suggested antelope in the middle ground share affinities with animals painted on prehistoric cave walls or described in pictographs.

3. For further discussion of this sketch, see essays by Lisa Strong and Kathleen A. Foster in this volume.

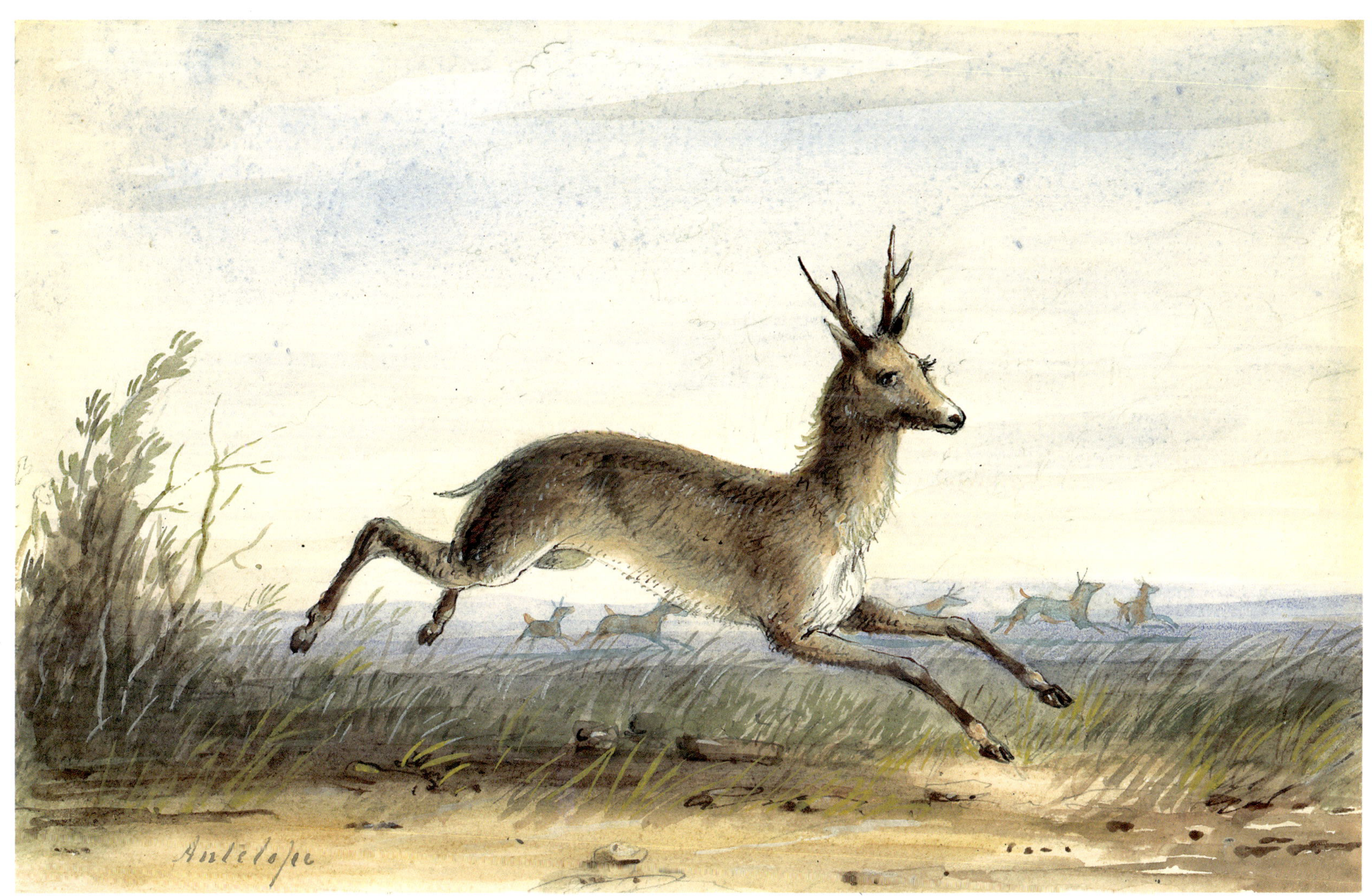
Antelope

7 *Indian Fort*

Ink wash, pen and ink, and pencil on cream wove paper, 5$^{3}/_{16}$ × 7 in. (13.2 × 17.8 cm). Inscribed lower right: Indian Fort. BAC 10288

ON THE TRAIL, MILLER WOULD HAVE SEEN A WIDE VARIETY OF INDIAN encampments, villages, and shelters. Among them was this structure, which he called an Indian fort. It is similar to a Pawnee Loup breastwork that Titian Ramsay Peale sketched on the Platte River when he was part of Major Stephen H. Long's expedition in 1820, but many Plains tribes created similar structures of logs, branches, and other natural detritus, to provide temporary shelter.[1]

There was little free time for Miller to sketch on the trail, so he often drew when the wagons halted at noontime for a meal and to rest.[2] *Indian Fort* may have been drawn during just such an interlude. One of Miller's approximately one hundred field sketches, it simply records a sight on the trail; it is not, in other words, a first draft of one of the many potential subjects Stewart frequently suggested to the artist.[3] It includes none of the editorializing of Miller's more elaborate compositions but, rather, appears as a memorandum.

Miller may have begun with a pencil sketch that, although slight, caused considerable indentations in the sheet, suggesting the page was originally part of a sketchbook.[4] He then suggested the bulk of the fort with gray and sepia wash. Lyrical lines of ink and dots of darker wash evoke the variety of the structure's organic materials. It is further animated by the array of branches that poke beyond its edges. Small areas of the cream-colored paper were left untouched to create the highlights. The shadowy entrance of the fort, defined by gradated tones of ink wash, appears at once welcoming and ominous. Miller only hints at the fort's locale and gives no indication of its size. Without a sense of scale, it appears as a lone creature. MCC

1. For Peale's image, see Kenneth Haltman, *Looking Close and Seeing Far: Samuel Seymour, Titian Ramsay Peale, and the Art of the Long Expedition, 1818–1823* (University Park: Pennsylvania State University, 2008), 23. On other Indian breastworks of the period, see "The Rocky Mountain Letters of Robert Campbell," originally published in the *National Atlas and Tuesday Morning Mail* (Philadelphia), vol. 1, nos. 14–19, 1 November–6 December 1836, at www.xmission.com/~drudy/mtman/html/camltrin.html.

2. Strong, "Images of Indian-White Contact," 36.

3. Miller used the same ink in the drawing and its inscription, suggesting he notated the subject for later reference. Perhaps he intended to employ it later, yet it does not otherwise appear in a known drawing. On Stewart's role in Miller's subjects, see DeVoto, *Across the Wide Missouri*, 21.

4. All but the right edge of the drawing have been cut, another indication the sheet may have originally been part of a sketchbook. Miller's original sketchbooks are now unlocated. Troccoli, *Miller: Watercolors*, 68. The type of paper with blue fibers on which the sketch appears is unique among the Bank of America's works by Miller.

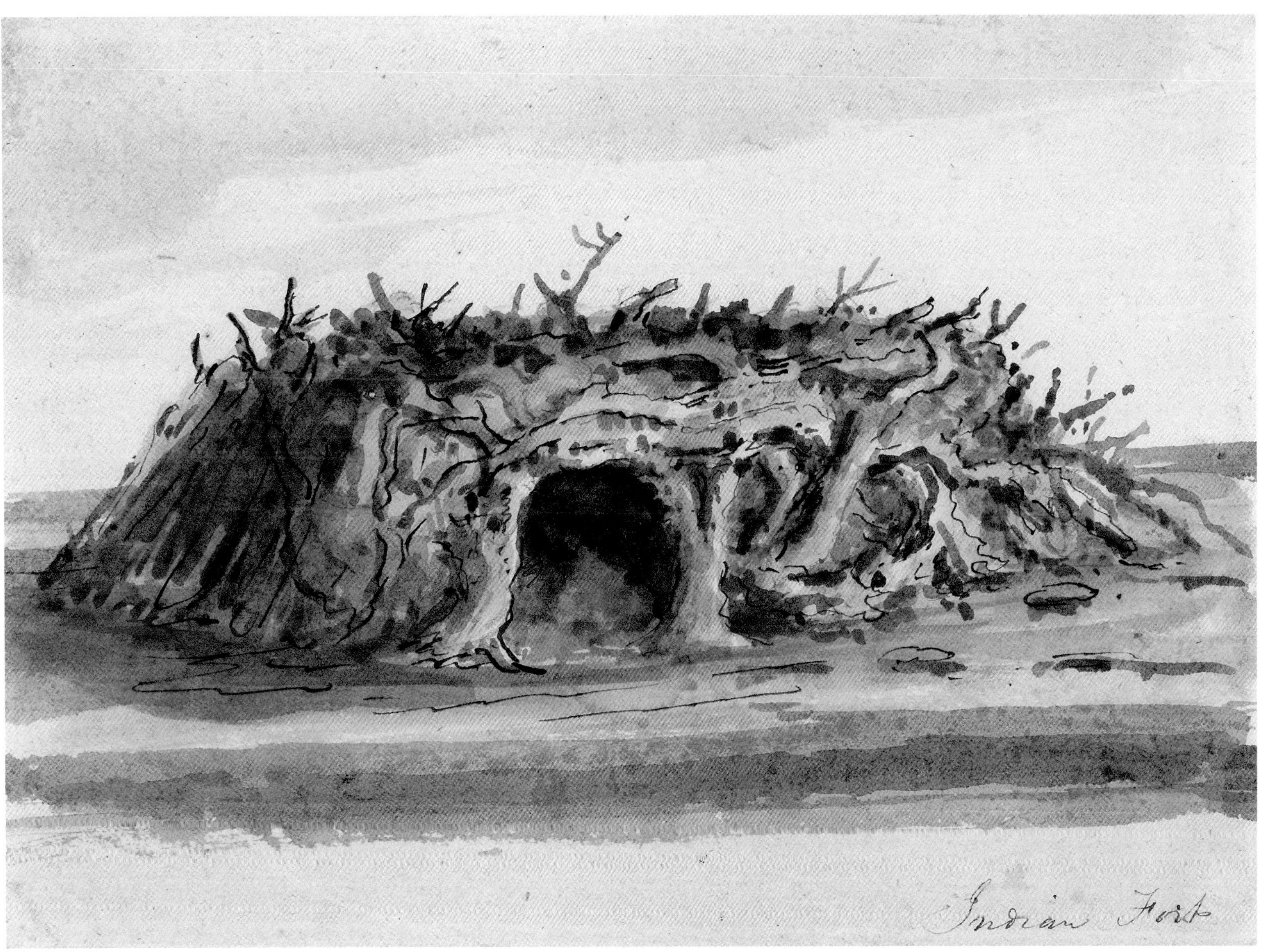
Indian Fort

8 *The Indian Guide*

Oil over white ground and graphite with patches of glossy coating on dark tan paper, 7 15/16 × 10 in. (20.2 × 25.4 cm). Signed with monogram, lower right: AJM. BAC 10307

THROUGHOUT HIS CAREER, MILLER FOCUSED ON THE EXCHANGE BETWEEN whites and Indians. *The Indian Guide*, one of only a small number of his works on paper executed in oil (see also cats. 1, 15, and 30), depicts an Indian giving directions to two seated figures, who are presumably lost. While *The Indian Guide* doubtless resonated with events and stories Miller surely knew firsthand, it more importantly follows literary and artistic conventions that place it squarely among nineteenth-century images of the Indian as noble savage, such as James Fenimore Cooper's Uncas in *Last of the Mohicans* (1826) and Charles Bird King's *Young Omahaw, War Eagle, Little Missouri, and Pawnees* (1822; Smithsonian American Art Museum).[1]

Beginning in the eighteenth century, the noble savage was understood to be the authentic natural man, dignified yet unencumbered by civilization, primitive but with an intelligence rooted in intuition and emotion.[2] The central figure in *The Indian Guide* is presented as just such a man. He appears unfettered and majestic, generous and virtuous, without specific tribal affiliation or evidence of the disease or forced removal endemic when Miller likely painted this image in the 1850s.

Familiar historic and contemporary art aided Miller in his construction of this ideal Indian. He borrowed the fundamental pose from George Catlin's majestic portraits, like that of the Mandan chief Máh-to-tóh-pa (1832; Smithsonian American Art Museum).[3] He accentuated the grounding of Catlin's work in ancient Roman portraiture by employing more exactly the classic orator's pose of such sculptures as *Aulus Metellus* (c. 90 BCE; Museo Archeologico Nazionale, Florence), which has long symbolized public service and intellectual strength. Miller outfitted the Indian man in a very splendid but generic costume of a long shirt and profusely decorated leggings more typical of a formal occasion than a chance meeting. Also, in keeping with much of his art, Miller essentially painted dark skin tones on Caucasian features, especially the high forehead and prominent nose, long recognized as a Roman type and associated with virtue.[4] Placed at the apex of the triangular arrangement of the three figures and silhouetted against the backdrop of the big sky of the open landscape, he towers over the hunters as a commanding yet sympathetic figure, a type of image to which Miller's patrons in the 1850s would have been attracted. MCC

1. Among works by Miller known today, it is nearly unique, retaining only a distant relationship to the Walters's watercolor *Trappers and Indians Communicating by Signs* (1858–60).

2. On the history and meanings of the myth of the noble savage, see Terry Jay Ellingson, *The Myth of the Noble Savage* (Berkeley: University of California Press, 2001).

3. Miller knew Catlin's art and was in contact with him in London when both artists were in residence. Alfred Jacob Miller to his brother, 10 February 1842, Bernard DeVoto Papers, Stanford University Libraries.

4. Troccoli, *Miller: Watercolors*, 7; and Julie Schimmel, "Inventing 'the Indian,'" in *The West as America: Reinterpreting Images of the Frontier, 1820–1920*, ed. William H. Truettner, exh. cat. (Washington, D.C.: Smithsonian Institution Press, 1991), 151.

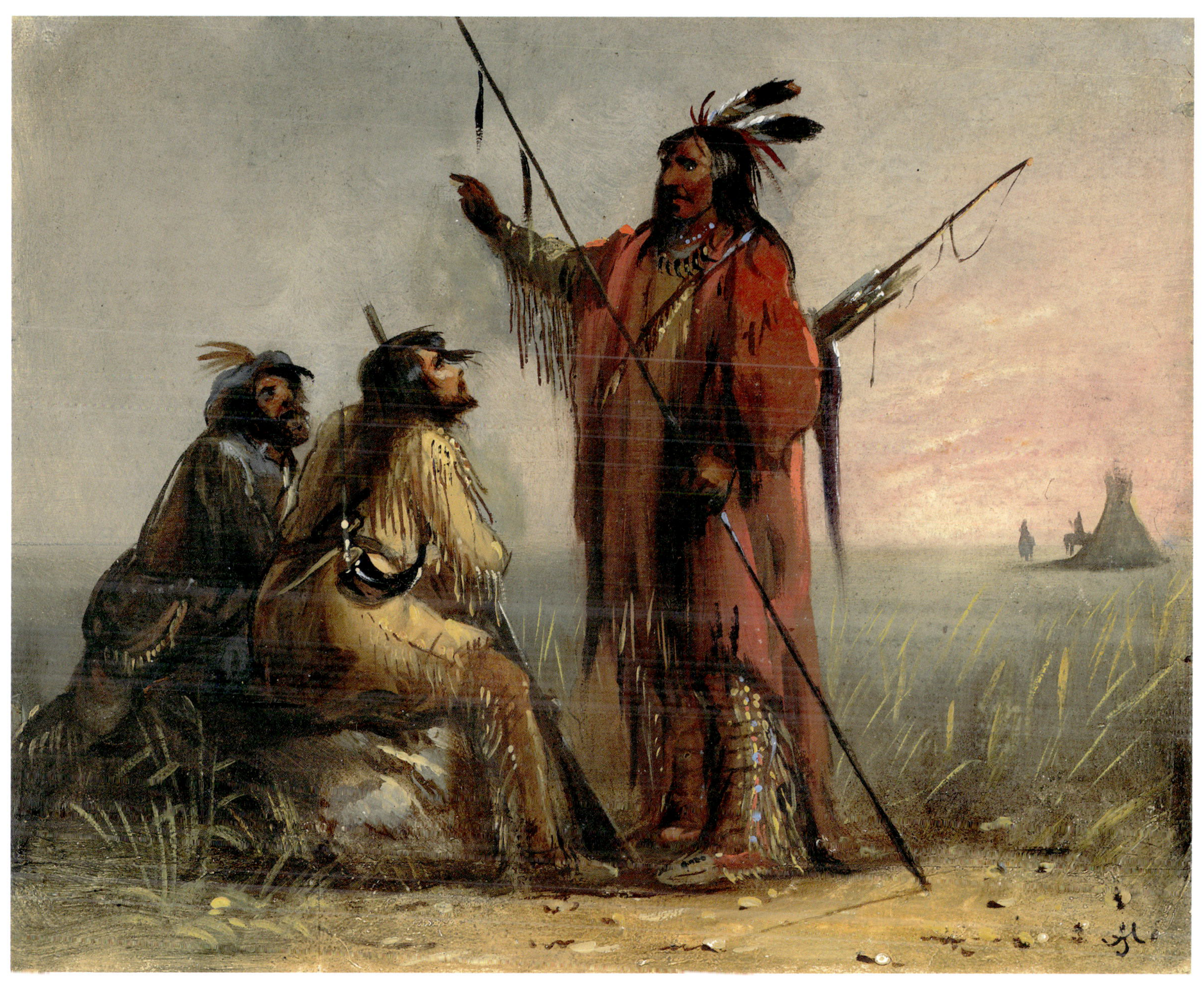

9 *Visit to an Indian Camp on the Border of a Lake*

Watercolor, gouache, ink, pencil, and glazes on thin tissue, lined, 8¹⁄₁₆ × 12³⁄₁₆ in. (20.5 × 31 cm). Signed with monogram, lower right: AJM; inscribed lower right: Visit to an Indian Camp / on the border of a Lake. BAC 10311

Visit to an Indian Camp on the Border of a Lake is one of many scenes in which Stewart is seen at leisure with Indians. His attraction to Indian life was due to more than just curiosity. He felt that Indians shared a certain status with Scottish aristocrats like himself. If Stewart was a member of the civilized nobility, Indians represented the "indigenous nobility." As Lisa Strong has pointed out, both culture groups made their livings from warfare and hunting, and "independence, honor, and freedom" marked their behavior.[1] Here, Miller depicted the Indian man and Stewart as visual equals. The pipe they share, an expression of goodwill, further cements their equivalence.

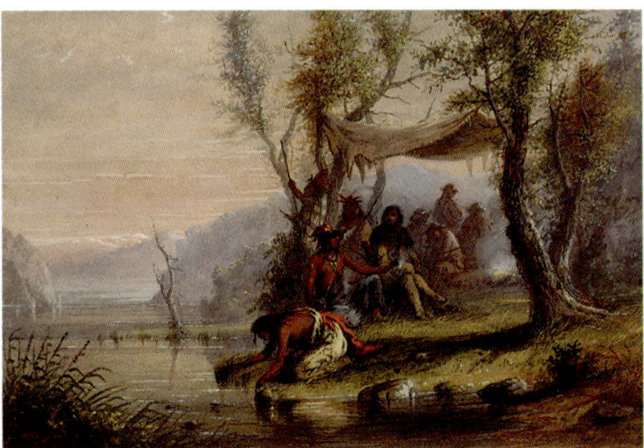

Figure 31. Alfred Jacob Miller, *Visit to an Indian Camp*, 1858–60. Watercolor on paper, 8¹⁵⁄₁₆ × 13³⁄₁₆ in. (22.7 × 33.5 cm). The Walters Art Museum, Baltimore

Miller may have created this image over several campaigns of work. Painted on thin tissue, it appears that he may have first traced in pencil and ink parts of the image from a sheet destined for Stewart's album. Outlines of trees and mountains that may have been traced are visible especially on the left side. The sketchy ink line of the landscape generally resembles that seen in drawings for Stewart such as *Repose at Mid-Day* (c. 1837; Amon Carter Museum) and *Visit to an Indian Encampment* (c. 1837; private collection).[2] A blue-gray wash over much of the surface including the inscription and monogram suggests the color work was accomplished later, as do the more generalized features of Stewart, who in earlier sketches is more individualized and slender.

Regardless of its precise genesis, *Visit to an Indian Camp on the Border of a Lake* looks like an intermediary step between two works. The right side is considerably more complete than the left and the anatomy of the figures is somewhat negligent. Even so, Miller included details—the cattails and grasses at the left, the fringe on Stewart's buckskin leggings—that enhance a sense of reality. Most noticeable, perhaps, is the woman kneeling at the stream's edge. Outlining her body in black ink, Miller calls attention to the curves of her figure. Although the story of Stewart's experience is clearly told in the middle ground, the Indian woman, an exotic type Miller features repeatedly, is the image's focal point (see cats. 22, 23). The work looks ahead to *Visit to an Indian Camp* (fig. 31). Although the two sheets are very similar, the action of the latter watercolor is pushed farther back, the landscape is more fully realized, and the figures are more resolved but also more generalized, including the woman who, no longer entirely outlined in black ink, is more integrated into the composition. These differences highlight the use of each work, the one in the bank's collection being a visual aid and the more complete image intended for contemplation. Even so, both works share an overall misty blue tone, which adds the mysteriousness with which Miller continually infused his art.[3] MCC

1. Strong, *Sentimental Journey*, 103–5.

2. Both works are reproduced in Tyler, *Miller: Artist on the Oregon Trail*, nos. 61A and 419.

3. Strong, "Images of Indian-White Contact," 22; and Miller, Journal, 56.

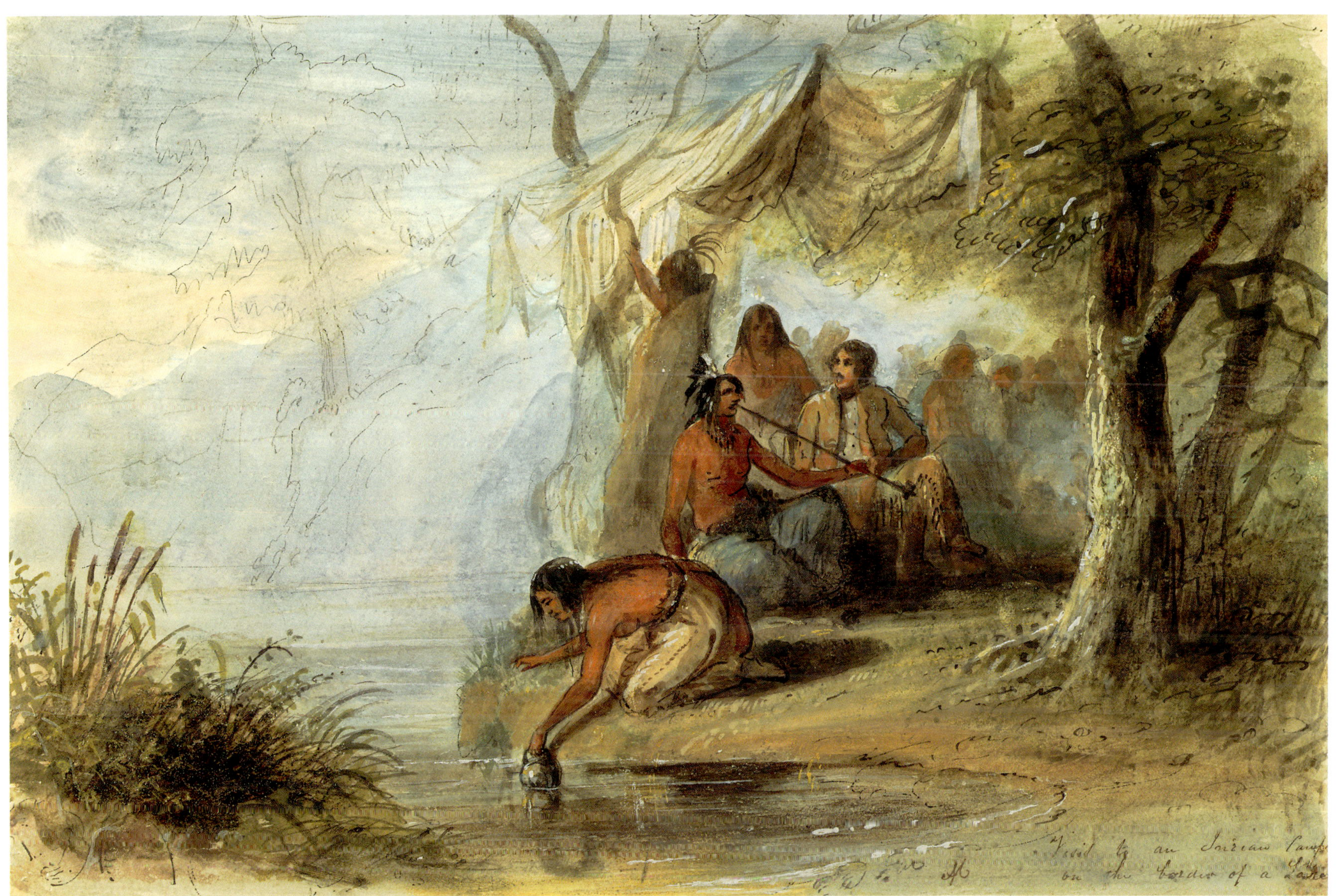
Visit to an Indian Camp
on the border of a Lake

10 *Elk Taking the Water*

Watercolor, gouache, ink, pencil, and gum glazes on cream or gray wove paper, 8⅛ × 12¹⁵⁄₁₆ in. (20.6 × 32.9 cm). Inscribed lower right: Elk Taking the Water. BAC 10314

Pressed by hunters, after a hard run, the Elk has here indiscreetly jumped into a stream too shallow for him to swim, which seals his fate. The enemy is hovering about him, one in the act of giving a "Coup de Pistolet," while others are in the background hurrying on with a ball in reserve if required.[1]

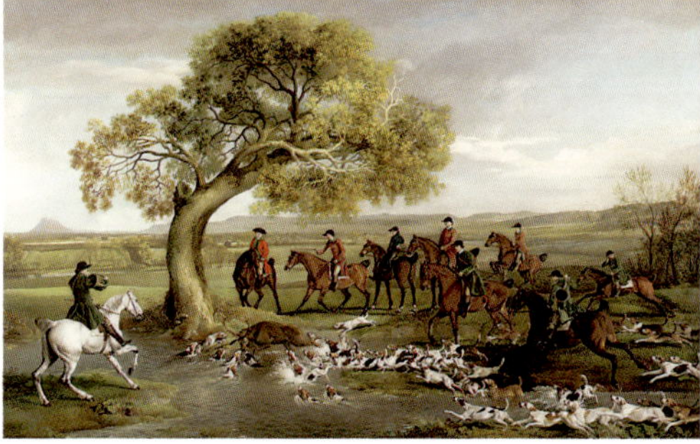

Figure 32. George Stubbs, *The Grosvenor Hunt*, 1762. Oil on canvas, 59 × 95 in. (150 × 241 cm). Private collection. Courtesy The Bridgeman Art Library, New York

The identity of the "enemy" responsible for "giving a 'Coup de Pistolet'" is not revealed in Miller's "Rough Draughts." However, it is probable that the man at the center of this composition, sporting fringed buckskin highlighted in yellow and sitting erect astride a white horse, is none other than Stewart. In attire, comportment, and choice of equine, this figure corresponds with other depictions of the Scottish adventurer in Miller's oeuvre.[2]

Stewart was an avid hunter, dispatching big game on three continents.[3] Hunting was a leisure pursuit with a venerable tradition among European noblemen, who often commissioned art to commemorate their exploits. In composition and treatment of the subject matter, Miller's hunting sketches pay tribute to this artistic pedigree. *Elk Taking the Water* shares affinities with the French Rococo artist Jean-Baptiste Oudry's paintings of the hunt and British sporting pictures by George Stubbs, especially *The Grosvenor Hunt* painted in 1762 (fig. 32) and published as an engraving by John Young in 1821.[4]

As was his practice, Miller combined a variety of methods in *Elk Taking the Water*. In addition to his habitual layering of media, he abraded the paper in the upper portion of the composition, increasing its ability to absorb the thin watercolor wash and enhancing the atmospheric qualities of the mottled sky.[5] He created textured bark on the trunk of the tree that frames the scene at the left by scraping the paper and then applying wash or tinted glaze. Miller also delicately scratched the dried washes of iron gall ink and watercolor in the foreground to expose the bare paper beneath. This action created rippling highlights on the surface of the stream that augment those evoked by touches of white gouache.

An incomplete pencil sketch dated 1831 on the verso depicts Christ flanked by two figures at the left and a profile head at the right. Miller may have drawn it while studying with Thomas Sully in Philadelphia. SFK

1. Miller, "Rough Draughts," no. 78, which relates to Ross, *The West of Miller*, opp. pl. 113.

2. Miller made at least three other sketches depicting this scene, including a now unlocated sketch for Stewart himself. Additionally, although not identical, the Bank of America's *Elk Taking the Water* has many correlations to *Lord Stewart Shooting the Elk* (c. 1859; Stark Museum of Art, Orange, Tex.).

3. For more on Stewart's international hunting expeditions, see Mae Reed Porter and Odessa Davenport, *Scotsman in Buckskin: Sir William Drummond Stewart and the Rocky Mountain Fur Trade* (New York: Hastings House, 1963).

4. I am grateful to my colleagues Ian Kennedy, Louis L. and Adelaide C. Ward Curator of European Painting and Sculpture, and Simon Kelly, Associate Curator of European Painting and Sculpture, both at the Nelson-Atkins Museum of Art, for suggesting these connections.

5. Some abrading or scraping also appears in cats. 3, 13, 16, 24, and 26. The renowned British artist J. M. W. Turner aggressively worked his watercolor paper toward the end of his career, a practice that may have influenced Miller.

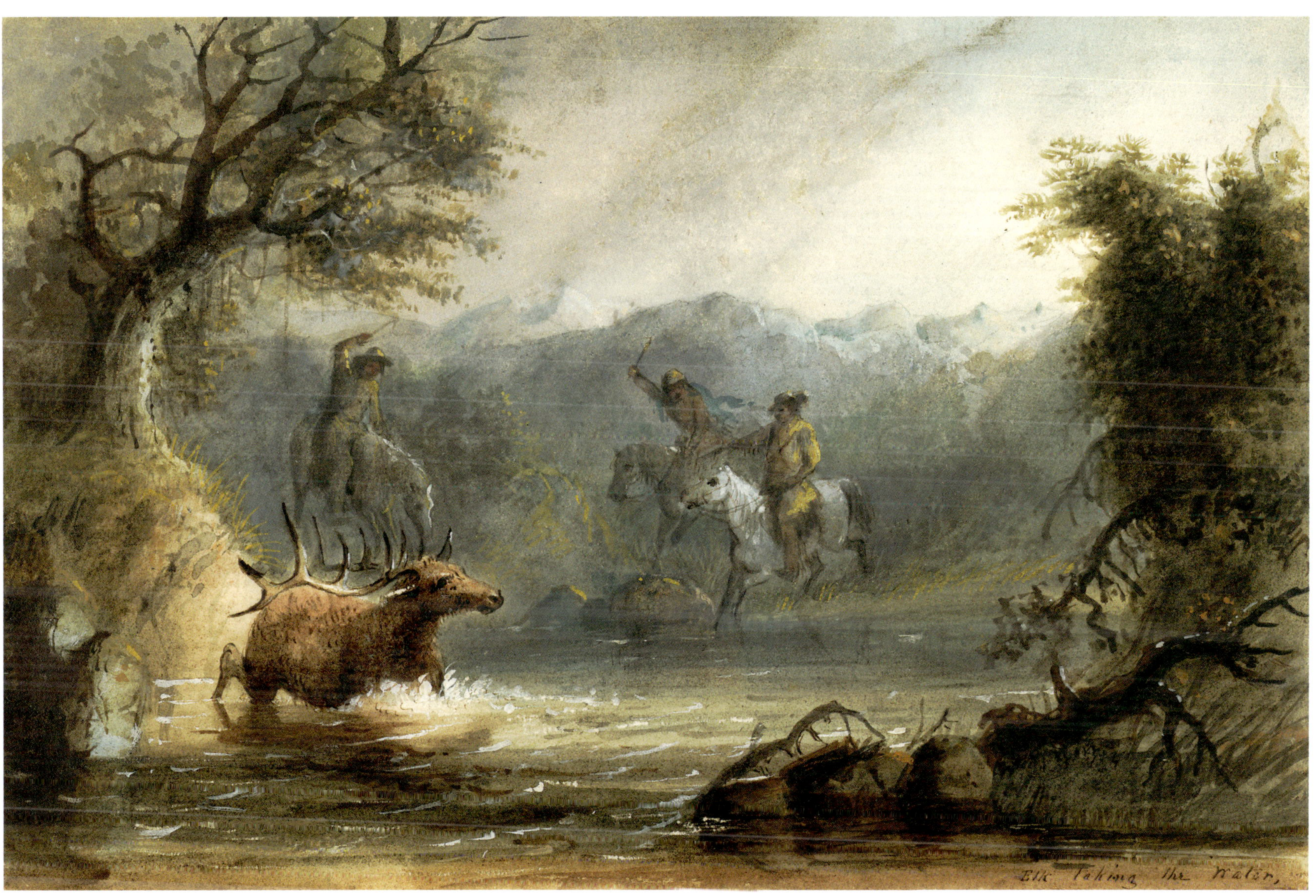
Elk taking the Water,

11 *Chase of the Grizzly Bear, Black Hills*

Watercolor, gouache, pencil, ink, and gum glazes on tissue mounted to card, 8⅝16 × 7¹³⁄16 in. (21.1 × 19.8 cm). Inscribed upper right: Black Hills; inscribed lower right: Hunting the Grissly [illegible].

BAC 10300

ALTHOUGH THE VISIT TO THE FUR TRAPPERS' RENDEZVOUS PROVIDED THE centerpiece of their trip west, Miller accompanied Stewart on numerous hunting excursions throughout their travels. Pursuing large game, including grizzly bear, was among the Scotsman's favorite forms of leisure activity. His hunting expeditions in the West mirrored the exotic game hunts he had enjoyed earlier in India and Turkey as well as his frequent forays in Scotland.

The importance of hunting for Stewart is reflected in the fact that the theme appears in more than one-quarter of the images Miller created for him. Throughout, Miller ensured Stewart was depicted in a way that not only recounted his adventures but reflected his Scottish aristocratic ideals that valued the sportsmanship and skill required. Stewart considered hunting a privilege of his class, since before 1832 only landowning British aristocrats could engage in the sport.[1] For the Indian accompanying Stewart, hunting could have had a number of associations; in addition to its purely practical function, it surely had a symbolic meaning.[2]

Like other sheets in the bank's collection (cats. 9, 12), this one suggests Miller began it by tracing on a sheet of tissue elements from one of Stewart's watercolors,[3] since the figure of Stewart almost exactly replicates that in one of the Scotsman's sheets (see fig. 17). The artist then attached the tracing to a thin card before applying color, some of which extends beyond the tissue border. The pencil sketching on top of as well as below the paint suggests multiple campaigns of work.[4] Miller alternated layers of watercolor and gouache with heavy graphite, especially in the lower right, where it describes the texture of the scrubby terrain.

The locale of *Chase of the Grizzly Bear* is the Laramie Mountains in eastern Wyoming.[5] The mountains form a backdrop against which Miller highlighted Stewart's considerable skill as his white horse jumps a ravine in hot pursuit of a bear, seen in the distance. The strong diagonal along which the hunters are arranged creates a sense of movement and energy that is underscored by the horses' flying legs and such details as the rider waving his quirt. In this sheet, Miller expanded the depth of the landscape even though he retained the earlier work's close-up perspective of the figures. This resulted in making Stewart and his companions more prominent, an aspect he adjusted for balance when he revisited the composition in *The Grizzly Bear* for William T. Walters.

MCC

1. Strong, *Sentimental Journey*, 93.

2. Each Plains Indian group assigned its own significance to the hunt. Because the Indian shown here is depicted in so general a fashion that his tribe cannot be identified, it is impossible to attach specific meaning here. Ibid., 99.

3. The composition for the initial image may have been inspired by canvases like Paul Bril's *Stag Hunt* (1590–95; Musée du Louvre, Paris), which Miller could have seen during his 1833–34 travels.

4. Two inscriptions executed in two different inks further suggest this process.

5. Miller called the area the Black Hills, but it is near the intersection of the Laramie and North Platte rivers. Tyler, *Miller: Artist on the Oregon Trail*, 28.

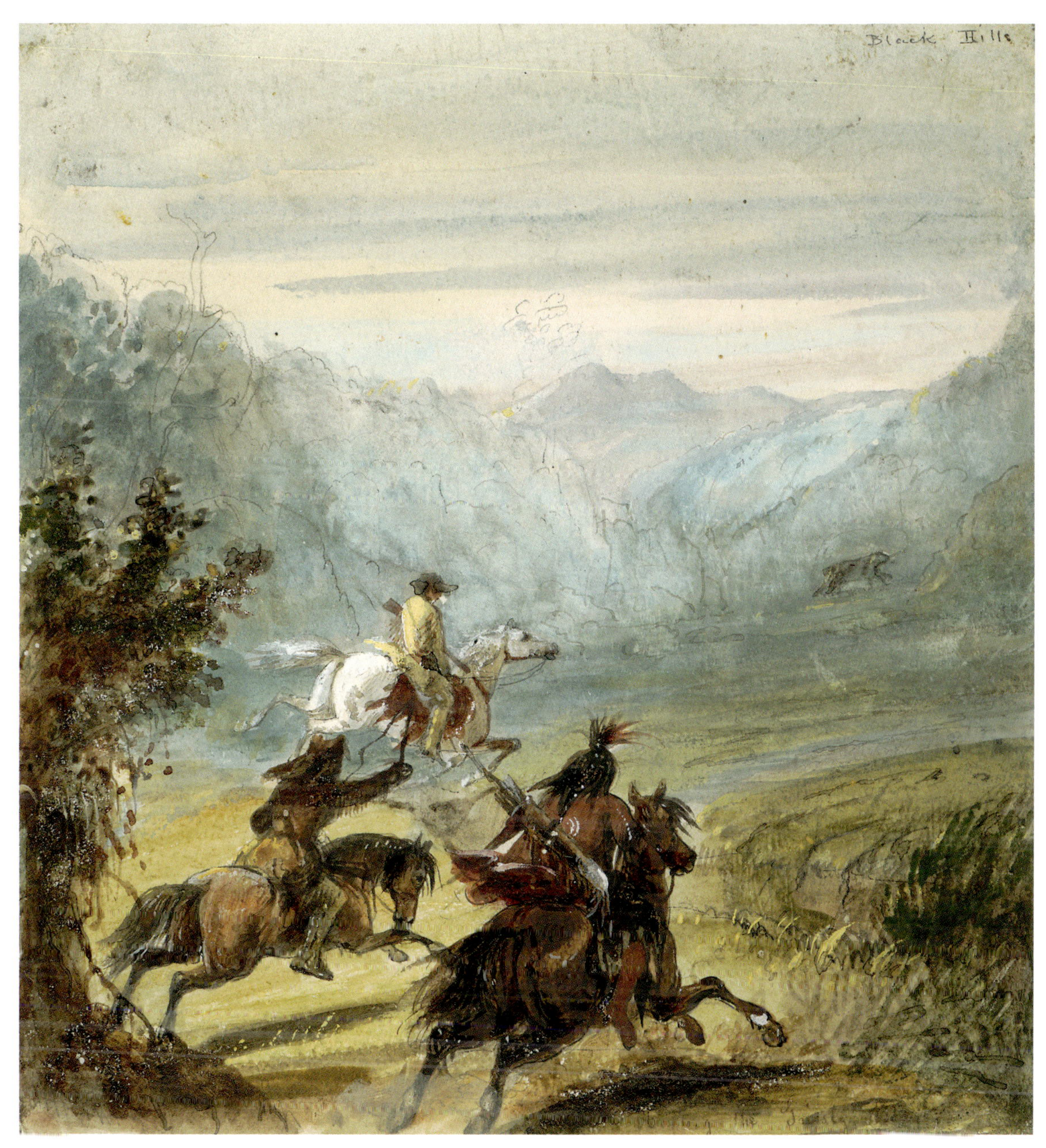
Black Hills

12 *Grizzly Bear Hunt*

Watercolor, gouache, iron gall ink, blue or gray ink, and pencil on tissue mounted to thin card, 7⅛ × 10⅞ in. (18.1 × 27.6 cm). Inscribed upper left: 107; inscribed upper right: Driving the Grissly Bear from his/ covert.—near Black Hills; inscribed on center of verso: 107. BAC 10316

"THE GRIZZLY BEAR IS THE ONLY REALLY FORMIDABLE QUADRUPED ON OUR continent," wrote Washington Irving in *Astoria*, his 1836 account of the Rocky Mountain fur trade.[1] The animals, which can weigh more than 1,500 pounds, are known for their tremendous strength and ferocity, making them among the most dangerous to hunt. Thus, as Miller recounted in a "Rough Draught" entry, hunting grizzlies necessitates having a skilled party that has the discipline to refrain from pressing the bruin too closely.[2]

Grizzly Bear Hunt is one of at least eleven grizzly-hunting images Miller painted. They include sketches for each of his three primary patrons as well as this image on tissue that, like *Visit to an Indian Camp on the Border of a Lake* and *Chase of the Grizzly Bear* (cats. 9, 11), seems to have provided an intermediary stage between a sketch for Stewart's album and one for Walters (see fig. 28).[3] This sheet, the most fully realized of the Bank of America works on tissue, also displays the greatest transformation of an image over time, noticeably replacing a party of Caucasian hunters with one of Indians. This shift in protagonists appears to have occurred in anticipation of the Walters sheet, which is the only other of the group to feature Indians.

In this sheet, the Indians, dressed more for war than hunting, flush a bear from his covert.[4] The oversize animal, which only generally resembles the titular beast, shoots out of thick foliage. Trees framing the scene compress and dramatize the action in a composition divided along a diagonal that separates the earthy tones of the foreground action from a hazy blue-green backdrop of a mountain landscape. The resulting stagelike composition and the animated black outlines around the figures enhance the tension between the Indian, bow pulled and red blanket streaming behind, and the bear. Aligned on parallel diagonals, the man on his flying horse and the beast are frozen at the anticipatory moment just before the arrow is released. Since grizzlies are known for attacking when wounded, the viewer is encouraged to ponder the bravery and courage of Indians and the possible variants of the narrative's outcome. MCC

1. Washington Irving, *Astoria, or Anecdotes of an Enterprise beyond the Rocky Mountains* (1836), ed. William H. Goetzmann (New York: J. B. Lippincott Company, 1961), 241–42.

2. "Rough Draughts," no. 107, a number that matches the inscription on the Bank of America collection sheet; an additional "Rough Draught" on the same topic is paired with the related Walters image in Ross, *The West of Miller*, opp. pl. 125.

3. The works are listed in Tyler, *Miller: Artist on the Oregon Trail*, nos. 141, 141A–B, 142, 142A–B, 143, 143A–C, 144, and 145.

4. I am grateful to my colleague Gaylord Torrence, Fred and Virginia Merrill Senior Curator of American Indian Art, The Nelson-Atkins Museum of Art, for the information on the figures' clothing.

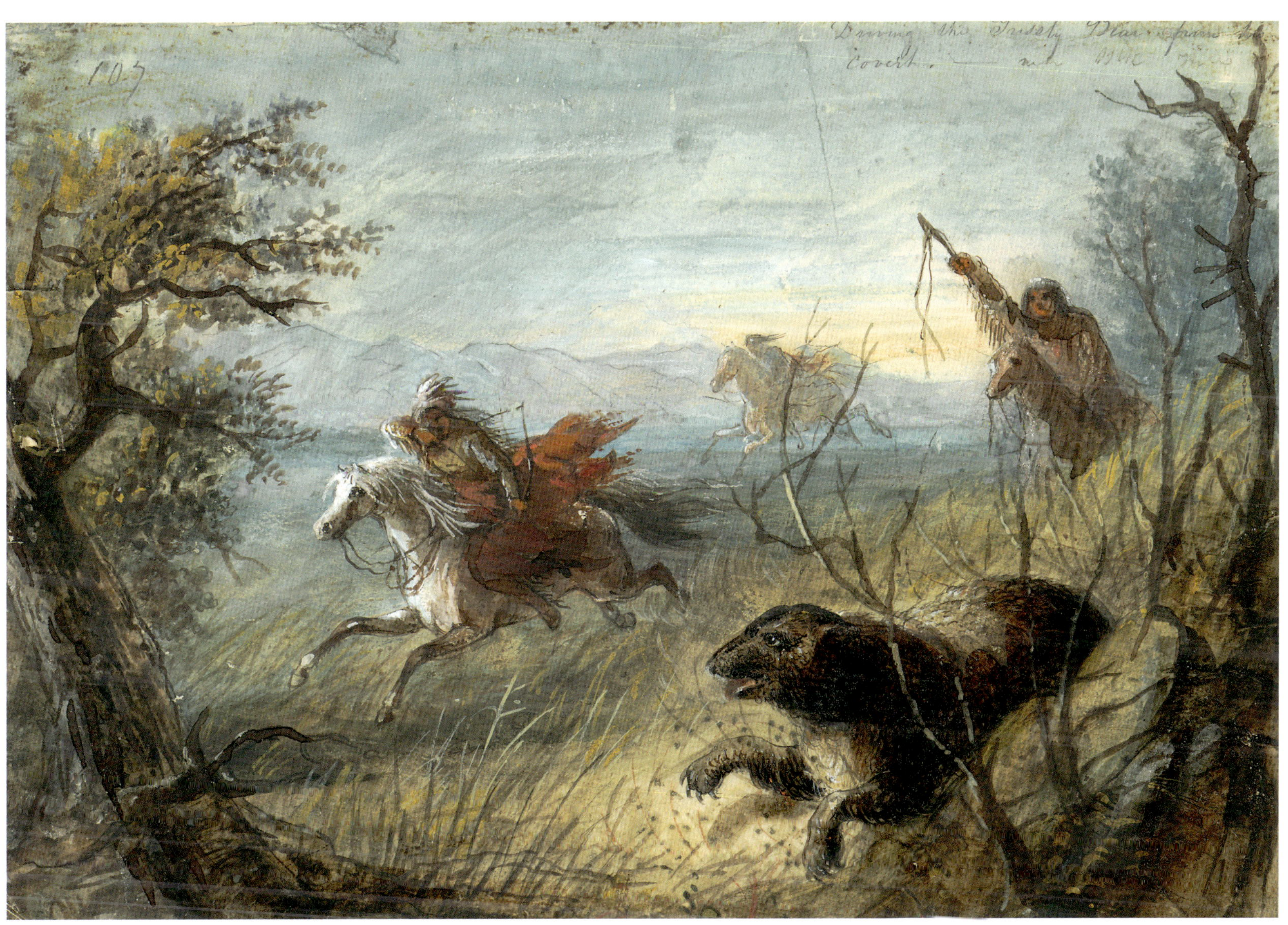
103
Driving the Grizzly Bear from the
covert.

13 *Buffalo Hunt, Black Hills*

Ink and/or watercolor wash, white gouache, pen and ink, brush and ink, and pencil on brown wove paper, 10⁵⁄₁₆ × 15¹¹⁄₁₆ in. (26.2 × 39.8 cm). Inscribed upper right: Buffalo Hunting/ in herds; inscribed lower right: Hunt of Buffalo / Black Hills. BAC 10292

BY THE LATE EIGHTEENTH CENTURY, MOST PLAINS INDIAN TRIBES HAD A singular dependence on buffalo, and their practical and spiritual lives revolved around the massive animals.[1] Buffalo hunts were collective efforts occurring in the summer and fall. They often entailed traveling considerable distances, setting up camp in enemy territories, and complex ritual ceremonies, even though the hunt itself was often brief in duration.[2]

Miller conjured the excitement of the activity in *Buffalo Hunt, Black Hills* in a composition organized around carefully placed vignettes. In the right foreground, Miller prominently depicted the height of a hunter's pursuit: lancing a buffalo while riding at a full gallop. The buffalo is delicately outlined in ink, and the texture of its fur indicated by scratches in the paper, but its massive body is given substance with brown wash and white highlights. Miller balanced the buffalo's substantial form against the graceful skill of the Indian rider, who guides his horse with his knees. The reach of both animals' legs and tails suggests the high speed of the chase, as does the opaque cloud of gray dust flying behind the buffalo. Along a line that zigzags across the lower half of the sheet, Miller depicted, from left to right, other aspects of a hunt: an Indian shooting a buffalo with a bow and arrow, others chasing the bulk of the herd into the distance, and a buffalo chasing two riders. Miller accomplished the suggestion of the massive herd by moving from generalized but realistic renderings of the buffalo in the center foreground to increasingly indistinct dots of brown wash that stretch across the Plains basin to the base of the mountains.

Miller depicted the wide-open space of the western plains with considerable skill. He accentuated their expanse by employing a high viewpoint, which may have been inspired by the epic battle paintings by Horace Vernet that Miller saw in Paris.[3] Using a medium-weight, moderately textured brown paper, he sketched in pencil the vast mountain landscape that fills the distance. A thin white wash across the mountains and lower sky adds an atmospheric effect. Gray wash with feathery white highlights above gently animates the sky, offering a peaceful, almost sublime, counterweight to the rush of activity below. MCC

1. Entry on buffalo, in *Encyclopedia of the Great Plains*, ed. David J. Wishart (Lincoln: Center for Great Plains Studies, University of Nebraska–Lincoln, 2004), 576–77; and Paul H. Carlson, *The Plains Indians* (College Station: Texas A&M University Press, 1998), 42.

2. Most Plains Indians preferred hunting buffalo with bow and arrow or lances, since the weapons were inexpensive and accurate. William Drummond Stewart and other white hunters, however, used guns, as is seen in *The Buffalo Hunt* (c. 1839; Philbrook Art Center, Tulsa, Okla.). On buffalo hunting, see Wishart, *Encyclopedia of the Great Plains*, 576–77.

3. See, for example, Horace Vernet, *The Battle of Valmy* (1826; The National Gallery, London), originally commissioned by the duc d'Orléans.

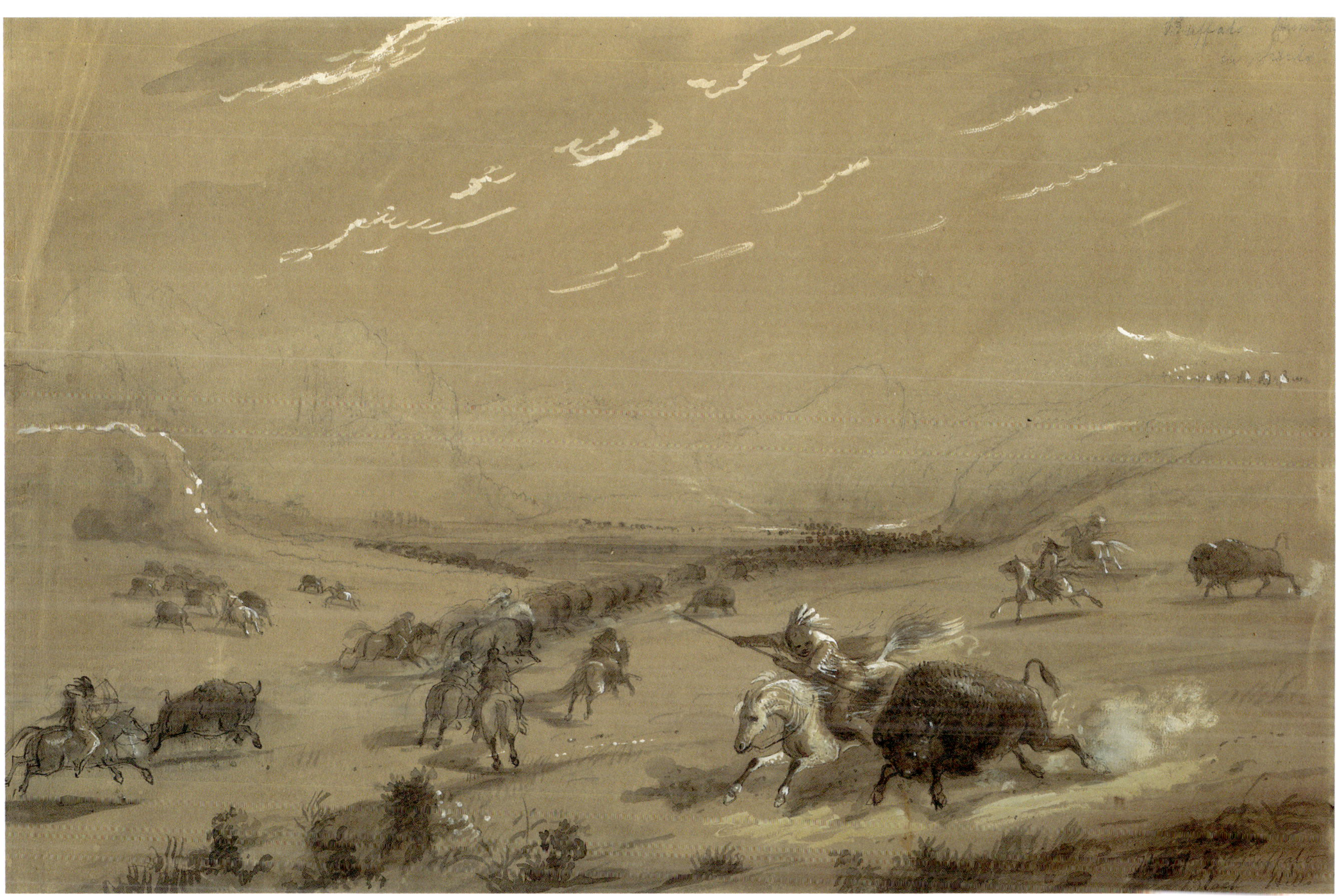

14 *Two Indians Killing a Buffalo*

Watercolor, gouache, and pencil on beige wove paper, 9⁵⁄₁₆ × 15⅞ in. (23.7 × 40.3 cm). Signed lower right: AJMiller. BAC 10294

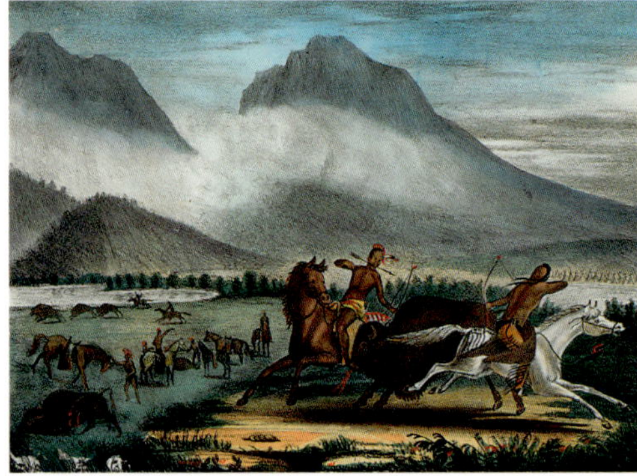

FIGURE 33. Peter S. Duval after Titian Ramsay Peale, *Buffaloe Hunt on the River Platte*, 1836. Hand-colored lithograph, in James Otto Lewis, *The Aboriginal Port Folio; or, a Collection of Portraits of the Most Celebrated Chiefs of the North American Indians* (Philadelphia: Lehman and Duval, 1836), fol. 10. Courtesy The New York Public Library

MILLER ILLUSTRATED INDIANS HUNTING BUFFALO NEARLY SEVENTY-FIVE TIMES. His interest in the subject matched that of many artists attracted to western subjects in the nineteenth century, from Titian Ramsay Peale and George Catlin in the 1830s to John Mix Stanley and Carl Wimar at midcentury, and Albert Bierstadt after the Civil War. *Two Indians Killing a Buffalo* closely recalls a widely circulated 1836 lithograph after Peale's *Buffaloe Hunt on the River Platte* (fig. 33) that may have served as Miller's model even though he had seen and heard stories of buffalo hunts himself.[1] Miller adopted Peale's basic composition, which features a buffalo sandwiched between two Indians on horseback poised to kill the animal. Miller, however, reduced the other hunting activity Peale depicted in the middle ground and employed a low horizon, which silhouettes the figures, their lances, and their regal Arabian-type mounts against the open sky and distant mountain landscape. The action is frozen at that moment when one horseman is about to deliver the death blow. The viewer's eyes are drawn to the bottom of an inverted triangle that points to the head of the exhausted buffalo, fallen to its knees. Miller selectively used white next to deep brown and black brushstrokes to highlight the horns, whites of the eyes, and nose, from which spills bright red blood. A wounded buffalo is a dangerous animal, yet Miller's artful arrangement of the Indians, their bodies twisted into graceful arabesques, helps belie any sense of endangerment and emphasizes the Indians' heroic abilities.

George Catlin wrote in 1841: "Nature has nowhere presented more beautiful and lovely scenes, than those of the vast prairies of the West . . . no nobler specimens than those who inhabit them – the *Indian* and the *buffalo*."[2] Miller celebrated in *Two Indians Killing a Buffalo* a Romantic notion of Native Americans' primitive nobility that lodged in many easterners' minds as bloody disputes and forced removal of Indians increased after 1840. Miller painted no fewer than seven versions of this composition, all remarkably similar (see fig. 14). Three of them are in oil, suggesting the import he attached to the subject.[3]

MCC

1. On Peale's image, see Kenneth Haltman, *Looking Close and Seeing Far: Samuel Seymour, Titian Ramsay Peale, and the Art of the Long Expedition, 1818–1823* (University Park: Pennsylvania State University, 2008), 197.

2. George Catlin, *North American Indians, Being Letters and Notes on Their Manners, Customs, Written during Eight Years Travels amongst the Wildest Tribes of Indians in America* (1841), quoted in Robert F. Berkhofer Jr., *The White Man's Indian: Images of the American Indian from Columbus to the Present* (New York: Alfred A. Knopf, 1978), 89.

3. They are *Buffalo Hunt* (n.d.; private collection), listed in Tyler, *Miller: Artist on the Oregon Trail*, no. 367B; *Buffalo Hunt with Lance* (1858; private collection), listed in Tyler, no. 367C; and *Buffalo Hunt* (n.d.; Amon Carter Museum).

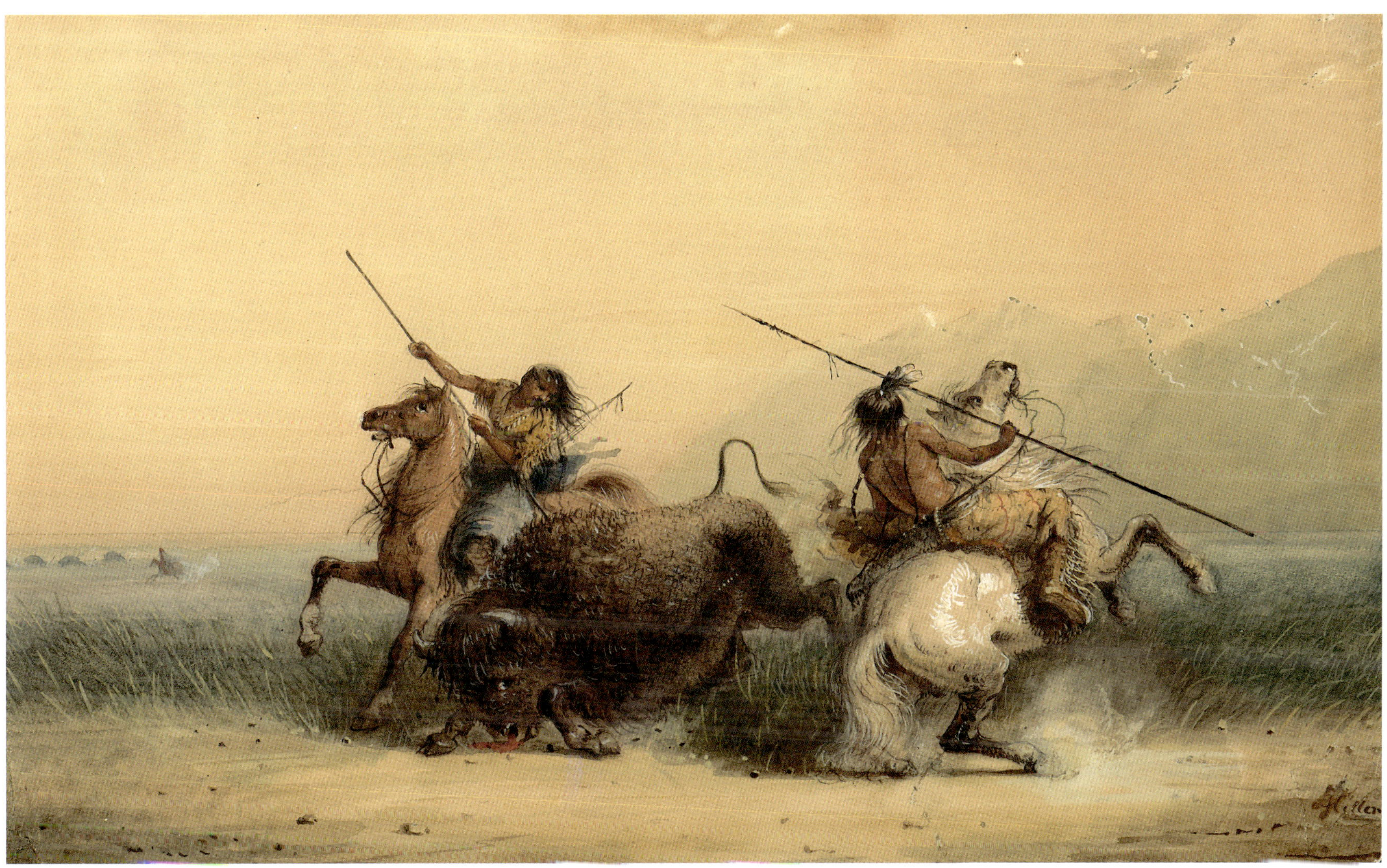

15 *Taking the Hump Rib*

Oil and glazes over ink, watercolor, and gouache on cream wove paper, 6⅞ × 9¹¹⁄₁₆ in. (17.5 × 24.6 cm). Signed with monogram, lower right: AJM; inscribed upper left: 65 Taking the Hump Rib. BAC 10302

WILLIAM DRUMMOND STEWART'S LOVE OF THE HUNT AND FASCINATION WITH buffalo surely motivated Miller to depict multiple episodes of the buffalo hunt narrative. *Taking the Hump Rib* features the end of the story: butchering the slain animal. When performed in Plains Indian fashion, as Antoine, Stewart's hunting guide, is shown doing here, the first cut is made along the buffalo's upper backbone. This allows the tastiest portion of meat—the hump rib—and the best fleece for making a robe to be removed without damage. Miller accurately positioned the buffalo on his knees,[1] a pose that offered the artist a solid mass around which to organize his composition, which also includes a horse rearing, likely upset by the smell of fresh blood; a pack mule waiting patiently to carry the meat to camp; and another of the party receiving a tomahawk from a mounted figure.[2] Dressed in buckskin, the man on horseback closely resembles Stewart, although his face is reduced to a few dark brushstrokes. Indeed, *Taking the Hump Rib*, which may have been a precursor to Walters's watercolor for the same subject, harkens back to *Butchering the Buffalo* (fig. 34), one of the large canvases Miller originally painted for Stewart.[3] In translating the image from a large canvas to the intimate scale of an album sheet, Miller lowered the viewpoint and cropped the foreground.

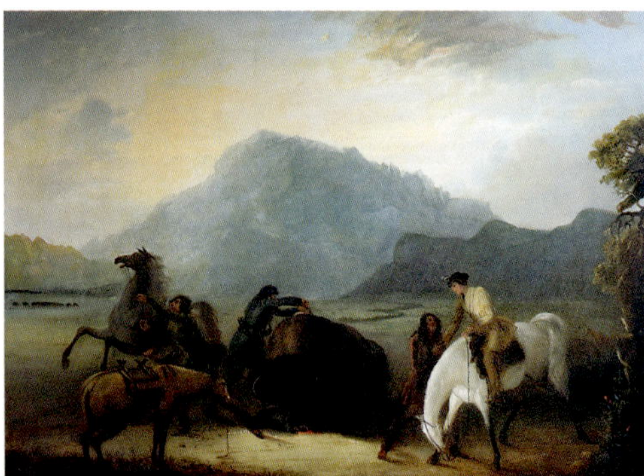

FIGURE 34. Alfred Jacob Miller, *Butchering the Buffalo*, c. 1839. Oil on canvas, 30 × 43 in. (76.2 × 109.2 cm). American Heritage Center, University of Wyoming, Laramie

As in the canvas for Stewart, Miller painted *Taking the Hump Rib* in oil. Thick paint covers the entire paper surface, but delicate, dry brushwork visible in the animals' manes and fur and the fringe on the men's clothing betrays his watercolor technique and penchant for fine details, which are more forthrightly evident in the Walters sheet.[4]

The sky, which is the area most different from *Butchering the Buffalo*, received the artist's greatest attention.[5] He applied yellow, peach, and salmon paint in long strokes and daubs of impasto, interweaving sunset colors that lighten as they reach the horizon. On the right, Miller suggested an oncoming storm with tones of gray-blue covering deep pinks. Reflected colored light skims across the landscape, the top of the buffalo, the shoulders and chest of the left-hand figure, Stewart and his horse, and the grassy foreground. The resulting overall warm glow adds a wistful pensiveness that may reflect Miller's growing concerns about the demise of Indian culture in the 1850s, when this sheet was likely executed.[6]

MCC

1. Miller describes the process and the buffalo's position in his "Rough Draughts," no. 100, which relates to Ross, *The West of Miller*, opp. pl. 85.

2. Miller identifies the object and notes the man will help with the slaughtering process. Ibid.

3. Typical of the artist's later renditions of the Scottish aristocrat, however, his body is stockier in the bank's image. The Walters's watercolor is reproduced in Ross, *The West of Miller*, pl. 85.

4. There may be water-based media on this sheet, but the thickness of the oil layer and areas of glaze coating on the dark colors prevent any definitive identification of aqueous materials.

5. Paint covers some of the edges of the sheet, indicating Miller continued to work after he trimmed the paper. At the top, the final paint layer stops short to reveal lighter tones underneath.

6. By the 1850s Miller was disturbed by the changes in the West. See Strong, "Images of Indian-White Contact," 41–43.

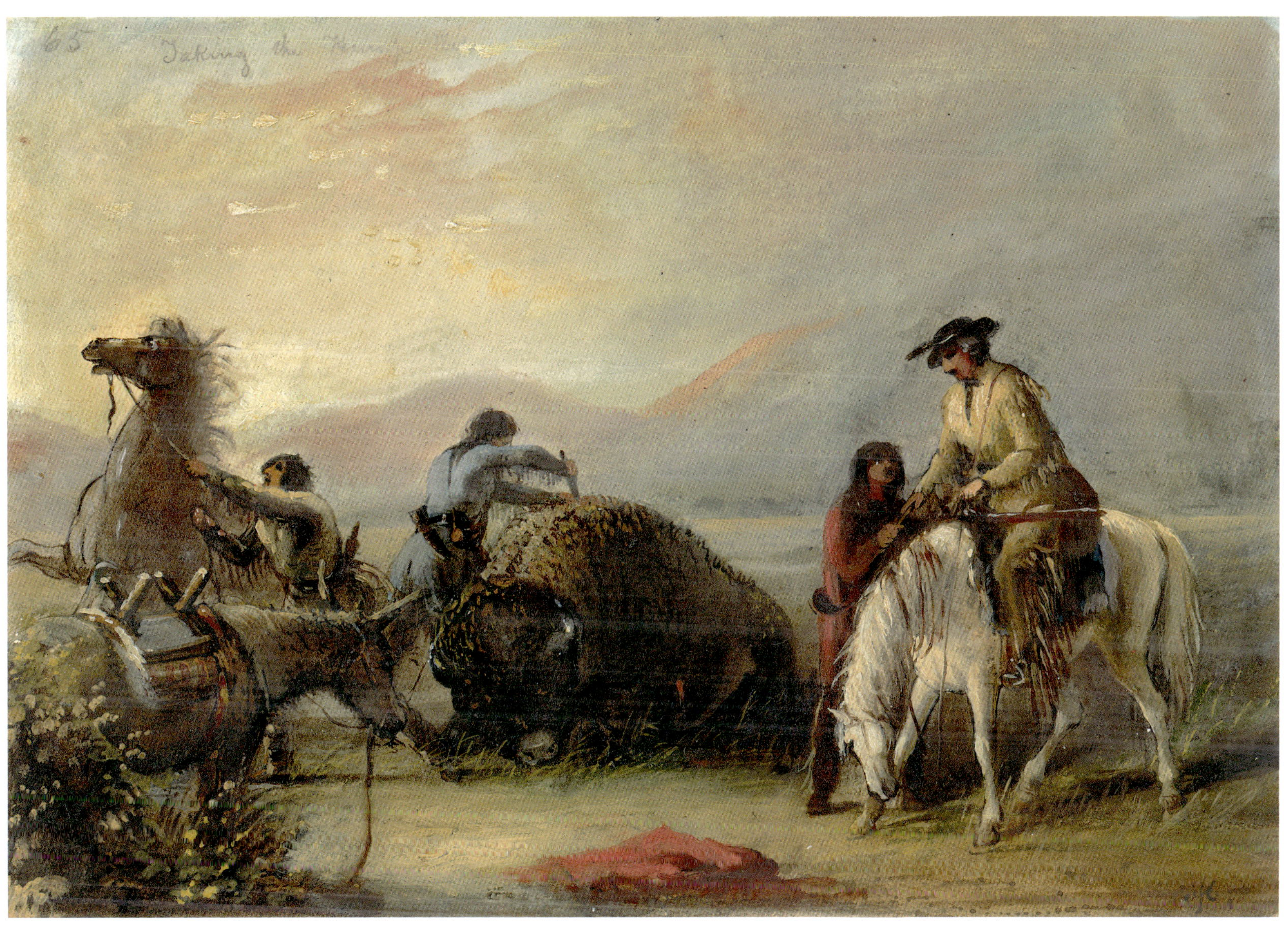

16 *Indian Boys (Children of the Snake Tribe)*

Watercolor, gouache, graphite, and ink on off-white wove paper, 6¾ × 8½ in. (17.1 × 21.6 cm). Inscribed lower right: Children of the Snake Tribe. BAC 10299

AGAINST A MOUNTAINOUS BACKDROP, A YOUNG ARCHER FROM THE SNAKE tribe draws back his bow, steadies his arrow, and takes aim while his seated companion watches attentively.[1] *Indian Boys (Children of the Snake Tribe)* is a tantalizing stand-alone image among Miller's western scenes. The viewer cannot see the target that is the focus of the boys' intense concentration. It is unclear whether they are stalking small game, like the youth in *Shooting the Prairie Dog* (fig. 35) or are engaged in a recreational test of their proficiency, as are the men in *Trial of Skill—with the Bow and Arrow* (see fig. 12). Miller drew three tepees with pencil in the middle ground of the composition, as if to imply that the boys are not far from camp.[2] His decision not to develop the details of the camp more fully contributes to the ambiguity of the context.

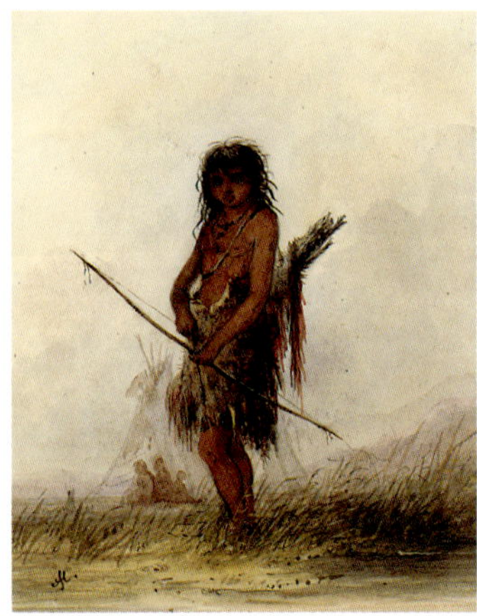

FIGURE 35. Alfred Jacob Miller, *Shooting the Prairie Dog*, 1837–38. Watercolor on paper, 6⁵⁄₁₆ × 5 in. (16 × 12.7 cm). Yale Collection of Western Americana, Beinecke Rare Book and Manuscript Library

This elusiveness allows Miller's indigenous archers to enjoy associations that transport them away from the West altogether. In sketches like *Indian Boys*, where bows and arrows figure prominently, there is an implicit reference to medieval enactors of chivalric deeds such as those promulgated by Sir Walter Scott in *Ivanhoe* (1819). Miller was an ardent reader of Scott. Quotes from the Scottish poet and novelist pepper his notes that accompanied his commission from William T. Walters.[3] Additionally, the artist's penchant to ascribe classical attributes to Indians in his writings supports a further relationship that crosses time and cultures, linking these Snake boys to the archer-heroes and deities of ancient myth such as Heracles and Apollo.[4]

Miller selected a British paper on which to render this conflation of connections inspired by his experiences in the American West.[5] Miller manipulated the high-quality paper both to alter and to enhance the composition. The paper surrounding the archer's extended arm and his arrow has been aggressively abraded—evidence of the erasure of an earlier effort. Likewise, Miller completely reworked the face of the seated boy after scraping away his initial attempt. The series of tiny white dots in the red-brown watercolor and gouache of the seated boy's neck and the standing boy's chest are pinpricks in the paper's surface that cleverly suggest beaded necklaces.[6] SFK

1. For a discussion of the use of the bow and arrow in American Indian culture, see Reginald Laubin, *American Indian Archery* (Norman: University of Oklahoma Press, 1980).

2. Were it not for these tepees (one immediately to the right of the archer's leg and a pair closer to the right edge of the composition), the sketch would lack a middle ground. The compositional space would plunge from the fully modeled boys and defined terrain in the foreground into the deep space of the background with its mountain range composed of thin pencil lines and overlapping areas of wash.

3. Strong, "Images of Indian-White Contact," 153; and Strong, *Sentimental Journey*, 99.

4. Miller, "Rough Draughts," nos. 35, 58, 84, and 133, which relate to Ross, *The West of Miller*, opp. pls. 64, 6, 145, and 147.

5. At its lower left, the paper is embossed "LONDON SUPERFINE." In the early nineteenth century, linen rags sold to London paper mills were ranked by quality into five categories, with London Superfine being the best. Thomas Martin, *The Circle of the Mechanical Arts* (London: Richard Rees, 1813), 467.

6. Miller painted over several of the pinpricks on the archer's chest with gouache.

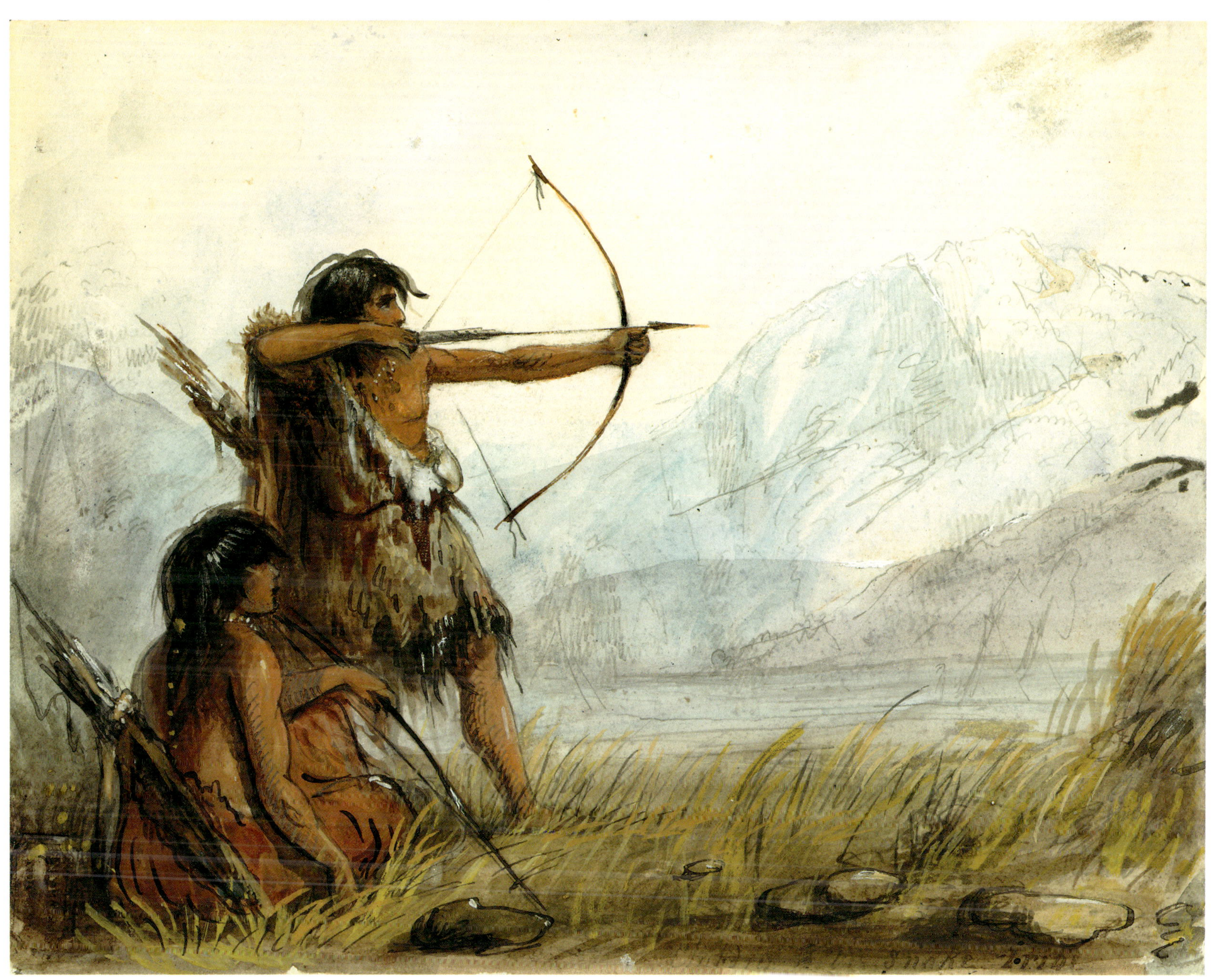

17 *Indian Village*

Watercolor, gouache, pencil, and glazes on beige wove paper, 8⁵⁄₁₆ × 11¾ in. (21.1 × 29.8 cm). BAC 10290

ON 23 APRIL 1837, AS MILLER, STEWART, AND THEIR ENTOURAGE PREPARED TO leave St. Louis, the artist wrote to his friend Brantz Mayer, an author and fellow Baltimorean. He described what lay ahead as "a new and wider field for both poet and painter—for if you can weave such beautiful garlands with the simplest flowers of Nature—what a subject her wild sons of the West present, intermixed with their legendary history."[1] *Indian Village* showcases Miller at his most poetic, having taken full advantage of the inspiration offered by "the simplest flowers of Nature," the "wild sons of the West." In the harmony and elegance of its stillness and quietude, this tableau is transcendent. No mere anecdote, *Indian Village* is a timeless emblem of the Romantic West.[2]

Miller achieved this quality through the sensitive treatment of his subject matter and skillful handling of his media. With the exceptions of the arresting figure who twists his torso to gaze out toward the viewer and the horse on which he rides, *Indian Village* is less heavily worked than many of the Bank of America sketches.[3] Although pencil underdrawing can be seen in the pair of figures and three horses, there are beautiful passages that lack any preliminary definition in graphite.[4] Aside from the pencil horizon line that bisects it, the large tepee is described completely in watercolor with gouache highlights. Because the trees at the right and two tepees in the background just left of center are likewise devoid of underdrawing, they impart to the sheet a freshness and spontaneity. Long, graceful strokes of blue, green, olive, and mauve watercolor deftly evoke the shallow water through which the horses slowly wade, while narrower, wavering lines suggest their reflections. The horses' movements cause only the slightest disruption in the water's calm surface. Miller conveyed this with exceptional facility through delicate, horizontal strokes of pale blue and white gouache and three, short diagonal lines—a subtle splash—at the main horse's foreleg. He rendered the reeds and grasses with a delicate calligraphic touch that is singular among the bank's sketches.

As more and more artists were lured by the promise inherent in the "new and wider field" of the West, idyllic images of Indian encampments near the shores of placid lakes or rivers grew increasingly popular. Painters such as Worthington Whittredge, Seth Eastman, Paul Kane, and Albert Bierstadt echoed the Edenic tone of Miller's *Indian Village*.

SFK

1. Alfred Jacob Miller to Brantz Mayer, Esq., 23 April 1837, quoted in Strong, *Sentimental Journey*, 31.

2. Although *Indian Village* is a unique image in Miller's oeuvre, serene scenes of Indians on horseback wading through shallow waters appear throughout his body of western work. See, for example, *Scene on "Big Sandy" River* (1858–60; The Walters Art Museum, Baltimore) and *River "Eau Sucré"—Indian Women* (n.d.; Gilcrease Museum, Tulsa, Okla.). Miller referred to the former as "a small slice of an Indian paradise." Ross, *The West of Miller*, opp. pl. 20.

3. This figure is built up with thicker watercolor than appears elsewhere in the sketch, with touches of gouache, ink, and what is likely a gelatin-based glaze.

4. The pencil underdrawing of the foremost figure reveals alterations in the position of his arms. Likewise, the underdrawing that defines the pack on the horse farthest away indicates a change in the shape and size of the bundle. Pencil was also used to indicate two tepees behind the large tepee at the right of the sketch.

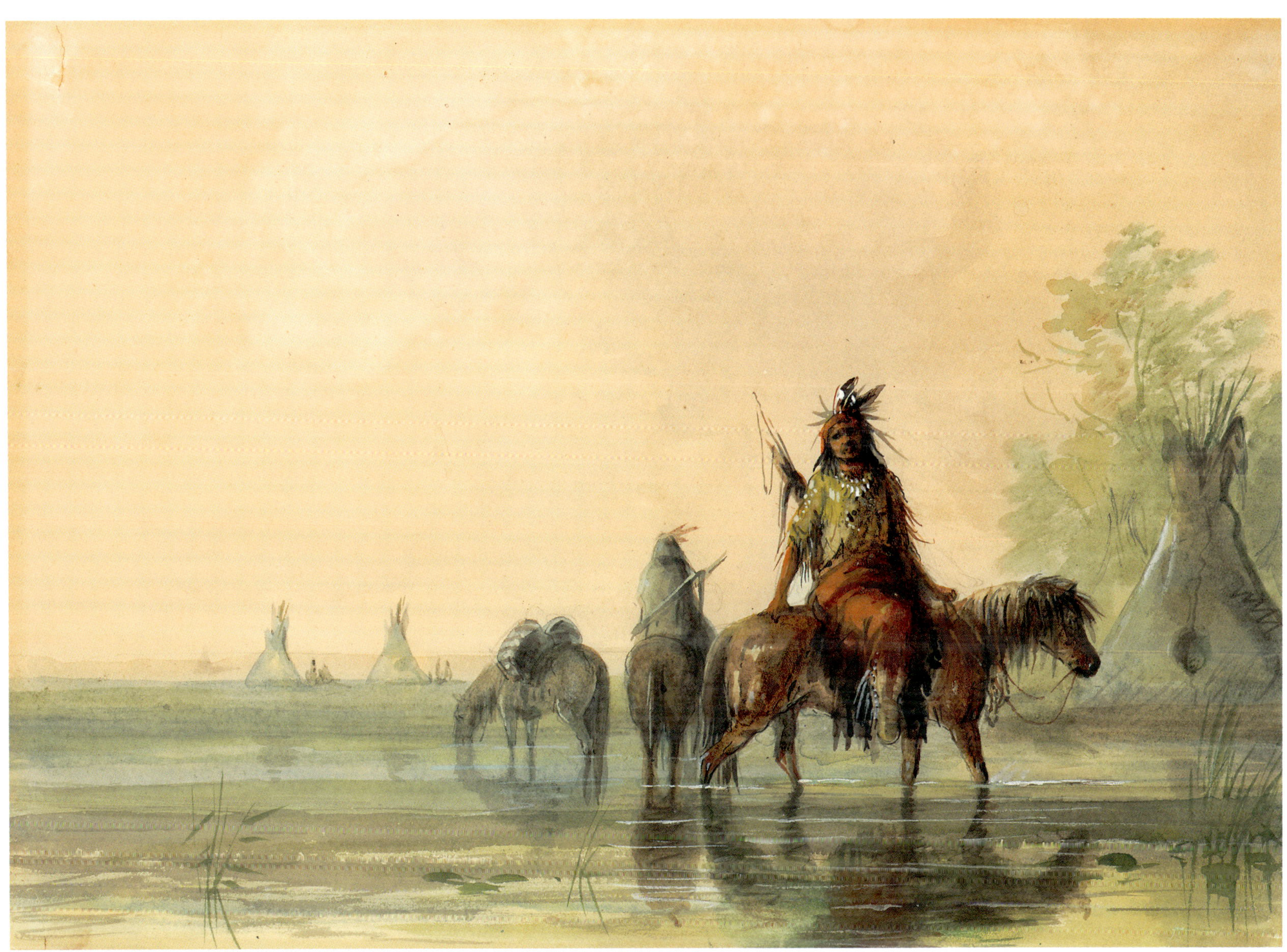

18 *Indian Lodges near the Missouri*

Watercolor and gouache over pencil on cream wove paper. 7⁵⁄₁₆ × 13⅛ in. (18.6 × 33.3 cm). Signed with monogram, lower left: AJM; inscribed upper right: 76; inscribed lower right: Indian Lodges—near the / Missouri. BAC 10297

PLAINS INDIAN DWELLINGS FASCINATED MANY EARLY-NINETEENTH-CENTURY Anglo-European artist-explorers and their patrons. Images of Indian architecture were integral to the western portfolios by Titian Ramsay Peale, George Catlin, Karl Bodmer, and Seth Eastman, as well as Miller. The indigenous architecture Miller encountered while traveling to and from the 1837 rendezvous was comparable in function as shelter and a locus for social interaction to the Federalist, Neoclassical, and Greek Revival styles popular in the early nineteenth century in his native Baltimore, though differing considerably in form. This intriguing distinction surely enhanced its appeal as a subject for artist and audience alike.[1] Miller's sketches in the Bank of America collection feature a variety of Indian refuges ranging from simple forts constructed of branches (see cat. 7), to portable tepees (see cat. 17), to the more substantial structures favored by seminomadic tribes seen in *Indian Lodges near the Missouri*.

It is unclear whether Miller witnessed this scene or whether it is an amalgam of imagination, artistic precedents, and on-the-trail experience. Earth lodges built by Plains agricultural societies first appeared in the western landscape around the year 700. The Mandan, Hidatsa, and Arikara built these circular structures with domed roofs pierced by an oculus near Missouri River tributaries in the Dakotas.[2] However, despite the suggestion of water at the lower right and Miller's inscription that locates these lodges near the Missouri, the route along which Stewart's caravan journeyed did not follow the Missouri River much past St. Louis.[3] Catlin, with whom Miller was acquainted, painted many depictions of Mandan dwellings that may have influenced this sketch, or at least inspired its title.[4]

The Pawnee, Omaha, Ponca, and Oto, through whose lands Miller did travel, also erected similar earth lodges on the central Plains of what is now Kansas and Nebraska.[5] The elongated, barrel-roofed, multifamily, bark- or reed-mat-covered dwelling in the middle ground, near the earth lodges, suggests a village of Omaha, Osage, or their eastern Plains neighbors more than it does a Mandan or Hidatsa community along the Missouri.[6] When Miller refined this sketch for the William T. Walters commission in 1858, he omitted the designator of place from the title, only to restore it nearly a decade later, when he painted the scene again for the Englishman Alexander Hargreaves Brown.[7] SFK

1. On Baltimore architecture, see William Barksdale Maynard, *Architecture in the United States, 1800–1850* (New Haven: Yale University Press, 2002), 11. See also Mary Ellen Hayward and Frank R. Shivers Jr., eds., *The Architecture of Baltimore: An Illustrated History* (Baltimore: Johns Hopkins University Press, 2004).

2. Peter Nabokov and Robert Easton, *Native American Architecture* (New York: Oxford University Press, 1989), 126.

3. Miller may have considered granting the river a more prominent role in this sketch. At the lower right, between the two large rocks, two figures drawn in pencil appear near the shore. Heightened with neither watercolor nor gouache, they remain ghostlike indicators of the artist's thought process.

4. For a discussion of the possible influence of Catlin's *Bird's Eye View of Mandan Village* on Miller's composition, see Lisa Strong's essay in this volume. When carefully compared with the earth lodges in Catlin's painting (see fig. 18), Miller's appear far less stylized. The slight slump of the mud roof of the central earth lodge in Miller's composition exhibits greater veracity than the idealized, hemispherical roofs rendered by Catlin. Peter Nabokov, e-mail to author, 20 May 2009.

5. Nabokov and Easton, *Native American Architecture*, 126 and 136.

6. Nabokov, e-mail to author, 20 May 2009.

7. For additional information regarding this sketch as preparation for *Indian Lodges* (1858–60) now at the Walters Art Museum, see Lisa Strong's essay in this volume.

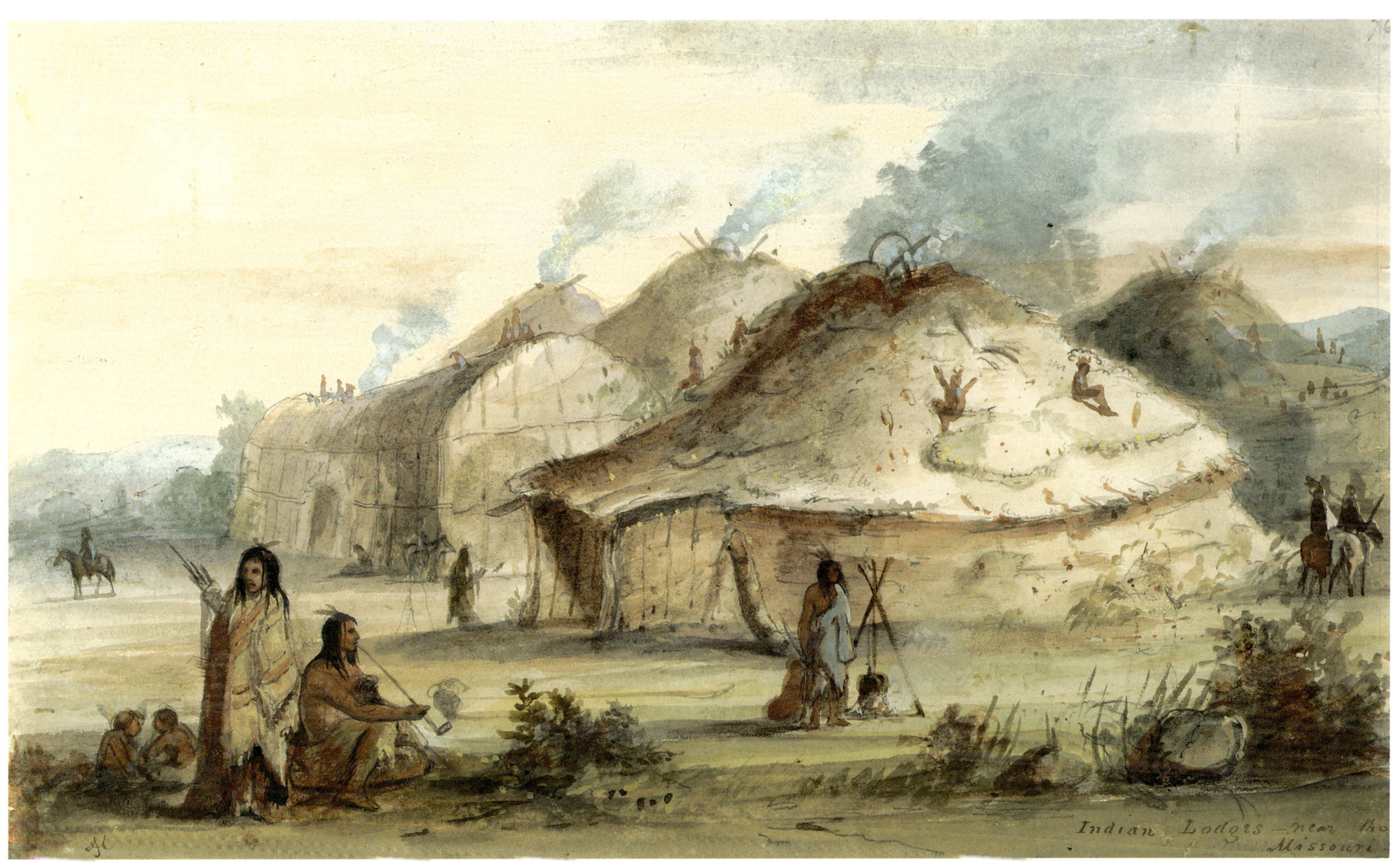
Indian Lodges — near the Missouri

19 *Indian Lodge on the Upper Missouri*

Gray and brown wash, graphite, and white gouache on brown paper mounted to rag board, $7\frac{15}{16} \times 12\frac{3}{16}$ in. (20.2 × 31 cm). Signed with monogram, lower edge, left of center: AJM; inscribed lower right: Indian Lodge on the Upper / Missouri. BAC 10291

Many of the Plains Indian cultures who preferred village life built earth lodges. These were usually constructed of central posts joined by crossbeams, like those Miller depicted in this drawing. Roof rafters on the interior, typically of cottonwood, radiated from a central smoke hole and rested on an outer ring of posts and beams. Side planks supported the walls. A circular form was common owing to its cosmic symbolic meaning for a number of tribes. Earth lodges, however, were not always only sacred spaces. They housed the varied activities of daily life as well as gatherings of all types.[1] Remarking on a similar image made for William T. Walters, Miller noted that the figures seated in a circle in the background were playing a favorite Indian game like the Anglo-European hunt the slipper.[2]

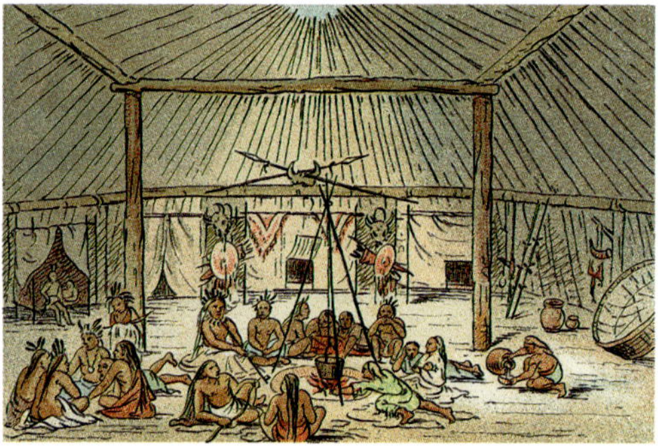

Figure 36. George Catlin, *Mandan Village, Upper Missouri*, from *The Manners, Customs, and Condition of the North American Indians* (London: the author, 1841), 1: pl. 46. Courtesy The Nelson-Atkins Museum of Art, Kansas City, Mo., Spencer Art Reference Library

Actual and artistic sources aided Miller in the making of *Indian Lodge on the Upper Missouri*. His primary inspiration appears to have been George Catlin's renditions of lodge interiors, notably *Mandan Village, Upper Missouri* (fig. 36), which was first published in 1841. Miller borrowed from Catlin the basic composition of several figure groupings arranged throughout a large interior. The architecture of Miller's lodge, however, is more consistent with the Pawnee style he likely saw in his travels along the Kansas and Little Blue rivers. Pawnee earth lodge architecture typically employed more than the four central poles preferred by the Mandan that Catlin pictured.[3]

More important, Miller and Catlin approached their subjects with opposing concerns. If Catlin was driven mainly by an interest in scientific observation and ethnographic recording, Miller's emphasis was on sentiment and capturing the emotional atmosphere of Indian life.[4] Using a brown paper that provided the primary tone of the image, he loosely articulated the shape and structure of the lodge with graphite and gray and brown wash. Highlights of white gouache create the rhythm of light and shadow across the space, animating it, drawing the viewer's eye from figure to figure, and picking out such details as the smoke rising from pipes, shields hanging from poles, the saddle in the foreground, and the baby in the cradleboard on the right. Without specifying either culture or locale, Miller suggests a peaceful communal enclave that diffuses any sense of the conflicts of the day.[5]

MCC

1. For information on Plains Indian earth lodge construction and interiors, see Peter Nabokov and Robert Easton, *Native American Architecture* (New York: Oxford University Press, 1989), 124–26.

2. Ross, *The West of Miller*, opp. pl. 196.

3. Nabokov and Easton, *Native American Architecture*, 136.

4. On the impetus for Catlin's art, see William H. Truettner, *Natural Man Observed: A Study of Catlin's Indian Gallery* (Washington, D.C.: Smithsonian Institution Press, 1979).

5. The brown paper has somewhat darkened over time. On Miller's other strategies that deflected the issue of conflict in his portraits, see Strong, "Images of Indian-White Contact," 57.

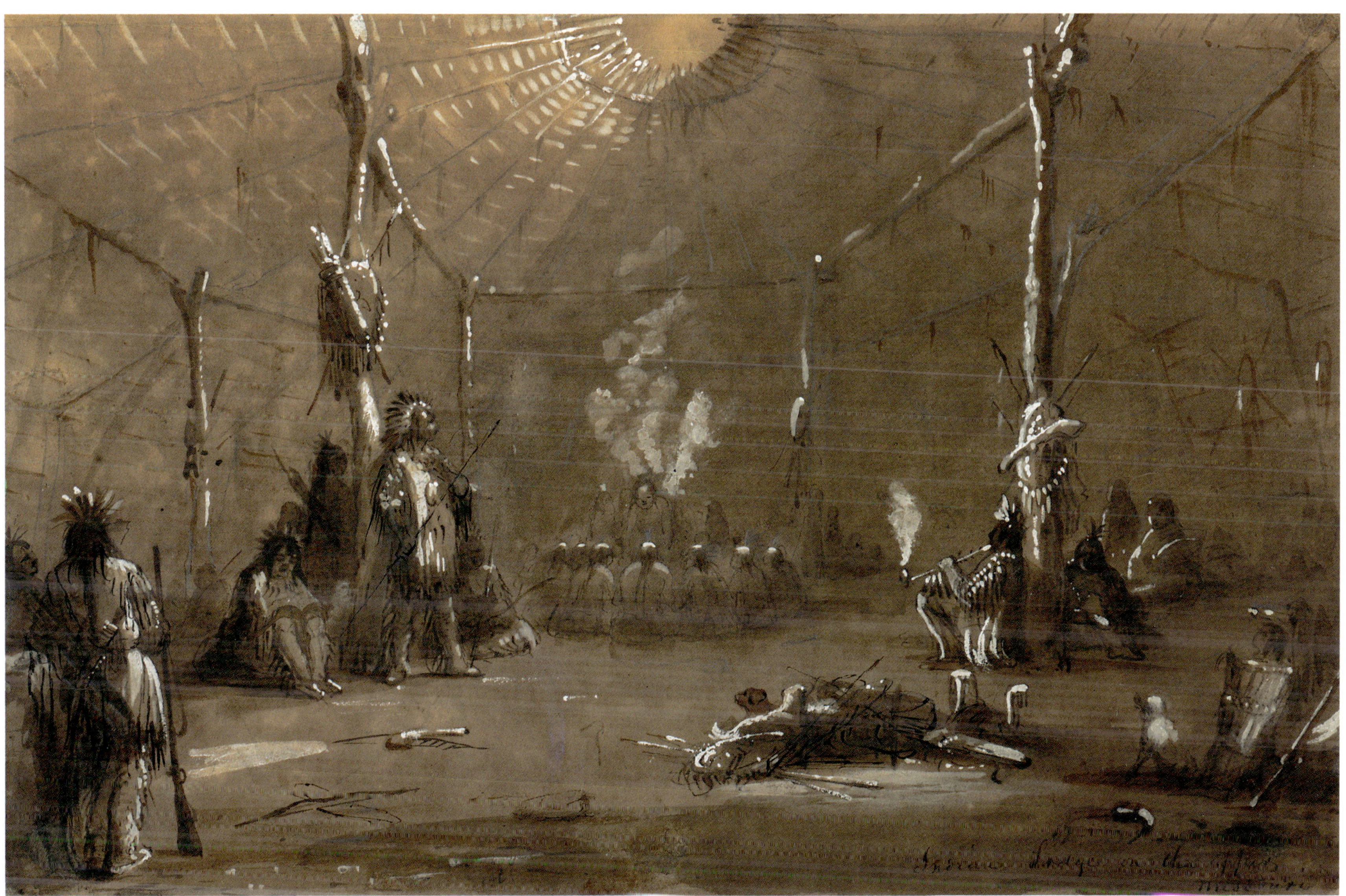

20 *Migration of the Pawnees*

Watercolor, gouache, gum glazes, and pencil on joined sheets of beige paper, 5 11/16 × 9 7/16 in. (14.4 × 24 cm). Inscribed upper right: Migration [illegible] aw [illegible]. BAC 10296

THE RHYTHM OF LIFE FOR THE PAWNEE WAS DETERMINED BY THE SEASONS. Throughout the spring and autumn, when crops were planted and harvested, the Pawnee lived in earth lodge communities (see cat. 19). Then, like many Great Plains tribes, during the summer and winter months, they abandoned their villages to follow the buffalo herds.[1] This ritual, spurred by what Miller termed "stern necessity, who rules her children with an iron rod," demanded that everyone and everything pull its share of the weight – quite literally.[2] In this sketch, spread across two joined sheets of rag paper of dissimilar thicknesses and textures, a procession of encumbered men, women, and children accompanied by horses, mules, and dogs dragging travois ascend a steep incline.

Miller revisited this image of seasonal migration four times. This sketch, with its joined sheets, extensive pencil underdrawing, and unfinished quality, is either his original conception or second attempt at the composition.[3] Most of the figures are rendered with thin, transparent watercolor and a dearth of detail. The exception is the woman enrobed in fringed buckskin who wears trade cloth leggings and carries a small child on her shoulder. Miller built up these figures with watercolor and gouache and applied gum glaze to saturate the pigment. This layering of media, the pair's larger scale relative to their fellow travelers, and Miller's increased attention to detail, exemplified by the minuscule strokes of white gouache that mimic stitching or beading on the woman's red leggings, heighten the figures' visual impact.[4]

Although Miller's depiction of women toting children and other heavy loads on foot while mounted men carry weapons in case of attack, accompanied by dogs as pack animals, is historically accurate, the mountainous terrain through which this migration occurs casts doubt on his identification of the tribe as Pawnee rather than Snake or Shoshone, who populated this sort of western topography.[5] Ethnographic exactitude was not Miller's aim, however. Instead, he excelled at wedding western subject matter with Romantic sensibilities, a fact underscored by his quotation from the English poet John Milton in his description of the composition: "The world is all before them where to choose / Their place of rest, and Providence their guide."[6] Miller's presentation of an exotic, seminomadic culture also had parallels with the concurrent vogue for Orientalist images of caravans roaming the deserts and grasslands of the Middle East and North Africa exploited by his European contemporaries such as Eugène Delacroix and Horace Vernet.[7]

SFK

1. Gene Weltfish, *The Lost Universe: Pawnee Life and Culture* (Lincoln, Nebr.: Bison Books, 1977), 7–8. See also David J. Wishart, ed., *Encyclopedia of the Great Plains Indians* (Lincoln: University of Nebraska–Lincoln, 2007), 205.

2. Miller, "Rough Draughts," no. 20, which relates to Ross, *The West of Miller*, opp. pl. 66.

3. The three works identified as directly related to the Bank of America's sketch are *Migration of the Pawnees* (n.d.; Western Americana Collection, Beinecke Rare Book and Manuscript Library, Yale University), *Snake Indians Migrating* (n.d.; Joslyn Art Museum, Omaha), and *Pawnee Indians Migrating* (1858–60; The Walters Art Museum, Baltimore). Although Miller altered the titles slightly and explored different media, the composition remained relatively consistent.

4. The prominence of the woman and child in this sketch is unique. In the three related works, the pair is more integrated into the group and their size closer to that of the other figures.

5. Weltfish, *The Lost Universe*, 140 and 143; William Brandon and Alvin M. Josephy, *The American Heritage Book of Indians* (New York: American Heritage, 1961), 351; and DeVoto, *Across the Wide Missouri*, caption for pl. 38. The related work at the Joslyn, although titled *Snake Indians Migrating*, does not bear an inscription by Miller and has been published as *Pawnee Indians Migrating*.

6. Miller, "Rough Draughts," no. 20, which relates to Ross, *The West of Miller*, opp. pl. 66. The lines Miller quotes are from the final stanza of Milton's epic *Paradise Lost* (1667).

7. Joan Carpenter Troccoli, *Painters and the American West: The Anschutz Collection* (Denver: Denver Art Museum, in association with Yale University Press, 2000), 195n2. It would have been difficult for Miller to avoid seeing such paintings while abroad in Paris and Rome between 1833 and 1834.

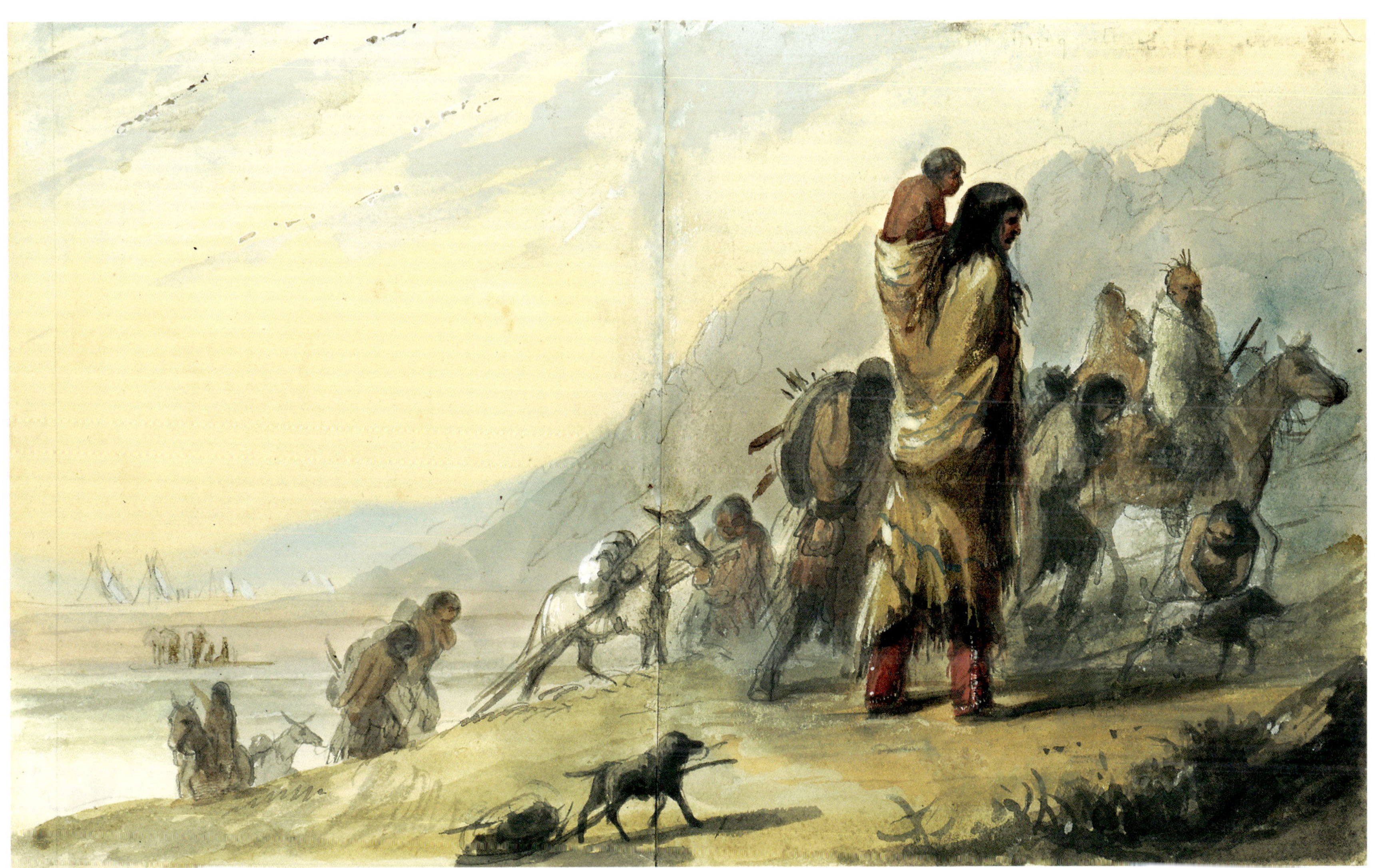

21 *Pawnee Indian Camp*

Watercolor, gouache, pen and ink, gum glazes, and pencil on thin beige card, 7¼ × 9³⁄₁₆ in. (18.4 × 23.3 cm). Inscribed upper right: 118; inscribed lower center: Pawnee Indian Camp. BAC 10304

Reclining against his beaver and buffalo packs, the warrior is enjoying his "dolce far niente" while smoking his Calumet. . . . At a little distance (screened from the sun by a blanket overhead) is seated his mild and patient help-mate, ready to receive his imperial orders, and execute them with cheerfulness. On the broad prairie beyond, his vassals encircle the camp fire, roasting their meat.

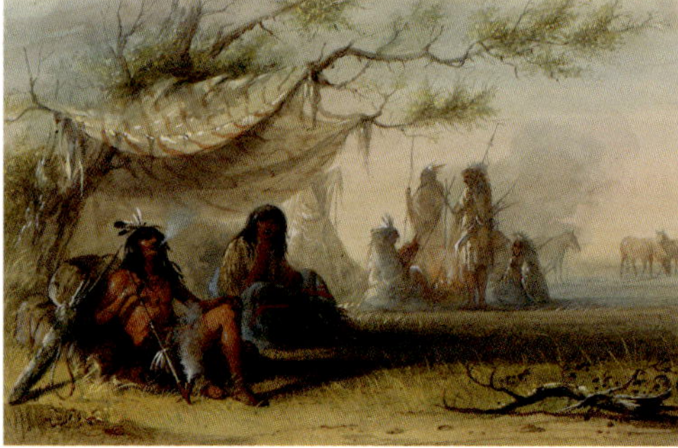

FIGURE 38. Alfred Jacob Miller, *Indian Encampment*, 1858–60. Watercolor on paper, 8⅝ × 13 in. (21.9 × 33 cm). The Walters Art Museum, Baltimore

This explication of *Pawnee Indian Camp*, which overtly casts the smoking protagonist as a member of the indigenous aristocracy, was written by Miller in his "Rough Draughts."[1] Many of Miller's sketches in the Bank of America collection can be matched to his notes based on their equivalence to the scene described in his text or their similarity to images in the William T. Walters albums (1858–60) with which Miller paired a more polished version of his commentary. However, the inscription "118" in the upper right corner of *Pawnee Indian Camp* definitively links this sketch with the text bearing the same number in Miller's "Rough Draughts."

Pawnee Indian Camp is itself, in effect, a rough draft. Artist changes are evident, an inscription along the top edge has been scraped away and painted over, and the level of detail and finish throughout is inconsistent. Miller also appears to have been testing a range of techniques. Transparent washes over and under strokes of watercolor are enhanced with opaque gouache atop fine black ink lines drawn with pen. Evenly brushed gum glaze saturates the deep tones of dark pigment in the "warrior," while a rich, red-tinted glaze emphasizes both the feathers adorning his headdress and the straps of his quiver. The lounging "warrior," defined more completely than his "vassals," who congregate at the right side of the composition, simultaneously showcases Miller's talents and suggests this is a work-in-progress. The figure's skillfully described upturned chin and the underside of his left foot are the epitome of sensitive draftsmanship. His left hand atop his knee, however, has been reworked and is rendered with much less proficiency. *Pawnee Indian Camp* may be a trial composition executed specifically in preparation for the Walters commission (fig. 37) or a sketch that Miller had in his studio but did not fully develop for a patron until the late 1850s.[2] SFK

1. Miller, "Rough Draughts," no. 118, which relates to Ross, *The West of Miller*, opp. pl. 115. *Dolce far niente* is Italian for carefree idleness or pleasant relaxation. For additional information about Miller and Stewart's understanding of the concept of indigenous aristocracy, see Troccoli, *Miller: Watercolors*, 10; and Strong, *Sentimental Journey*, 88 and 103–5.

2. In addition to making minor changes to the composition when he painted it for Walters, including increasing the degree of detail and describing the scene from a vantage point slightly farther away, Miller also amended the title from *Pawnee Indian Camp* to the less precise *Indian Encampment*. Miller never identified the Indians as Pawnee in his "Rough Draughts" or in the notes he composed for Walters. There is not enough ethnographic specificity in either sketch to classify them as Pawnee, or any other tribe.

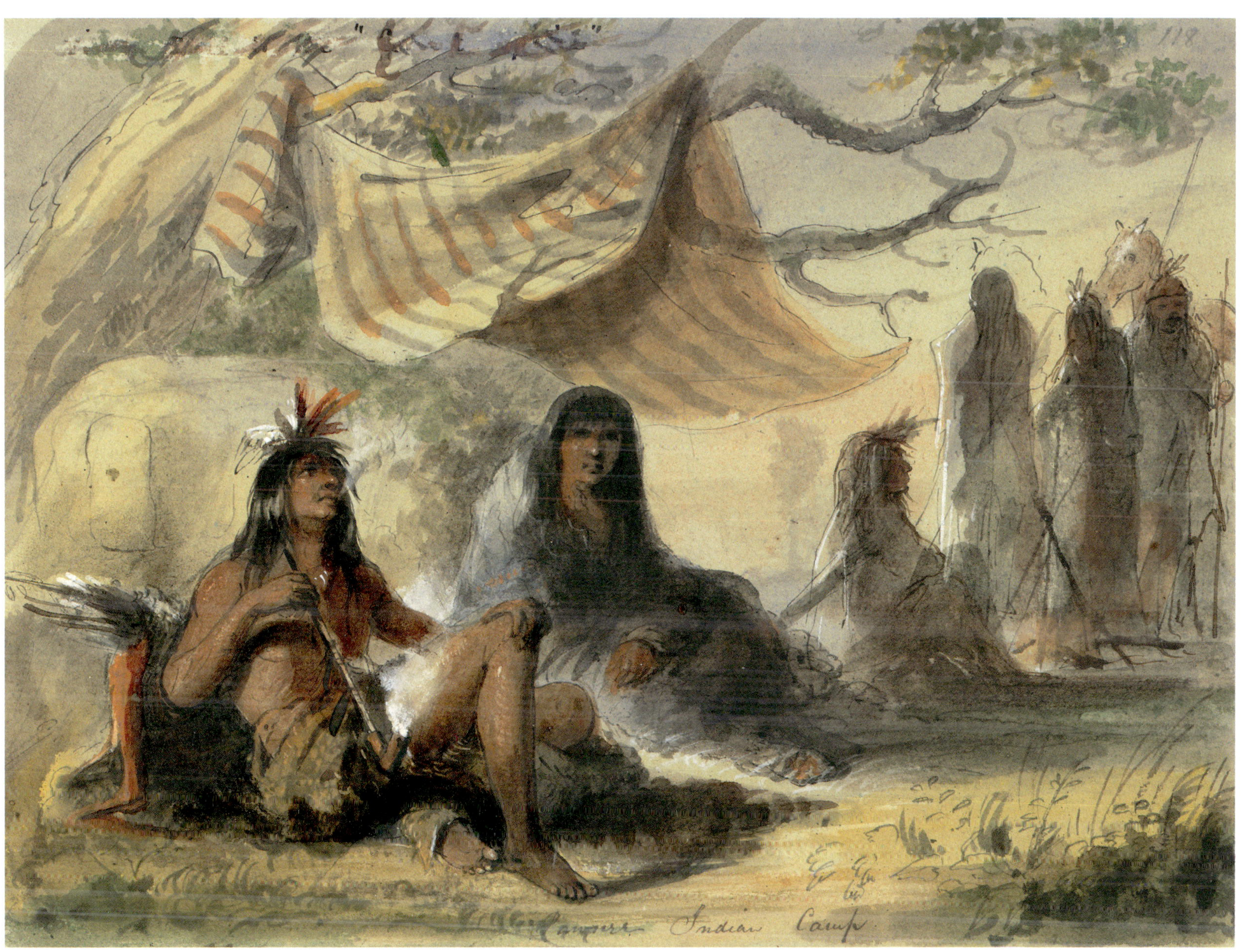

22 *Indian Women, Snake Tribe, Oregon*

Pen and ink, watercolor, gouache, ink, and gelatin glazes on cream wove rag paper, 8 × 10 in. (20.3 × 25.4 cm). Inscribed upper right: Indian Women / Snake Tribe / Oregon. BAC 10312

MANY OF THE SKETCHES THAT MILLER BASED ON HIS WESTERN EXPERIENCE depict indigenous people whom the artist broadly identified as "Indians." Just as frequently, he inscribed his compositions with titles that denote their specific tribes.[1] The inscription that Miller appended to this tranquil sketch distinguishes the two women as members of the Snake tribe, who inhabited the Oregon Territory. Despite this explicit appellation, Miller omitted overt ethnographic detail in favor of generic idealization.[2] Rather than reflecting a documentary impulse, *Indian Women, Snake Tribe, Oregon* encourages fantasy. To achieve this result, Miller invoked eighteenth-century French Rococo conventions and shrewdly adapted them to correspond to a western setting. The young Snake women, in harmony with their Arcadian surroundings, ably stand in for obligatory peasants or requisite shepherdesses that appear in the paintings of Jean-Antoine Watteau, for example. The irregularly shaped tree at the center that gracefully arches to form a bower over the pair creates an appealing frame-within-a-frame, a common device in Rococo compositions. The suggestion of a tepee at the left edge of the composition, more readily identifiable in the fully realized version of the scene Miller painted for William T. Walters between 1858 and 1860, serves as a fitting substitute for ancient ruins that frequently embellish Rococo paintings.[3]

Miller employed myriad watercolor techniques to transplant French artistic traditions to the western plains. He layered thin washes of color and applied loose, transparent brushwork on top of fine, looping ink lines that read as both foliage and clouds. Thicker ink lines define the women's hair, outline their limbs, and, in the case of the woman in front, accentuate the fringe of her buckskin garments. White gouache creates highlights on the buckskin, the tree branches, and the water. As in *Elk Taking the Water* (cat. 10), Miller scratched the paper, at lower right, to mimic the reflection of light on the water's surface. He brushed heavy, brown-toned glaze over the figures' skin. Red-toned glaze deepens the hue of the blanket that envelops the woman demurely crouching behind her companion, who languidly draws water from the placid stream.[4] SFK

1. Based on Miller's inscriptions, representatives of the Kansas, Blackfoot, Sioux, Shoshone, Delaware, Nez Percé, Crow, Flathead, Arikara, Pawnee, Arapahoe, and Snake tribes populate his art. For a comprehensive record of the known depictions of American Indians by Miller, see Karen Dewees Reynolds and William R. Johnston, "Catalogue Raisonné," in Tyler, *Miller: Artist on the Oregon Trail*, 201–446.

2. For further examples of this tendency in Miller's art, see Troccoli, *Miller: Watercolors*, 30.

3. Not only is the tepee more prominent in the Walters composition, *Indian Encampment on the Eau Sucre River* (1858–60), but the baby in the cradleboard propped against a tree just behind and to the left of the women and the dog that lies nearby are described with greater clarity. Miller also included more of the canoe in the Walters watercolor. Although the title does not associate the women with a particular tribe, it identifies the location of the setting more precisely than the inscription on the bank's sketch.

4. Miller had difficulty determining the position of the figures. Remnants of the right foot of the woman wrapped in the red blanket show through her companion's left hand and extend to the water's edge. The hand on which the woman in buckskin supports herself appears to have originally been half an inch to the left.

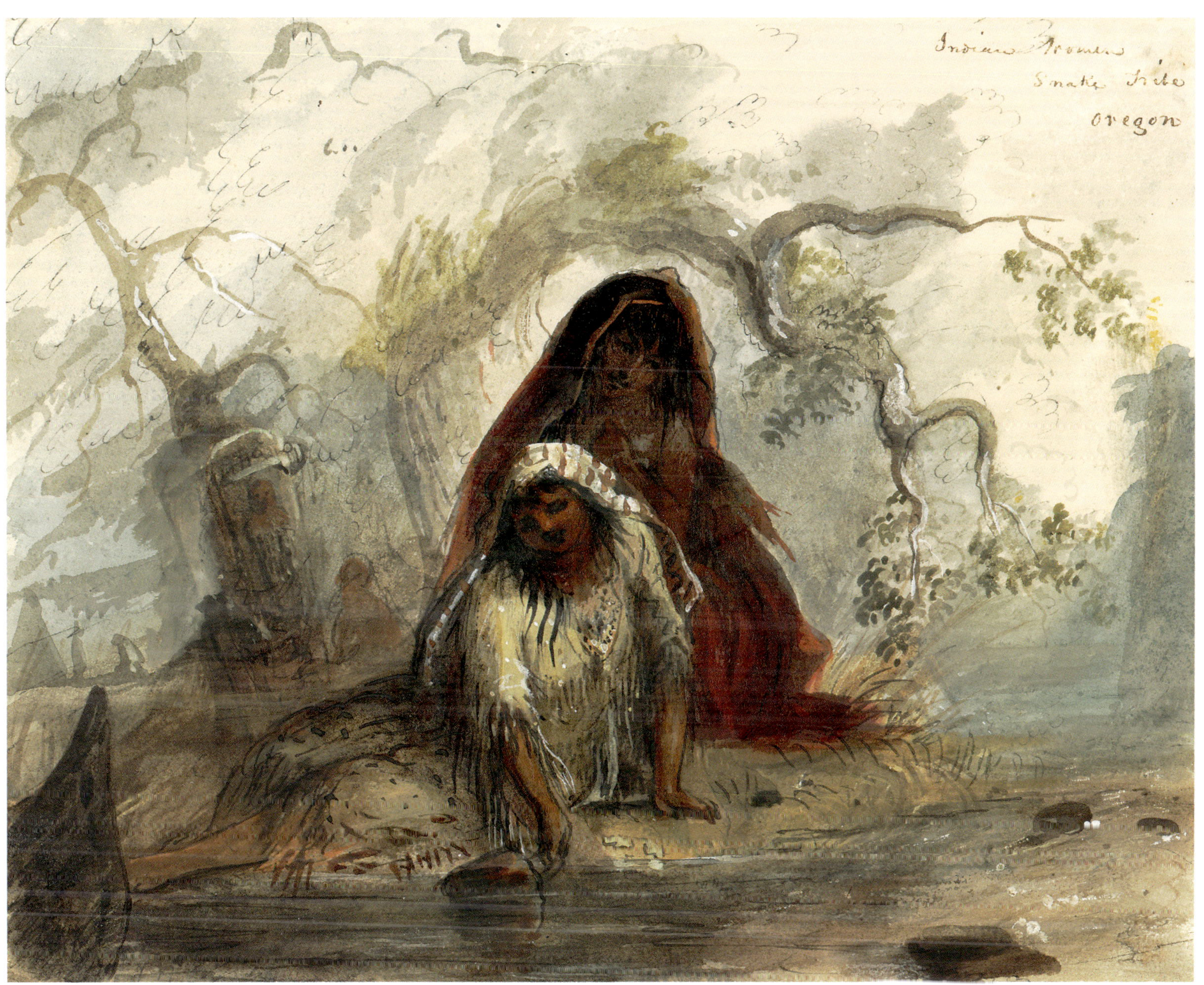
Indian Women
Snake Tribe
Oregon

23 *Snake Female Reposing*

Watercolor, gouache, ink, and gum glazes on Whatman drawing board, 6¼ × 10⅜ in. (15.9 × 26.4 cm). Signed with monogram, lower left: AJM; inscribed upper left: X; inscribed lower right: Snake Female—Reposing. BAC 10310

IN SPITE OF ITS SEEMINGLY STRAIGHTFORWARD SUBJECT MATTER, *SNAKE Female Reposing* draws on a rich array of traditions. A young Indian woman, silhouetted against the glow of the setting sun, slumbers peacefully atop a buffalo skin on the bank of a stream. Miller's treatment of his subject allies her with a sorority of recumbent women artfully posed to emphasize their contours and enhance their allure. This sensual sisterhood includes paintings and sculptures of lolling nymphs and lounging goddesses that Miller would have seen in the galleries of the Louvre and Musée de Luxembourg in Paris and at the Palazzo Borghese in Rome. While he was abroad between 1833 and 1834, contemporary paintings of exotic odalisques by artists such as Eugène Delacroix were growing in popularity as well. Such paintings frequently cast women as passive objects for voyeuristic delectation and possibly inspired the spirit of this sketch.[1]

Although *Snake Female Reposing* may offer private pleasures, this sketch and the four other compositions that directly relate to it also resonate more broadly.[2] They adhere to a practice in art and literature of representing the New World that dates to its "discovery" by the Europeans. America, an exotic land perceived by would-be colonizers as inviting conquest, was often personified as an Indian maiden.[3] For Miller, his patron Stewart, and others such as William T. Walters who also owned a version of this sketch, the West *was* a new and foreign world, and the Snake woman may have embodied a range of Romantic fantasies associated with it.

Technically, *Snake Female Reposing* shares similarities with *Indian Women, Snake Tribe, Oregon* (cat. 22). Both compositions lack the pencil underdrawing seen in the majority of the bank's sketches and feature an extensive use of ink and glaze. For this sketch, Miller applied black ink with both pen and brush. The medium appears beneath and on top of the layers of transparent watercolor and opaque gouache that build up the figure and the striped canopy that rhymes her graceful, if anatomically impossible, pose. Gum glaze adds luster to the woman's dark hair, saturates her red sash, deepens the shadow she casts, and darkens the soles of her feet. White pigment mixed with thin watercolor enhances the atmosphere of the background and heightens the dreamlike quality of this intimate sketch. SFK

1. For more on the links between trends in Orientalism and Miller's paintings of Indian women, see Troccoli, *Miller: Watercolors*, 10–12; and Jennifer McLerran, "Trappers' Brides and Country Wives: Native American Women in the Paintings of Alfred Jacob Miller," *American Indian Culture and Research Journal* 18, no. 2 (1994): 10–17.

2. For Stewart, who owned a watercolor and an oil painting related to this sketch (both unlocated), Miller's art undoubtedly revived, if not embellished, memories. The oil, *Indian Belle Reclining* (1840), hung in the Scotsman's bedchamber at Murthly Castle, a room adorned with a mélange of Near Eastern and American Indian trappings, where Stewart reportedly slept on buffalo skins. Strong, "Images of Indian-White Contact," 180. The two other related works, *Indian Woman Sleeping* (n.d.) and *Indian Girl Reposing* (1858–60), are now in the collections of the Gilcrease Museum and the Walters Art Museum, respectively. The Gilcrease image depicts the figure in a supine posture.

3. See E. McClung Fleming, "The American Image as Indian Princess, 1765–1783," *Winterthur Portfolio* 2 (1965): 65–81; and Rayna Green, "The Pocahontas Perplex: The Image of Indian Women in American Culture," *Massachusetts Review* 16 (Autumn 1975): 710–20. See also McLerran, "Trappers' Brides and Country Wives," 4–5.

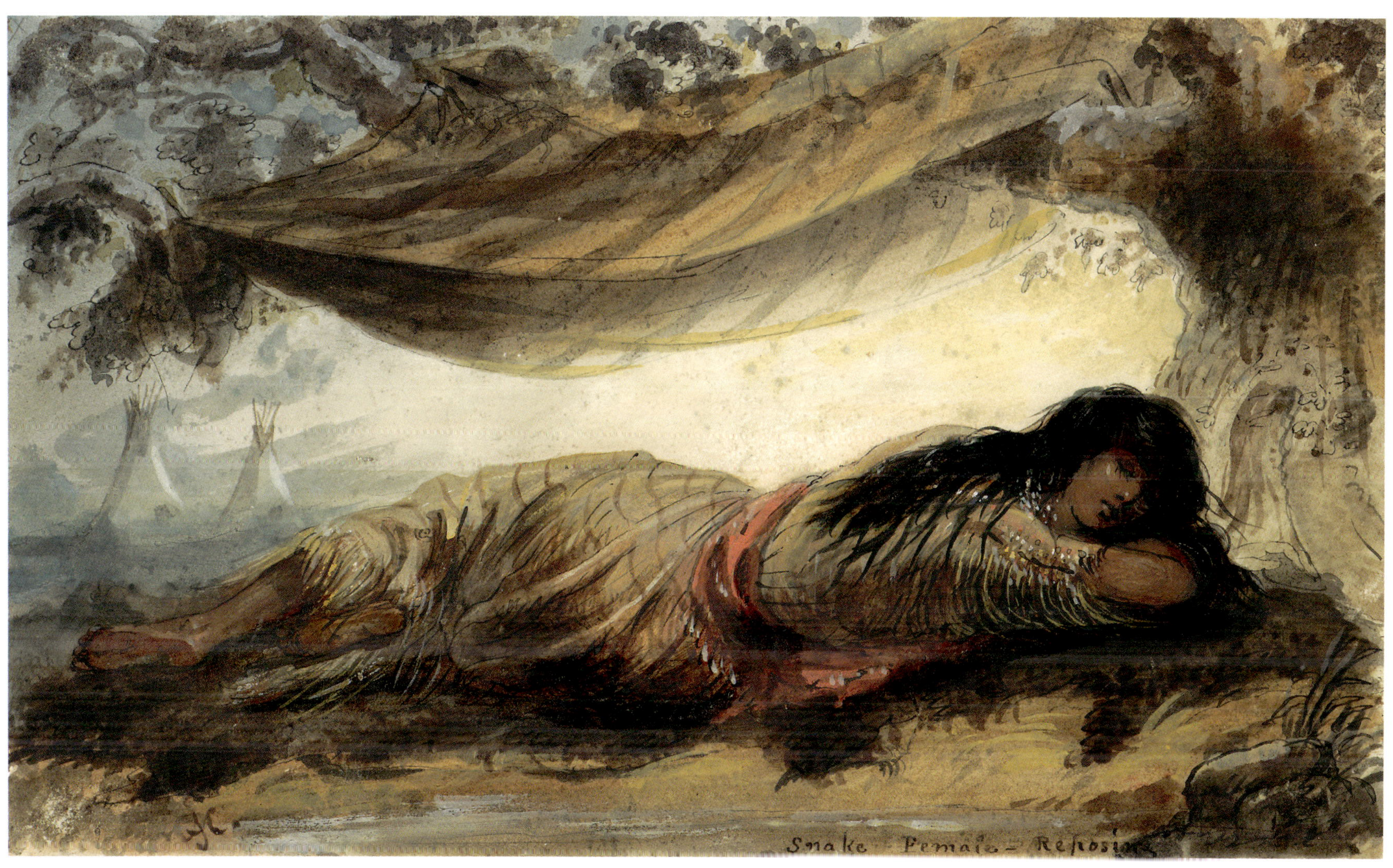
Snake - Female - Reposing

24 *Chimney Rock near Scott's Bluff*

Watercolor, gouache, graphite, ink, and gum glazes on off-white wove paper, 9⅜ × 12⅞ in. (23.8 × 32.7 cm). Inscribed lower left: The 'Chimney' Rock/near Scott's Bluff. BAC 10298

PURE LANDSCAPE DID NOT GENERALLY INTEREST MILLER AS A SUBJECT FOR his art. Even though views of the West figure prominently in much of his work and were popular with his patrons, nature mainly provided the backdrop against which William Drummond Stewart's adventures unfolded (see cats. 11, 12). In *Chimney Rock near Scott's Bluff*, although there are four small figures on horseback in the foreground, the massive rock formation dominates the sheet. The artist's attraction to the clay and sandstone monolith is not surprising. Chimney Rock, nine hundred miles west of St. Louis in today's western Nebraska, marked the end of the prairie and the beginning of the Rockies. First seen by whites in 1813 and visible for three or four days in advance of arriving at its base, it was an important landmark for travelers going west in the nineteenth century.[1] Miller, in 1837, was yet among a still small number of white men who had encountered it. Washington Irving brought it to wider public attention with the publication of *The Adventures of Captain Bonneville* that same year.

Chimney Rock is one of just a few of Miller's watercolors that hews closely to topographic fidelity. The artist first drew the distinctive shape, seen head-on in the center of the sheet, in a wavering pencil line that captures the craggy edges of the eroded rock. Its facets are further described with a combination of thin, opaque terra-cotta and patches of yellow along with energetic strokes of pencil that lie both underneath and on top of the watercolor. With opaque white and peachy pink, Miller indicated the sunlight hitting the left edge of the spire, while darker shadows fall on the right side of the rock's base. The movement of the sky, shown by smooth watery washes of peach at the left and more textured blue and gray ones on the right, further animates the sheet. Overall, Miller's method generally replicates the size, shape, and geology of Chimney Rock and the experience of viewing it as the sun sets, but it also suggests the artist's recognition of the privilege to be among the first white men to experience this extraordinary landscape.[2] MCC

1. In 1813 employees of the Astoria Fur Company were the first whites to see Chimney Rock. Howard Lamar, "An Overview of Western Expansion," in *The West as America: Reinterpreting Images of the Frontier, 1820–1920*, ed. William H. Truettner, exh. cat. (Washington, D.C.: Smithsonian Institution Press, 1991), 5–8; and Merrill J. Mattes, *The Great Platte River Road: The Covered Wagon Mainline via Fort Kearney to Fort Laramie* (Lincoln: Nebraska State Historical Society, 1969), 384.

2. Ron Tyler, "Alfred Jacob Miller and Sir William Drummond Stewart," in Tyler, *Miller: Artist on the Oregon Trail*, 34.

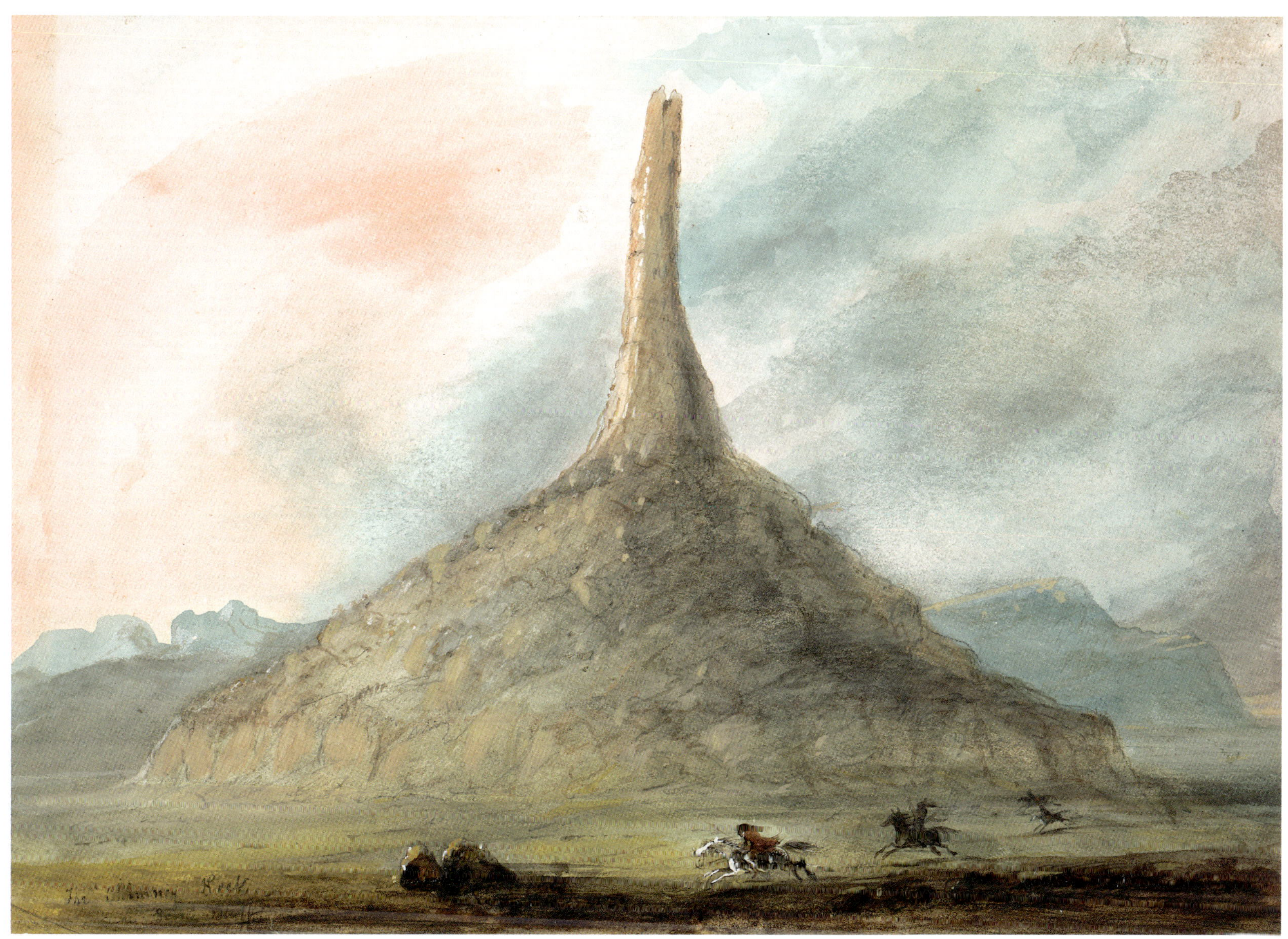

25 *Rocky Formations near the Nebraska or Platte River*

Watercolor, gouache, graphite, ink, and gum glazes on beige wove paper, 7⁹⁄₁₆ × 11⁵⁄₁₆ in. (19.2 cm × 28.7 cm). Inscribed upper left: 128; inscribed upper right: Rocky Formations near the / Nebraska or Platte River.
BAC 10305

THE IMPRECISE LOCALE MILLER INSCRIBED ON THIS SHEET — "NEAR the Nebraska or Platte River" — suggests this dramatic yet congenial scene was drawn from the artist's memory some years after his journey west.[1] It also is testament to Miller's interest in depicting the character of that landscape and its deeper associations rather than its precise geology or specific sites. While the scene is surely rooted in the artist's experience, his depiction of Indians, in miniature scale, galloping across the verdant plain in the shadow of the large rocks points to his sympathy with the mid-nineteenth-century Romantic assumption of native people's closeness to nature.[2]

In *Rocky Formations*, the carefully balanced arrangement of natural scenery and the use of alternating light and shade and suggestions of textures indicate the artist's debt to the eighteenth-century English concept of the picturesque landscape.[3] Here, the composition is built around two prominent rocky monoliths, set on slight diagonals to the picture plane. Pencil drawing over the green, pink, and blue washes as well as thicker strokes and dots of yellow, orange, and white define their craggy forms and rough-hewn surfaces across which light and shadow gently dance.

J. M. W. Turner also offered Miller important artistic models. Miller saw Turner's paintings in London in 1842 and had the opportunity again in the United States in 1857–58, when British watercolors were on view in New York and Philadelphia. He also would have had easy access to a broad range of Turner's prints.[4] Miller especially admired the Englishman's lavish atmospheric effects, evident here and even more so in *War Path* (cat. 30), yet he seems also to have desired to emulate Turner's ability to plumb nature's deeper significance.[5] Emphasizing the solidity of the formations and juxtaposing them against an open sky and a high mountain backdrop, Miller endowed the scene inspired by the landscape near Laramie with his initial wonder at their endurance beyond anything in human history.[6]

MCC

1. Its similarity to *Formation of Rock* (1858–60; The Walters Art Museum, Baltimore) indicates it may have been painted in connection with the Walters commission.

2. Herman J. Viola with H. B. Crothers and Maureen Hannan, "The American Indian Genre Paintings of Catlin, Stanley, Wimar, Eastman, and Miller," in *American Frontier Life: Early Western Paintings and Prints*, exh. cat. (New York: Abbeville Press, 1987), 163.

3. See Bruce Robertson, "The Picturesque Traveler in America," in Edward Nygren and Robertson, *Views and Visions: American Landscape before 1830*, exh. cat. (Washington, D.C.: Corcoran Gallery of Art, 1986), 189–211, esp. 189–90.

4. On Turner's influence in America at midcentury, see Kathleen A. Foster, "The Pre-Raphaelite Medium: Ruskin, Turner, and American Watercolor," in Linda S. Ferber and William H. Gerdts, *The New Path: Ruskin and the American Pre-Raphaelites*, exh. cat. (Brooklyn: Brooklyn Museum, 1985), 79–107, esp. 82–83. For a study of Turner's influence in America more broadly, see Franklin Kelly, "Turner and America," in *J. M. W. Turner*, ed. Ian Warrell, exh. cat. (London: Tate Publishing, 2007), 231–46.

5. Miller, Journal, 57; and Kelly, "Turner and America," 235.

6. Ross, *The West of Miller*, opp. pl. 87.

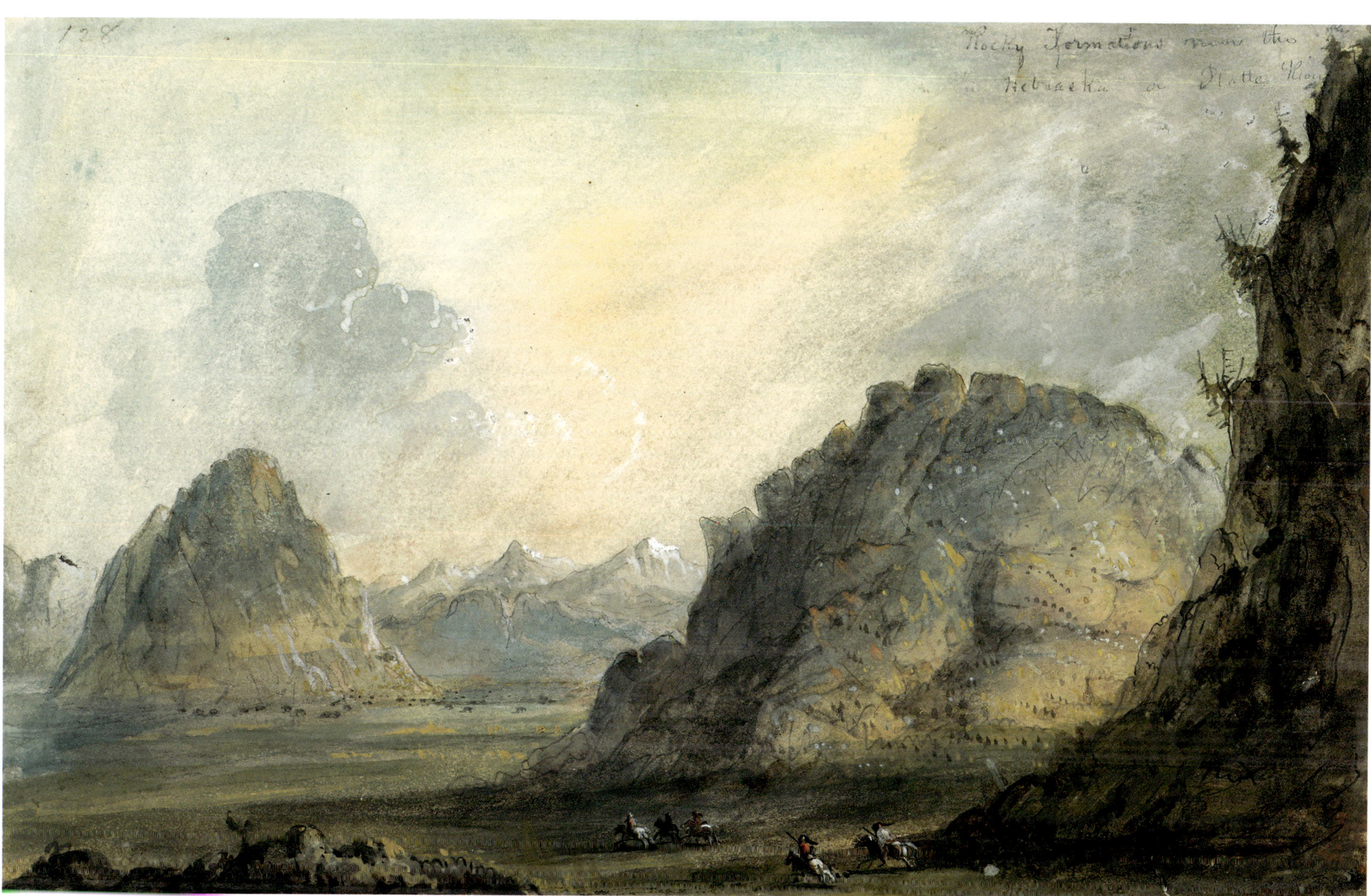
128
Rocky Formations near the
Nebraska or Platte

26 *Stampede of Wild Horses*

Watercolor, gouache, graphite, and gum glazes on off-white wove paper, 6 × 8 15/16 in. (15.2 × 22.7 cm). Inscribed upper right: Stampede of Wild Horses.
BAC 10303

ALTHOUGH CELEBRATED AS ICONS OF THE UNFETTERED WEST, WILD HORSES are not an indigenous species. Instead, they are feral descendants of Arabian stock introduced to this continent by Spanish explorers in the sixteenth century. Even so, so-called wild horses suggested to the Romantic imagination that the West was a locale where an Anglo-European pedigree could be cast off in favor of a natural life of unrestrained freedom.[1] According to Miller, atypical was the man traveling with Stewart's caravan who was not awed by herds of wild horses glimpsed along their route: "Among the wild animals of the west, none gave us so much pleasure or caused such excitement. . . . The beauty and symmetry of their forms, their wild and spirited action, long sweeping manes and tails, variety of colour, and fleetness of motion, all combine to call forth admiration from the most stoical."[2]

Stampede of Wild Horses allows those unable to partake directly of the "pleasure" and "excitement" elicited by such an encounter to experience vicariously the grandeur. In the shadow of a mountainous panorama, created with pencil underdrawing still evident, and beneath a subtle, arched frame of sky evoked through a controlled, delicate wash, Miller captured the horses' agility and uncommon beauty as they thunder through a valley washed in earth tones.[3] As in his depiction of antelope (see cat. 6), Miller employed the factually inaccurate artistic convention known as the flying gallop to suggest that the horses are running at full speed. Differing hues of brown, gray, black, red-brown, and white gouache both showcase the range of coloration of horses known to thrive in the West and also differentiate the animals as they charge en masse.[4] Fittingly, the horses closest to the picture plane are the most detailed. In addition to touches of white gouache that highlight muzzles, legs, hooves, and forelocks, pinpricks in the paper emphasize manes and anatomical details as minute as a nostril. Miller also employed this pinprick technique to add highlights to the distant mountain range, at the base of which he scratched fine, horizontal lines. He brushed thin gum glaze over the dark horses, foreground washes, and the trunks of the trees that bracket the left side of the composition. This prominent stand of trees serves as a *repoussoir* and amplifies the illusion of deep spatial recession Miller so successfully achieved in this sketch. SFK

1. Richard W. Slatta, *The Mythical West: An Encyclopedia of Legend, Lore, and Popular Culture* (Santa Barbara, Calif.: ABC-CLIO, 2001), 366. For more on contemporaneous beliefs regarding wild horses and their Arabian ancestry, see Strong, *Sentimental Journey*, 27 and 30–31. In addition to *Stampede of Wild Horses* and the two directly related sketches (Gilcrease Museum, Tulsa, Okla., and The Walters Art Museum, Baltimore), wild horses appear in Miller's art numerous times.

2. Miller, "Rough Draughts," no. 144, which relates to Ross, *The West of Miller*, opp. pl. 92.

3. Although it is tempting to consider the tangle of eleven legs associated with the pair of horses on the left of the white horse at the lower center as Miller's effort to convey motion, the multitude of limbs is more likely the remnant of an artist's change.

4. Hope Ryden, *America's Last Wild Horses: The Classic Study of the Mustangs – Their Pivotal Role in the History of the West, Their Return to the Wild, and the Ongoing Efforts to Preserve Them* (Guilford, Conn.: Lyons Press, 2005), 117.

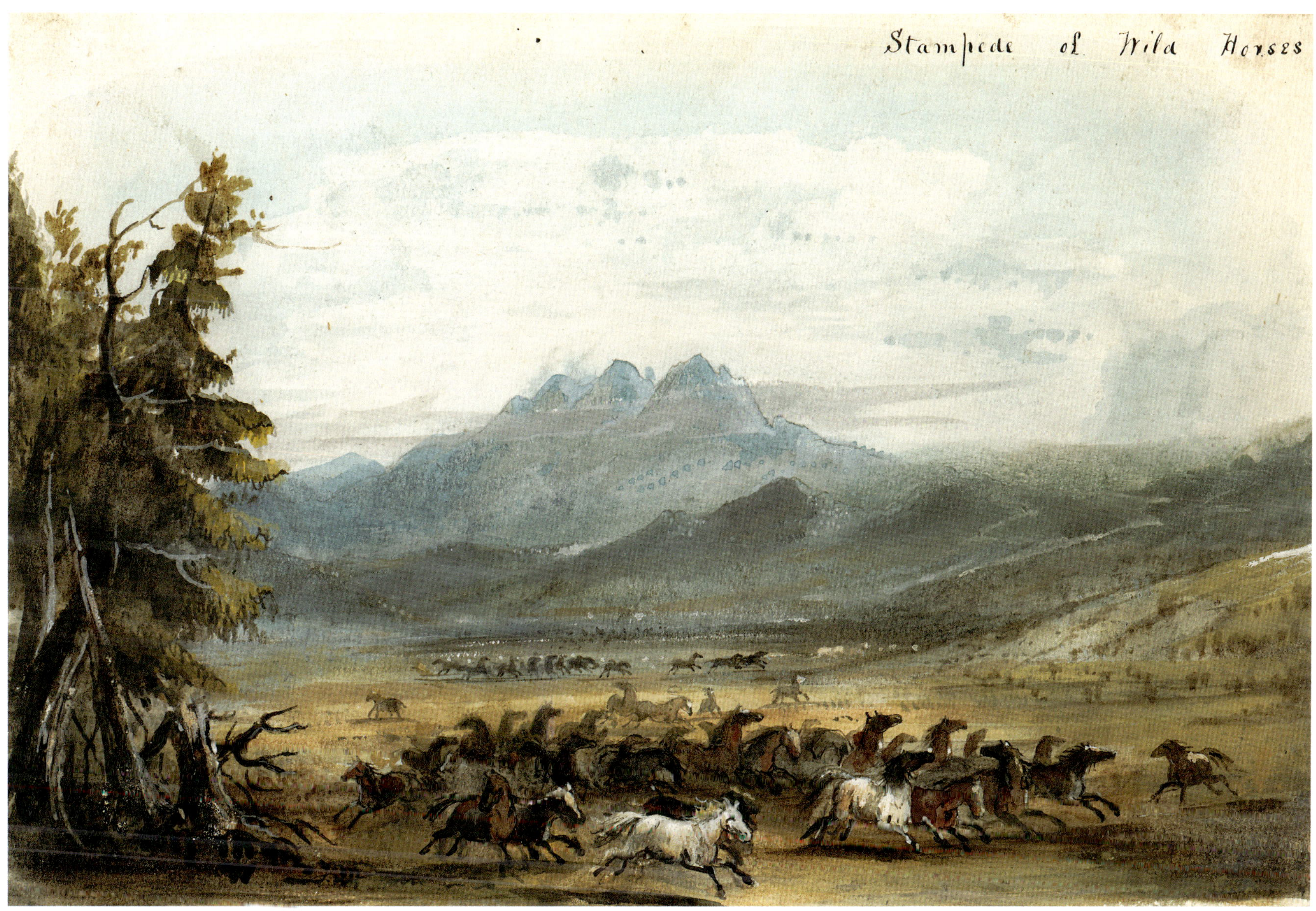
Stampede of Wild Horses

27 *Sioux Setting Out on an Expedition to Capture Wild Horses*

Watercolor, gouache, pen and ink, graphite, and gum glazes on smooth bristol board, 7 11/16 × 12 1/16 in. (19.5 × 30.6 cm). Inscribed lower right: Sioux Setting out on an Expedition / to capture Wild horses. BAC 10301

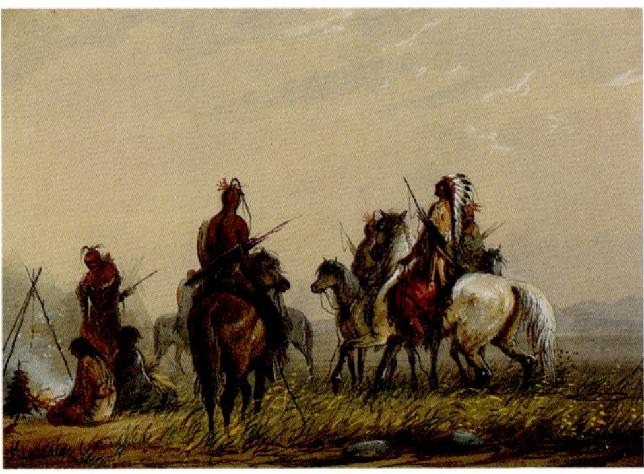

FIGURE 38. Alfred Jacob Miller, *Expedition to Capture Wild Horses – Sioux*, 1858–60. Watercolor on paper, 8 7/16 × 12 in. (21.4 × 30.5 cm). The Walters Art Museum, Baltimore

HORSES WERE SYNONYMOUS WITH WEALTH AND INFLUENCE FOR MANY OF the Plains tribes Miller encountered during his excursion west in 1837.[1] According to the artist, when the number of horses a man possessed dwindled, it became necessary to "call around him his 'good men and true,' with lariats and tackle in good order, and set out on a foray to catch these valuable animals."[2] Such a summons is the subject of *Sioux Setting Out on an Expedition to Capture Wild Horses*.

Amid these preparations, a spiked ball-head club occupies a conspicuous position in the foreground. The weapon, formidable in hand-to-hand combat, would have served little purpose in the acquisition of wild horses. However, if the leader of the pursuit opted not to limit the mission "to the strict letter of the wild-horse question," the club could be a beneficial addition to his arsenal. "Why should he trouble himself to look after wild horses, when tame ones may be had at the trifling cost of a little pounding?"[3] In Miller's sketch, the club anchors an inverted triangle whose angles are punctuated by objects that connote Indianness.[4] Its upper left corner is defined by the quiver on the back of the figure turned away from the viewer.[5] A striking feathered headdress, a forerunner of the iconic eagle bonnet worn by Central Plains tribes, establishes the third point of the triangle. The headdress, like the club, is an inappropriate accoutrement for the task at hand as described by the inscription. However, Miller's artistic license amplifies the resonance of this sketch as a quintessential Indian and, by extension, western picture.[6]

When, in 1858, William T. Walters commissioned two hundred watercolors from Miller, this sketch was among the compositions the artist reworked (fig. 38). Although Miller's notes that accompany the resulting portfolio allude to the use of a club when purloining enemies' horses, the weapon so prominently featured in the Bank of America's sketch is absent in the later composition.

SFK

1. Paul Howard Carlson, *The Plains Indians* (College Station: Texas A&M University Press, 1998), 46.

2. Ross, *The West of Miller*, opp. pl. 169.

3. Ibid.

4. It is possible that Miller saw a club like this one at the St. Louis home of Captain William Clark. Miller recalled that Clark showed them his Indian "trophies," including war clubs. Miller, postscript to preface of "Rough Draughts."

5. White lead on the quiver and its mirror image to the right has discolored to a peach tonality.

6. The liberties that Miller took extend to the title as well. The scalp locks worn by the men call into question their identity as Sioux. This distinct hairstyle may instead mark them as members of the Pawnee tribe. Ronald P. Koch, *Dress Clothing of the Plains Indians* (Norman: University of Oklahoma, 1982), 89. I am grateful to Gaylord Torrence, Fred and Virginia Merrill Senior Curator of American Indian Art, The Nelson-Atkins Museum of Art, for his suggestion that Miller inaccurately identified the men as Sioux and for his clarification regarding details pertaining to the ball-head club and headdress.

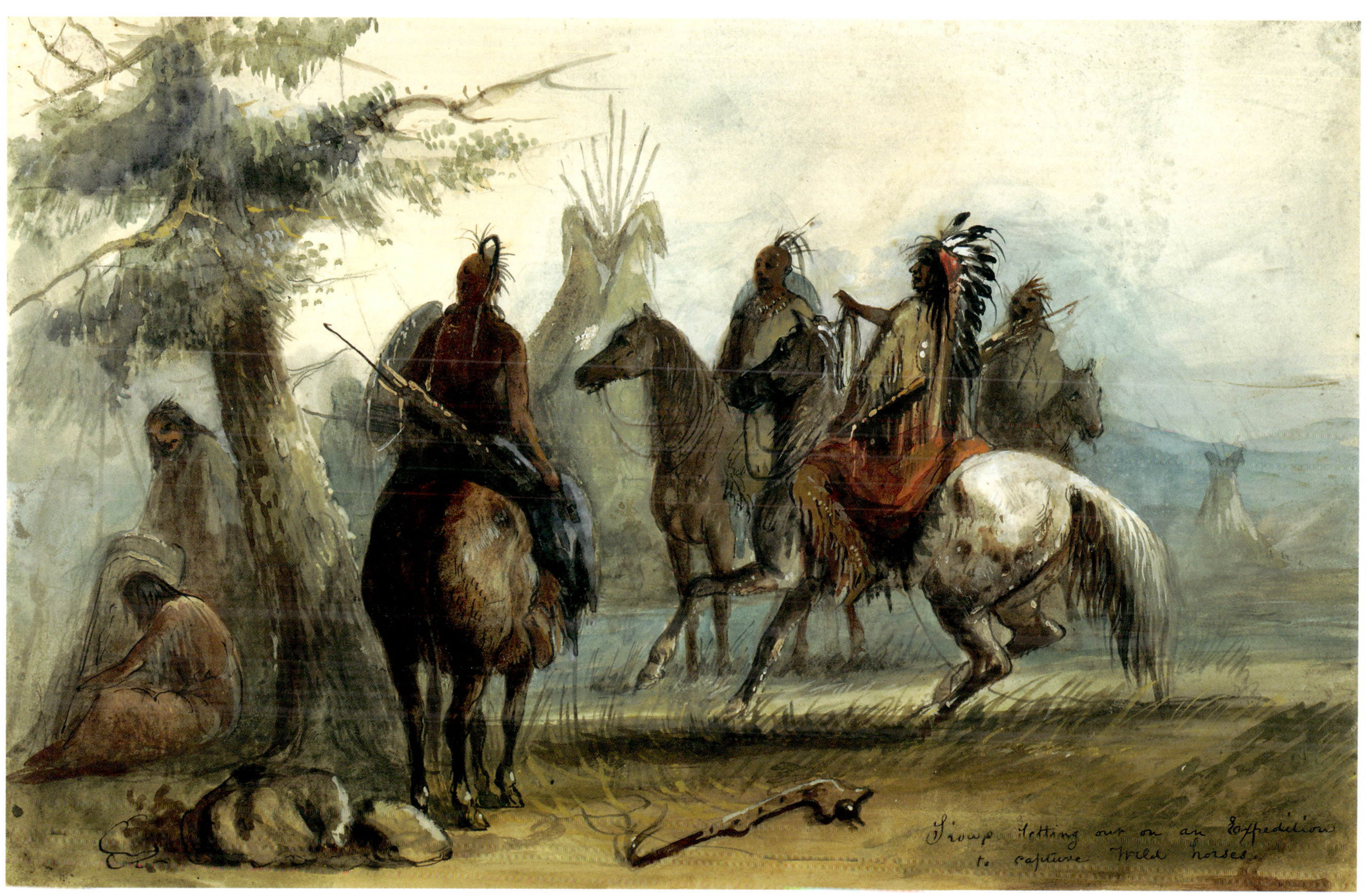
Sioux setting out on an Expedition
to capture Wild horses.

28 *Indian Women Watching a Battle*

Watercolor, gouache, pencil, ink, and glazes on Reynolds board, 7⁷⁄₁₆ × 8³⁄₁₆ in. (18.9 × 20.8 cm). BAC 10295

IN THE DECADES THAT FOLLOWED HIS WESTERN EXPEDITION AS THE RESIDENT artist with Stewart's caravan, Miller repeatedly reworked select images inspired by the trip. *Indian Women Watching a Battle*, by contrast, is a unique composition.

This sketch depicts six Indian women silhouetted against a mountainous backdrop. They are stationed on a rocky promontory markedly similar to the outcropping in *Watching the Caravan* (cat. 2). From this elevated vantage point, they witness a barely discernible skirmish being waged in the far distance. Despite the diversity of the women's reactions to this battle – ranging from interest to anguish – their figures merge to form a single pyramidal unit. Miller built up their interlocking forms with a harmonious palette of thickly brushed watercolor and gouache. He defined and augmented their basic shapes with thin strokes of brown and black ink applied with a pen, while using small touches of white gouache mixed with wash for costume ornament and highlights. Selectively applied glaze saturates and deepens the pigments, particularly in the huddling trio who, turning away from the conflict, conveys palpable distress.

The emotional response elicited by this sketch has equivalents in the sentiment provoked by contemporary, highly Romantic, so-called dying race imagery. During the 1840s and 1850s, artists such as Tomkins Matteson and John Mix Stanley (fig. 39) dramatized the fate of indigenous people affected by westward expansion by painting them isolated and pushed to the brink of the Pacific Ocean.[1] The affinities in both feeling and form that Miller's *Indian Women Watching a Battle* share with such paintings extend even to the distant landscape awash in blue, a color dictated by the conventions of atmospheric perspective but one that also resembles water.

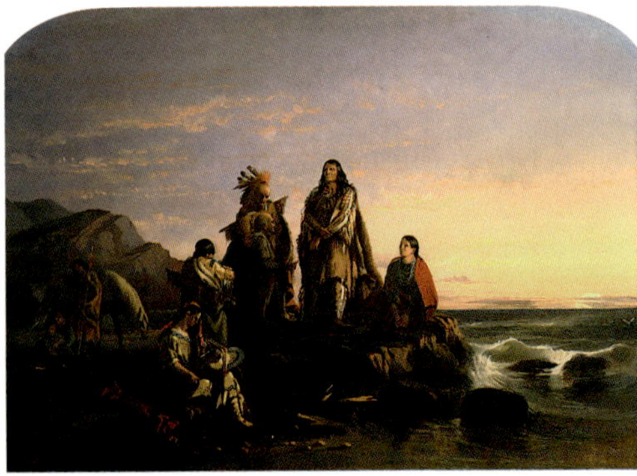

FIGURE 39. John Mix Stanley, *The Last of Their Race*, 1857. Oil on canvas, 43 × 60 in. (109.2 × 152.4 cm). Buffalo Bill Historical Center, Cody, Wyoming; Museum Purchase, 5.75

Miller executed this poetic sketch on a thin, high-quality drawing board that he trimmed roughly square to emphasize the figural group.[2] The board was manufactured by the British papermaking firm Reynolds and Son, whose trademark is prominently embossed in the upper left corner. Trade journals of the period recommended Reynolds Abraded Surface Drawing Boards as ideal for both drawing in pencil and working with colored pigments, making it an apt choice for Miller, who was prone to mixing media.[3]

SFK

1. Robert F. Berkhofer Jr., *The White Man's Indian: Images of the American Indian from Columbus to the Present* (New York: Alfred A. Knopf, 1978), 88 and 144; and Julie Schimmel, "Inventing 'the Indian,'" in *The West as America: Reinterpreting Images of the Frontier, 1820–1920*, ed. William H. Truettner, exh. cat. (Washington, D.C.: Smithsonian Institution Press, 1991), 168–69.

2. The support has been irregularly cut, and unfinished cut lines are visible. The nearly square format of this sketch is rare in Miller's body of western art.

3. "Drawing Paper and Boards," *Mechanics' Magazine, Museum, Register, Journal, and Gazette* (London), 17, no. 467 (21 July 1832): 263.

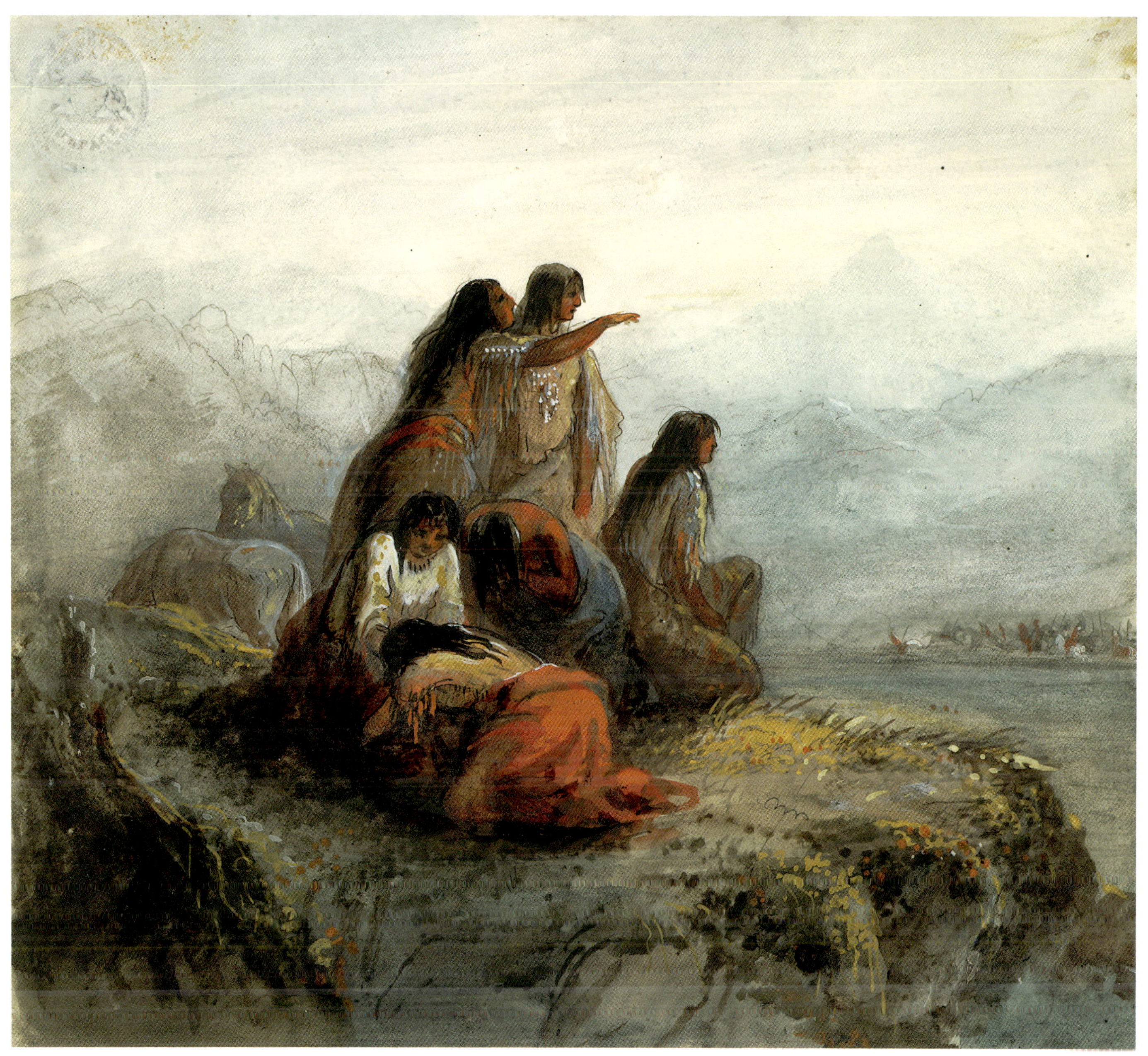

29 *On the Warpath—Running Fight*

Brown and gray wash, white and yellow gouache, black pen and ink, pencil, and chalk on brown paper, mounted to rag board, 8⅛ × 11¹⁄₁₆ in. (20.6 × 28.1 cm). Signed with monogram, lower right: AJM. BAC 10293

30 *War Path*

Oil and glazes over graphite, ink, and possibly watercolor on cream wove paper, 9 × 12¼ in. (22.9 × 31.1 cm). Signed with monogram, lower right: AJM. BAC 10309

When a tribe of Indians has a grievance either through loss of any of their men, or of depredations committed against them, the chiefs summon their young warriors, arm, dress, and paint themselves elaborately and set out on the war path. All this threatens mischief, and it is by no means a pleasant thing to meet them under such circumstances, unless you have an able escort.[1]

Miller wrote this account with the sort of conviction usually derived from firsthand experience. However, it is believed that the artist never witnessed Indian warfare. Instead, he was privy to tales told along the trail or while at the rendezvous, where multiple tribes converged and accounts of hostilities were surely traded.[2] In the absence of direct experience, such reports may have inspired *On the Warpath—Running Fight* and *War Path*, as well as five other directly related works.[3]

Although it is fairly certain that Miller did not observe Indian combat, he may have seen—albeit in less antagonistic contexts—the daring maneuver that he dramatically portrayed. When members of the Snake tribe arrived at the rendezvous one day after Miller and Stewart, their entrance was marked by a spectacle. Apparently, young braves broke ranks with the procession "in pursuit of an imaginary Sioux, hanging by their heels on the far side of their horses, shooting arrows under their necks."[4] Miller was also likely familiar with George Catlin's interpretation of this evasive tactic through the print *Comanche Feats of Horsemanship*, first published in 1841. The explication that accompanied the engraving described in detail this particularly precarious "stratagem of war."[5]

Whether campfire stories, a mock skirmish, or artistic precedents contributed to the impetus for *On the Warpath—Running Fight* and *War Path*, their content reflects a mid-nineteenth-century vogue for Indian imagery. During the 1840s and 1850s, Indians were an artistic and literary staple featured in portfolios, a plethora of illustrated books, and prints.[6] Like his contemporary F. O. C. Darley, who published a popular volume of tableaux titled *Scenes in Indian Life* (1843), Miller approached his subject with theatricality and emphasized the height of action while implying a thrilling narrative with which viewers could readily engage.

In *On the Warpath—Running Fight*, nuances of line convincingly convey the speed with which the pale horse charges while its intrepid rider clings to its neck. Short strokes of white and yellow gouache and black ink create compelling details such as the horse's flying mane and tail, the fluttering fringe of the Indian's leggings, his wind-whipped

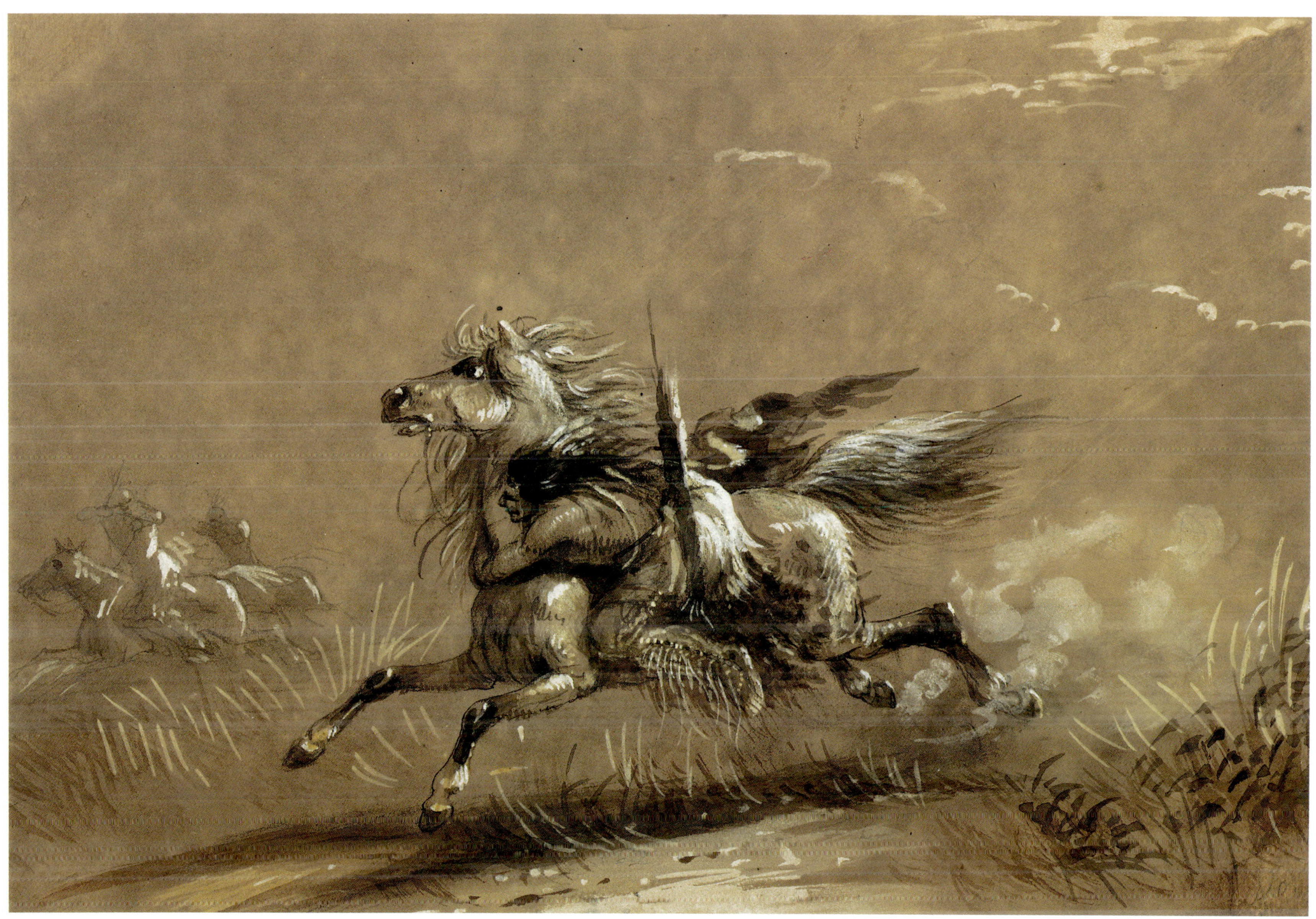

blanket, and flowing hair. Among the seven works that share this gripping motif, this is the sole example in which the Indian has long hair, rather than a scalp lock. It is also the only version in which his weapons of choice are arrows.

His counterpart in *War Path* wields only a large knife tucked into a belt that secures the red blanket wrapped around his waist.[7] *War Path* may date to approximately the same period as *Snake and Sioux Indians on Warpath* (fig. 40) and echoes its look and feel, but technical analysis and infrared reflectography reveal that a distinctly different composition lies beneath the finished image. The main figure originally had long hair, wore a quiver, and leaned forward over the neck of his horse while shielding his eyes with his hand. Just behind him, a second Indian, also with long hair and possibly brandishing a spear, is similarly hidden beneath the layer of ground. In oil on paper, *War Path*, like *Departure of the Caravan* (see cat. 1), melds Miller's two primary modes of production – intimate sketches on paper and larger oils – with which he earned distinction as an artist romancing the West. SFK

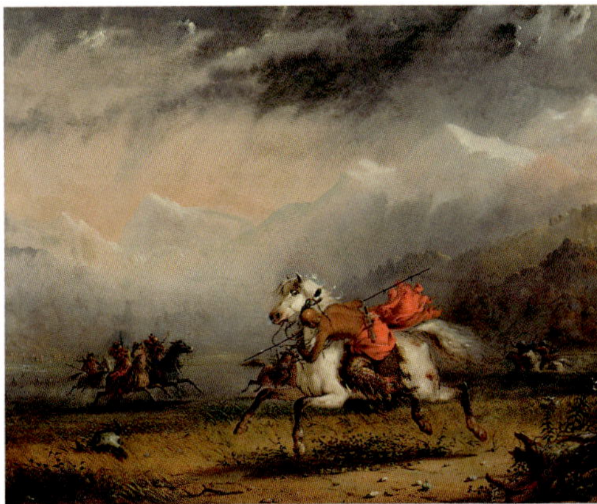

FIGURE 40. Alfred Jacob Miller, *Snake and Sioux Indians on Warpath*, 1856. Oil on canvas, 29 × 36 in. (73.7 × 91.5 cm). Gilcrease Museum, Tulsa, Oklahoma

1. Ross, *The West of Miller*, opp. pl. 61.

2. Ron Tyler, "Alfred Jacob Miller and Sir William Drummond Stewart," in Tyler, *Miller: Artist on the Oregon Trail*, 33. Joan Troccoli likens Miller's images of warring Indians to Delacroix's depictions of Arabian battles, in that neither artist directly experienced what they painted. Troccoli, *Miller: Watercolors*, 12.

3. See Tyler, *Miller: Artist on the Oregon Trail*, nos. 379, 379A–C, and 379F. It is difficult to determine the sequence of these works, as they do not necessarily represent a linear evolution.

4. DeVoto, *Across the Wide Missouri*, 322.

5. George Catlin, *The Manners, Customs, and Condition of the North American Indians* (London: the artist, 1841), 2:65–66 and pl. 167. Miller's "Rough Draught" for *Dodging an Arrow (Crows)* (1858–60; The Walters Art Museum, Baltimore) is quite similar to Catlin's notes. Miller, "Rough Draughts," no. 62, which relates to Ross, *The West of Miller*, opp. pl. 134.

6. See Bernard Reilly Jr., "The Prints of Life in the West, 1840–60," in *American Frontier Life: Early Western Paintings and Prints* (New York: Abbeville Press, 1987), 170–72; Robert F. Berkhofer Jr., *The White Man's Indian: Images of the American Indian from Columbus to the Present* (New York: Alfred A. Knopf, 1978), 95; and *Currier and Ives: A Catalogue Raisonné* (Detroit: Gale Research Company, 1985).

7. This red blanket, the small black-dyed buckskin pouch adorned with red quillwork that the Indian wears around his neck, and his German silver ball-and-cone earrings suggest that he may be a member of the Pawnee tribe. I thank my colleague Gaylord Torrence, Fred and Virginia Merrill Senior Curator of American Indian Art, The Nelson-Atkins Museum of Art, for pointing out these identifying details.

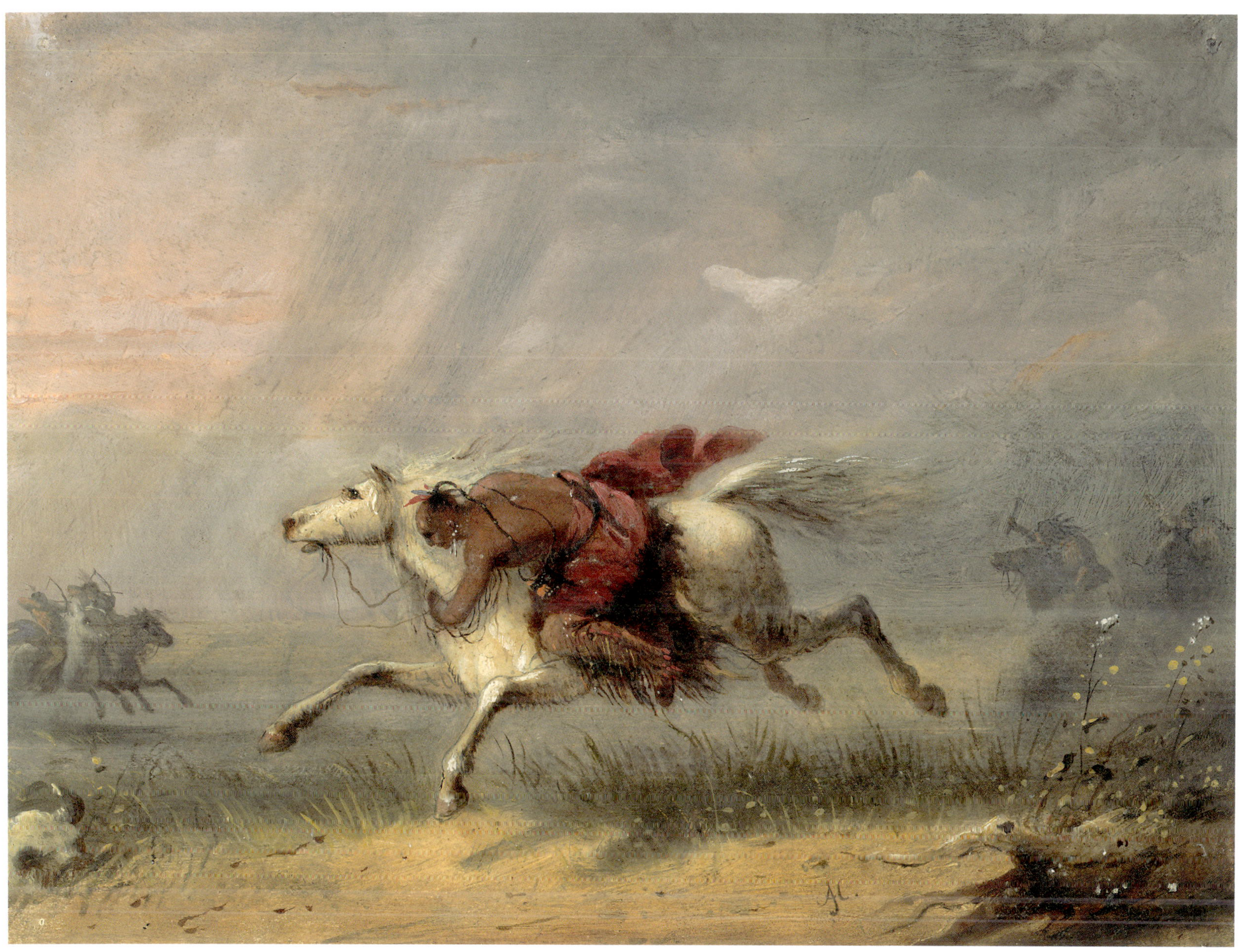

Photograph Credits

Photographs for illustrations have for the most part been provided by the owners of the individual works of art.

All works by Alfred Jacob Miller in the Bank of America collection were photographed by John Lamberton with the exception of Fig. 10.

Figs. 3, 10, 18, 36: Tiffany Matson

Fig. 33: © Rare Books Division, The New York Public Library, Astor, Lenox and Tilden Foundations

Fig. 17: © Sheldon Museum of Art

Frontispiece and figs. 6, 7, 8, 12, 26, 28, 31, 37, 38: © The Walters Art Museum, Baltimore